# CASE STUDIES IN EARLY CHILDHOOD EDUCATION

## IMPLEMENTING DEVELOPMENTALLY APPROPRIATE PRACTICES

**Rachel Ozretich**

*Linn-Benton Community College*

**Linda Burt**

*Oregon State University, Emerita*

**Susan Doescher**

*Linn-Benton Community College*

**Martha Foster**

*Linn-Benton Community College*

**Merrill**

Boston   Columbus   Indianapolis   New York   San Francisco   Upper Saddle River
Amsterdam   Cape Town   Dubai   London   Madrid   Milan   Munich   Paris   Montreal   Toronto
Delhi   Mexico City   São Paulo   Sydney   Hong Kong   Seoul   Singapore   Taipei   Tokyo

KH

**Library of Congress Cataloging-in-Publication Data**

Case studies in early childhood education : implementing developmentally appropriate practices /
Rachel Ozretich ... [et al.].
    p. cm.
  ISBN-13: 978-0-13-502603-8
  ISBN-10: 0-13-502603-2
  1. Early childhood education—Case studies.    I. Ozretich, Rachel A.
  LB1139.23.C385 2009
  372.21—dc22

                                                                2009002676


**Vice President and Executive Publisher:** Jeffery W. Johnston
**Acquisitions Editor:** Julie Peters
**Editorial Assistant:** Tiffany Bitzel
**Production Manager:** Wanda Rockwell
**Creative Director:** Jayne Conte
**Cover Design:** Bruce Kenselaar
**Cover Photo:** Jupiter Images
**Full-Service Project Management/Composition:** Aptara®, Inc.
**Printer/Binder:** Courier Companies
**Director of Marketing:** Quinn Perkson
**Marketing Manager:** Erica DeLuca
**Marketing Coordinator:** Brian Mounts

**Pearson**® is a registered trademark of Pearson plc
**Merrill**® is a registered trademark of Pearson Education, Inc.

Pearson Education Ltd., London
Pearson Education Singapore Pte. Ltd.
Pearson Education Canada, Ltd.
Pearson Education—Japan
Pearson Education Australia Pty. Limited

Pearson Education North Asia Ltd., Hong Kong
Pearson Educación de Mexico, S.A. de C.V.
Pearson Education Malaysia Pte. Ltd.
Pearson Education Upper Saddle River, New Jersey

**Merrill**
is an imprint of

www.pearsonhighered.com

10 9 8 7 6 5 4 3 2
ISBN-13: 978-0-13-502603-8
ISBN-10:    0-13-502603-2

1/21/11

# ABOUT THE AUTHORS

From left, Rachel Ozretich, Linda Burt, Susan Doescher, Martha Foster

## Rachel Ozretich

Rachel Ozretich has been a preschool teacher, college instructor, researcher, evaluator, consultant, and policy analyst in early childhood education, parenting education, and family policy for the past 25 years. She has coauthored many research-based publications in the fields of early childhood education, family policy, results accountability, and parenting education and has presented numerous workshops at both state and national conferences. She has taught classes of infants, toddlers, preschool children, elementary school children, and parents. She holds a Master's degree in human development and family studies from Oregon State University and an earlier Master's degree in oceanography from the University of Washington. She is a Certified Family Life Educator and has recently taught early childhood education practicum classes for preservice teachers at Oregon State University and Linn-Benton Community College. She and her husband have two adult sons and two granddaughters. Currently, she teaches college students, works as a consultant, and writes a newspaper column on parenting.

## Linda Burt

Linda Burt, Ph.D., is Faculty Emerita at Oregon State University. She has taught classes in early childhood curriculum development, advised undergraduate students in their coursework, and supervised early childhood education practica in community programs for infants through kindergarten children. Her articles and presentations have focused on the development of a scale measuring developmentally appropriate practice by what teachers do and what children do in the early primary classroom setting.[1] Later articles and presentations have described observational research of preservice teachers' interactions with children in multicultural settings. During her career in early childhood education, she has developed course curricula and workshops for both preservice and inservice early childhood teachers. She continues to mentor and support undergraduate interns and practicum students in community early childhood settings and their experiences with developmentally appropriate practice. The foundation of her later experiences has been greatly enriched by the years she spent working with high-risk children and families in early childhood settings, and at home with her husband, raising two daughters.

### Susan Doescher

Susan Doescher is a faculty member in the Education/Child and Family Studies Department of Linn-Benton Community College (LBCC) in Albany, Oregon. She is the Director of the LBCC Early Education Partnership program, funded by a federal Early Childhood Educator Professional Development grant. This 3-year early literacy project provides professional development for teachers and child care providers in Oregon's Linn and Benton counties. Susan's 30 years of experience include teaching in parent cooperative programs; university infant, toddler, and preschool laboratory schools; community child care centers; and a private kindergarten. Her university teaching and research have encompassed the areas of social and emotional development and early childhood professional development. She has written numerous cooperative extension publications and professional journal articles and is currently teaching college classes in early literacy, early childhood development, and curriculum. Susan holds a Master's degree from Michigan State University in early childhood education and a Ph.D. from Oregon State University in child development. She and her husband are presently raising their high school daughter, Kara.

### Martha Foster

Martha Foster has taught in the classroom for 38 years, working with infants, toddlers, and preschool children. During most of these years she has worked in laboratory schools, modeling and guiding preservice teachers, or in parent cooperatives, helping parents as they explore effective ways of relating to their children. She has worked in half-day preschools and full-day child care programs in settings located in urban areas in the West and Mid-West and in rural Appalachian Virginia. Currently, she is teaching classes for the Education/Child and Family Studies Department of Linn-Benton Community College in Albany, Oregon. In addition, she conducts training for child care providers and mentors community college students to support their development of appropriate and effective teaching practices. Martha holds a Master's degree from Pacific Oaks College. Storytelling has been a sustaining thread throughout her career and from this experience, Martha has learned to value the power of the story to teach, both as an educator and as a parent.

---

[1]Burt, L., Sugawara, A., & Wright, D. (1993). A scale of primary classroom practices (SPCP). *Early Childhood Development and Care, 84,* 19–36.

# PREFACE

Research informs us of the positive impact high-quality early childhood care and educational experiences have on children and their future well-being. It also tells us that poor quality of care environments can be harmful to young children. Quality of care matters, and it is closely related to developmentally appropriate practice (DAP) and ethical conduct on the part of each early childhood care and education teacher professional.

## PURPOSE OF THIS BOOK

Although students in the early childhood field are encouraged and advised to adopt practices that are developmentally appropriate, clearly there is some confusion about how to actually implement these practices once the students are in a setting with real children. If students are observing classrooms in the community, they may miss being exposed to appropriate practice models, and may even learn and adopt unsuitable practices, thinking that they are developmentally appropriate. The purpose of this book is to provide readers with examples of actual encounters they might have if they were able to observe classes in many different developmentally appropriate settings and listen in on some of the teachers' thought processes. This book will provide a bridge between what is learned through traditional pedagogy and what is actually practiced in the vast array of developmentally appropriate early childhood care and education settings that exist in the United States.

## AUDIENCE

This book is intended primarily as a textbook for students in early childhood education. It may also be used as a companion text for many different early childhood education courses for preservice teachers in which discussions of case studies may be used to help translate general ideas into concrete examples. It is particularly useful for practicum students and interns. It may also serve as a resource for inservice trainings or as a self-study resource for professional development systems.

## ORGANIZATION

The case studies are written about children from diverse families and their teachers working in various settings with different age groups, from infants and toddlers to the early elementary years. The questions following the case studies are designed to stimulate student reflection and class discussion about the reasoning behind the decisions teachers make, the consequences of using specific practices, and the ethical bases for making decisions. Just as in the real world, some cases are brief and are resolved quickly and others require more of the teacher's time and energy. In this book, the latter type of case is broken into multiple parts, each with its own focus; however, knowledge of what has come before each part is essential to understanding it. The strategies presented should be considered good examples of DAP rather than rigid recipes for the only correct way to handle a situation. Students are encouraged to use these strategies and also develop their own creative ways of supporting individual and developmental growth in the children with whom they work.

   We invite the reader to experience some typical situations and how they are handled, for the most part, by those we consider master teachers. Most of these cases present strategies we believe to be developmentally appropriate. However, there are also cases that portray certain situations that students may find in some work settings but that are not as appropriate. As you read through these cases, we urge you to think critically about the strategies used. Do they reflect developmentally appropriate practice as outlined in the National Association for the Education of Young Children (NAEYC) Position Statement on Developmentally Appropriate Practice? Do they consider ethical guidelines as discussed in NAEYC's Code of Ethical Conduct? What are the important specific or practical elements that make a strategy appropriate? Can you determine how you might expand on the strategies or use them in your setting and what impact they might have on the children?

In the 2009 NAEYC Position Statement, one of three important challenges is "recognizing teacher knowledge and decision making as vital to educational effectiveness" (p. 2).[1] Each day that teachers are in the classroom or child care setting, there are continuous decisions to be made about arranging materials, making curriculum plans, and interacting with children and parents. Teachers need to use their knowledge about DAP when making each decision and must constantly check its appropriateness by observing what the consequences are for children. The more the spirit of developmentally appropriate practice becomes a part of teachers' deep thinking, the easier and more effective the daily decisions become. For instance, once teachers truly understand and believe that it is essential to respect children's emotions and ability to learn, it becomes easier to take the time to work through a problem-solving solution rather than to brusquely send a child to "time-out." At the same time, once teachers have taken the time to respectfully problem solve with children and experience how effective it can be, it reinforces the commitment of teachers to the importance of treating each child with warmth and respect.

## QUESTIONS FOR REFLECTION

The process of applying DAP on a very practical level requires practice with day-to-day classroom decisions. To encourage students to practice their skills in decision making while reading through these cases, we have provided questions for reflection after each brief case study or section of an extended case study.

Our intension is to provide questions that may be understood and answered by students with a broad range of backgrounds in early childhood education. Students require little prior training to understand and answer these questions. More advanced questions are included in the Instructor's Manual. Faculty may choose to ask the student to focus on specific questions according to the objectives of the course or for other reasons.

In addition to specific questions after each case, the reader is encouraged to consider some general questions that contribute to the analysis of the cases, as follows.

1. What is the main focus of the case? Are there other subtopics that also support the main focus?
2. What is the relevant information that is given? What additional information would be useful to learn?
3. What age is involved in this case? Would the strategies demonstrated be useful with other ages? If not, what kinds of changes would need to be made and why?
4. Does this case raise issues with which I feel uncomfortable? Why? Does it give information that allows me to feel more comfortable or do I need more information?

As you read through these cases, listen to the words that teachers actually say, follow the process as teachers make their decisions, and witness the impact the strategies have on children. By truly incorporating developmentally appropriate practice in all of our decisions every day with children, we will have an important, beneficial effect on the positive development of children and their learning.

---

[1]Copple, C., & Bredekamp, S. (Eds.). (2009). *Developmentally appropriate practice in early childhood programs serving children from birth through age 8.* Washington, DC: National Association for the Education of Young Children.

## FEATURES

Many of the Questions for Reflection are followed by numbers and letters that provide the reader with the specific locations of:

1. The most relevant 2009 DAP guidelines, which can be purchased as part of a text[2] or accessed at http://www.naeyc.org/about/positions/dap.asp, and
2. The most relevant items in the NAEYC Code of Ethical Conduct and Statement of Commitment (2003) which can be accessed at http://www.naeyc.org/about/positions/ethical_conduct.asp.

## NAMES

As required by our profession's Code of Ethical Conduct (Code), we have changed the names in each case study to protect confidentiality. In addition, we refer to the early care and education provider as "teacher," in line with the profession's recognition that children learn not only from their first and primary teachers, their parents, but also from all early childhood professionals who work with them and facilitate their everyday experiences. We refer to the teachers by their first names, except in certain elementary school situations in which the children are typically expected to use titles when addressing their teachers; parents often imitate their children in this practice.

In using first names, we mean no disrespect to the teacher. Instead, we see both teacher and child as deserving of respect, and we want to enhance teacher–child relationships by avoiding the psychological barrier the expected use of a title may present, especially during the early years.

## SOURCES OF THE CASE STUDIES

The case studies in this book were based largely on our own experiences and on observations and interviews with other early childhood care and education teachers.

## ACKNOWLEDGMENTS

We would especially like to thank the following professionals for their important contributions: Cindy Bond, Janet Cover, Mary Hands, Susie Nelson, and Carol Young. We would like to thank the following reviewers for their input along the way: Velynda Cameron, *University of Missouri, Columbia*; Patricia Cantor, *Plymouth State University*; Sharon Carter, *Davidson County Community College*; Lauren Cummins, *Youngstown State University*; Muriel K. Rand, *New Jersey City University*; Marjorie Kostelnik, *University of Nebraska, Lincoln*; Jennifer M. Johnson, *Vance-Granville Community College*; Kathy Morrison, *University of Texas, Tyler*; Carol Patrick, *Eastern Kentucky University*; and Margarita Pérez, *Worcester State College*.

We would like to thank all of the children, families, college students, friends, family members, and professional colleagues who also made important contributions and from whom we continue to learn every day, and the Old World Deli in Corvallis for hosting our weekly meetings. We also wish to acknowledge our own children, families, colleagues, and friends who have nurtured and supported us through the process of writing this book. We would especially like to thank Julie Peters, our editor.

*Rachel Ozretich, Linda Burt,*
*Susan Doescher, and Martha Foster*

---

[2]Copple, C., & Bredekamp, S. (Eds.). (2009). *Developmentally appropriate practice in early childhood programs serving children from birth through age 8*. Washington, DC: National Association for the Education of Young Children.

# CONTENTS

**Note:** Every effort has been made to provide accurate and current Internet information in this book. However, the Internet and information posted on it are constantly changing; it is inevitable that some of the Internet addresses listed in this textbook will change.

## Matrix of Cases

| Case Number | Age Ranges | | | | | | Developmentally Appropriate Practice Dimensions | | | | | Ethical Responsibilities to: | | | | Diversity |
| --- | --- | --- | --- | --- | --- | --- | --- | --- | --- | --- | --- | --- | --- | --- | --- | --- |
| | Infants | Toddlers | 2 years | 3–5 years | Kindergarten | Early Elementary | 1 Caring Community | 2 Teaching | 3 Curriculum | 4 Assessment | 5 Families | 1 Children | 2 Families | 3 Colleagues | 4 Communities | |
| 1 | X | | | | | | X | X | X | | X | X | X | | | X |
| 2 | X | | | | | | X | X | X | | X | | | | | X |
| 3 | | X | | | | | | | X | X | X | | | | | X |
| 4 | | X | | | | | | X | X | | | | | | | |
| 5 | | | X | | | | X | X | | | | | | | | |
| 6 | | | X | | | | X | | X | | X | X | X | | | X |
| 7 | | | X | | | X | | X | X | X | X | X | X | | | |
| 8 | | | | X | | | X | X | | | | X | | | | |
| 9 | | | | X | | | X | X | X | | X | | X | | | |
| 10 | | | | X | | | | X | | | | | | | | |
| 11 | | | | X | | | | X | X | | | | | | | |
| 12 | | | | X | | | | X | | | | X | | | | |
| 13 | | | | X | | | X | X | X | | | X | | | | X |
| 14 | | | | X | | | X | X | X | | X | X | X | | | |
| 15 | | | | X | | | X | X | | | | X | | | | |
| 16 | | | | X | | | | X | X | | X | X | X | | | |
| 17 | | | | X | | | X | | | X | X | X | X | X | | |
| 18 | | | | X | | | | X | | | X | | X | | | |
| 19 | | | | X | | | | | | | | X | | X | X | |
| 20 | | | | X | | | | X | X | | | | | | | |
| 21 | | | | X | | | | X | | X | | X | X | | | |
| 22 | | | | | X | | X | X | | | | | | | | |
| 23 | | | | | X | | X | X | X | X | X | X | X | | | X |
| 24 | | | | | | X | | X | | | X | X | X | | | |
| 25 | | | | | | X | X | X | | | X | X | X | X | | |
| 26 | | | | | | X | X | X | X | | X | | X | | | X |
| 27 | | | | | | X | X | X | X | X | X | X | X | | | X |
| 28 | | | | | | X | X | X | | X | X | X | X | | | |

# CASE

# 1

# Caring for Infants

Shawna is sitting in a gliding chair holding 4-month-old Deshi as she feeds him a bottle of breast milk that his mother provided that morning. She gently stares into his eyes, patting him softly and saying in a quiet crooning voice, "Isn't that milk good? Your mama brought that milk for you because she knew you liked it. Yes, she did. Yes, she did. Your mama loves you very much." Deshi focuses on his bottle and Shawna takes a moment to look around the infant room that is part of a larger child care center that serves children from ages 6 weeks to 6 years. In her room, there are currently six children enrolled, aged 4 to 10 months. Shawna notices that Andrew (6 months) has spit up on the mat where he is lying beneath an arch of dangling rings. She looks to see if her assistant teacher, Ronnie, can wipe it up.

Ronnie has just finished changing Ada (7 months old) and brings her over to sit with a support pillow at her back on the floor by a gallon-size clear container and some colorful soft blocks to put into it. She cleans up the mat that Andrew is on, laughing with him as he bats at the rings hanging down. She sits between Andrew and Ada so that she can talk with them about what they are doing. "Oh you are putting lots of blocks in the jar, Ada. There is a red one and a green one. . . ." Ada stops and listens to the rings making a tingling sound as Andrew connects with them. "You hear those rings that Andrew is touching," Ronnie says, and then looks over at Andrew who is smiling. "You hit those rings, Andrew. They made a sound . . . ding, ding, ding." Andrew watches her as she talks and then turns back so he can reach for the rings again.

Deshi's eyes are starting to close as he lies in Shawna's arms. His mouth loses its grip on the nipple of the bottle as he falls asleep. Shawna begins to pull the nipple out of his mouth but he quickly starts sucking again. She leaves it in his mouth, patting him gently for a few more moments, and then when his toothless mouth once more releases the bottle, she removes it slowly. He smacks his lips a few times and then settles into a deeper sleep as they sit rocking for a little while longer. She puts him down on his back in his small crib. Attached to his crib is a 5-by-7-inch photograph of Deshi's mother and father, where he can see it when he wakes up.

Shawna goes back to the gliding chair that is next to the chair occupied by Natalya, who is nursing her 8-month-old son, Sasha. She works close by and enjoys coming over a few times a day to nurse and play with her son for short periods. She is singing in Russian to Sasha as he stares into her eyes and holds her finger. Natalya is remembering the first child care center she visited before finding this one. It was such a contrast. The caregivers talked to each other most of the time and didn't seem to even know how to talk to, nurture, or play with the babies. They had four baby swings all in a row and they were all kept occupied. The babies seemed to have such blank looks on their faces that it terrified her. It seemed that if a baby fussed, the caregivers ignored them or fed them or put them in a swing or in a crib without any

1

toys to interest them. The room décor itself was depressing. She is so happy that she has found this child care center with Shawna and Ronnie. The difference is like night and day.

"That is a beautiful song, Natalya," comments Shawna. "Yes, it is Russian," Natalya tells her. "My mama sings this song for me when I am little." "I think it is so important that Sasha hears all those Russian language sounds when he is still little. I am glad that you are speaking Russian as well as English with him at home. It will be very good for him to know both languages," Shawna tells her. "I'm so glad you say that, because lady who takes care of Sasha before, she says 'No Russian!' She says Sasha can't learn English if he is hearing Russian," shares Natalya. "Oh, no. It is good for him to hear both English and Russian sounds. If you speak to him in Russian and we speak in English here at the Center, then he is getting lots of important language sounds. Children's brains are pretty amazing. Once those sounds are in there, their brains can sort them out into Russian language and English language. Really amazing! The important part is letting Sasha hear all those sounds over and over. It also helps to have those sounds connected to people important to him. That makes him want to pay attention more," Shawna assures her. "You know, that lady did not speak much English with Sasha either. I think mostly she likes it when the babies are all quiet. She puts them in cribs so she does not have to talk much to them. I like when I hear you talk to babies," Natalya confides as she burps Sasha on her shoulder.

Shawna turns to see 10-month-old Olivia arriving in the arms of her father, Troy, who is in a bit of a rush. Shawna goes over to greet them as they come in. As she reaches her arms out to Olivia, Olivia turns and tucks her head into her father's shoulder. Shawna says, "Oh, I see you are not quite ready to say good-bye to your father yet." She takes the diaper bag from Troy and puts it in Olivia's cubby, so that he can give Olivia some last good-bye cuddles. "We are all a little tired today," Troy shares with her. "Olivia's grandma had a birthday last night and the whole family had a celebration. Lots of aunts, uncles, and cousins!" He quickly fills out a daily information sheet and then turns to Olivia, saying "I've got to go now, Livie," as he puts Olivia in Shawna's arms.

Olivia fusses mildly as he leaves. Shawna is swaying and singing a "Good-bye Daddy" song quietly as she holds Olivia so that she can see her father walk out of the door. Olivia is still whimpering when her father is no longer visible and Shawna carries her over to the CD player. She selects a CD that Olivia's parents brought in that has music on it that she has heard at home. As she prepares to play the CD, Shawna talks to Olivia about what she is doing. When she starts the CD, Olivia turns her head to the speakers and stops fussing. Shawna continues to talk to her and hold her, swaying to the music for a few more moments until Olivia starts looking around the room. Shawna puts her down by a low table on which is taped a freezer bag filled with blue water and colored sequins. Olivia stands, steadying herself with one hand, and slaps at the bag with the other. She stares as the sequins scatter and then she slaps it again, laughing at the results.

Xavier (7 months old), who has been asleep in his crib, starts to stir. He wakes up slowly and begins to talk aloud to himself, practicing his new sounds, kicking his feet, and playing with his voice. After about 10 minutes, he rolls over and sits up in his crib, looking around at the room and people. He lifts his arms toward Shawna, and Ronnie, seeing that Shawna is engaged with Andrew and Ada, goes over to Xavier and says, "Hello there, Xavier. Did you have a good sleep? Are you ready to get up, Xavier?" Xavier lifts his arms up toward her. "I think you are ready to get up and come and see all the children."

As she holds him up, she points to all of the children playing. "Look there is Ada and Andrew, and Deshi is still asleep. Shhhh," she says quietly. Moving more into the center of the room, she points to the gliding chairs. "Look. There is Sasha with his mother, Natalya. I think that Natalya is getting ready to go now. And look who is here." Ronnie lowers herself down onto the floor, still holding Xavier. "Look Xavier, Olivia has crawled over to see you. Hi, Olivia, Xavier just woke up." Xavier turns his face away from Olivia when she tries to get very close, making "ah, ah" noises. "I guess he is not ready to play yet, Olivia," Ronnie explains. Then patting his back she turns to Xavier, saying, "Are you still sleepy, Xavier?" He nestles closer into her shoulder for a moment, then turns to look at Olivia again. Ronnie rubs

Olivia's back as she kneels by her, looking up at Xavier. Xavier starts to smile at Olivia, pointing a finger out to her. "Do you think he is ready now, Olivia? Thank you so much for waiting until Xavier was ready to play!" Olivia looks at Xavier and then at Ronnie, and then crawls away. "Bye-bye, Olivia," Ronnie says, looking at Xavier as he watches her move away.

Natalya is getting ready to leave. Shawna has moved to a low couch where she is sitting with Ada, looking at a book. Natalya kisses Sasha and settles him into Shawna's lap. Natalya goes to the door and takes off the special slippers visitors to the room are asked to wear in order to keep the floor clean for the infants. "Dosvadanya, Sasha," she says as she waves good-bye. "Dosvadanya," repeats Shawna as she waves. "Your mama is going now, but here is your blanket that smells just like your mama does. Dosvadanya, Mama." When Natalya is out of sight, Sasha is content to lean back holding the blanket and to look at the book Shawna is holding. "Baa, baa Black Sheep, have you any wool," she sings. The children reach out and touch the fuzzy material on the picture of the sheep. "Yes, there is the fuzzy black sheep with the fuzzy black wool."

As they continue to look at the book, Xavier starts to cry and chews on his hand. Ronnie comes, lifts him, and carries him around for a few minutes, bouncing him gently in her arms and singing a rhythmic song. He giggles and is quiet for 5 minutes or so. Then his giggles turn into a cry and Ronnie takes him over to the charts that parents fill out each morning and looks for the last time Xavier ate. "Oh, it says you didn't eat much when you got up this morning. I bet you are hungry now." From across the room, Shawna looks up from the book and says that she thinks Ada might be hungry too. Ronnie brings Xavier over to Shawna while she goes to prepare some cereal for him and Ada.

Ronnie puts both Ada and Xavier into low feeding chairs and adjusts their bibs so that they are comfortable. She talks to them as she washes her hands and gets the meal set up, telling them what she is doing and that she has some good food for them. Ada watches intently as Ronnie stirs the cereal, tapping her tray and vocalizing "ab, ab." Xavier starts crying with impatience, and Ada's face starts to look like she will join in with him. "Oh, you are very hungry, Xavier. I have some food for you right now! But first I am going to wash off your hands very quickly." She sings a mealtime song as she washes both Ada's and Xavier's hands with separate washcloths and they stop crying to listen. Ronnie sits in front of them in a low chair with their bowls of cereal. She brings the small spoonful of cereal close to Xavier's mouth, then touches it to his lips as he starts to cry again. He stops and smacks his lips as he realizes there is food there. "Yes, there is cereal here for you. Do you want some more?" Ronnie waits a moment while Xavier opens his mouth and then she places the full spoon in it. While he is eating the spoonful, Ronnie turns slightly so that she is facing Ada and also offers her a spoonful of cereal from her spoon and bowl. Ronnie continues talking to the children and watching their cues for when they are ready for another mouthful. When they have eaten enough, Ronnie makes a note of what and when they ate on the communication sheet, which parents read when they pick up their child. After washing their hands and faces, she sets some toys on their trays while she finishes cleaning up the dishes.

When Ronnie is settled with the children on the floor again, Shawna takes Andrew over to the changing table. "Let's get a new diaper for you," she says, as she covers the mat with a new paper cover before laying him gently down. "I need to get my gloves on," she says as she slides them on, then puts her hands down low by Andrew's hand so he can grab it feeling the different texture. Andrew begins "talking" with several different sounds. Ronnie talks back to him, imitating his sounds, sometimes changing the inflection in her voice as if she is asking him a question. Andrew continues his talking, then waits for Ronnie to reply, then talks some more. It is a game he has just learned how to play. When the diaper change is complete and her hands are washed, she takes time to give Andrew's bare legs, belly, and arms a gentle but firm massage while humming a gentle tune. Andrew watches Shawna's eyes and laughs, kicking his legs and moving his arms when she is done. She brings him back to the floor and places him on his tummy near a couple of toys.

Olivia crawls over to Shawna as she sits down by Andrew. She is focused on Shawna's lap and bumps Andrew on her way to it. He starts to cry. Shawna picks him up and says, "Oh Andrew, did that hurt you or startle you? Perhaps both, huh? That's okay, that's okay, Andrew. Olivia didn't mean to bump you, did you Olivia? Olivia's just feeling excited. You will be more careful next time, won't you Olivia?" Andrew becomes calms and Shawna sits him back down next to her. He goes back to mouthing his toy. "It looks like Andrew is feeling better now. Did you want to sit in my lap, Olivia?" Olivia moves into Shawna's lap where she sits for a few moments before she "cruises" over toward the bulletin board. She steadies herself with one hand on the sofa and then reaches out to a conveniently placed big foam cube. As Olivia cruises around the cube she comes to a set of foam steps that she crawls up. She sits up on her knees and smiles back at Shawna. "You are up on top now, Olivia!" states Shawna. Olivia claps her hands and triumphantly exclaims "gaah!" Shawna moves closer to her as she twists around back on her hands and knees and crawls down a ramp to the floor. Olivia finds herself by the wall where large family photographs are posted close to the floor. She babbles as she crawls along in front of the pictures. "Look, Olivia. Here is a picture of your grandma," says Shawna. "Your daddy said that grandma had a birthday last night. Did you sing . . . happy birthday to you, happy birthday to you?" Shawna sings while clapping hands as Olivia does, too. Olivia turns back to look at more pictures.

An aide appears to give Shawna a morning break. She reflects that as usual this has been a busy morning. When she used to work with older children, she always had her day basically planned out. But now she focuses on being flexible and ready to meet the needs of the children as they are presented. She enjoys how she and Ronnie can work together, moving quickly to respond to a child but also taking time to fully engage that child. They always make sure that each of the children is in someone's care. She smiles as she thinks about how tired her voice is from talking with these young children, but she has seen how important it is to them to have words, music, and other sounds to listen to, interspersed with short quiet periods when they can experiment and exercise their own vocalizations, expanding their development and learning. She may take a break, but she will be glad to be back, ready to respond some more and to help them use words and sounds and playful interactions to build their connections to the world.

## QUESTIONS

1. Why do Shawna and Ronnie speak with the children even though they are not developmentally ready to speak themselves? List some specific examples and what the different benefits might be? DAP 2G(1,2)

2. What are some of the strategies Shawna and Ronnie use to build a sense of trust in these infants? DAP 1E(1,2,3,4); CODE I-1.4

3. Why does Shawna encourage Natalya to speak Russian with her son Sasha? DAP 2J(2), 5B,E; CODE I-1.10

4. Why do Shawna and Ronnie use children's names frequently when talking to them individually or about others in the group? DAP 1A, 1E(2)

5. Most of the teachers' interactions with infants need to be spontaneous and responsive to immediate cues rather than planned ahead. Describe some instances in which Shawna or Ronnie respond to a cue and build on it spontaneously. DAP 2B(1,2), 2F(4), 3D(2), 3F

6. Describe ways in which Shawna and Ronnie set up the environment so that it is responsive to children's needs. DAP 2E(1,4), 3F

7. What are some of the techniques Ronnie and Shawna use to keep the infants from crying out of boredom?

8. After a busy session with infants, why is it important for a teacher to take a break? What are the benefits to the children?

# CASE

## 2   Mason in Two Different Environments (Infants)

Critter House, one of the few child care centers in a small rural town, is located in an old two-story house with three small classrooms and a kitchen on the first floor and offices and storage space on the second floor. Children, ages 6 weeks to 5 years, are divided into infant, toddler, and preschool rooms. Mason, age 6 months, has been in the infant room with teachers Henry and Gale and seven other infants since he was 6 weeks old.

Wilma, the director of Critter House, has been running the center for 12 years. She hires family members as staff, all of whom have had their own children and love children. Wilma doesn't have a lot of money for toys, but often gets materials and equipment from garage sales or friends whose children have outgrown them. She believes that the children are well cared for by providing nutritious meals, appropriate rest, and love.

Mason is an only child living with his family who just moved to town about 6 months ago so that his dad could attend school. Mom, Cynthia, works full time as a nurse at the local hospital and dad, Yashar, is an engineering student at the university. Yashar comes from Iran and often speaks both Farsi and English to Mason at home so that he can learn both languages. Cynthia is quite busy working full time, taking care of their small apartment and family, and helping her elderly mother who lives in the same town.

Henry and Gale noticed how active Mason was the first few months they had him in their care. He constantly seemed to wiggle his arms and legs and he began rolling over early. Lately, though, Mason's motor development has slowed down. He seems to hold his body still much of the time and doesn't attempt to creep or crawl.

The two teachers agree that it is a challenge to keep Mason content. He watches others in the room and smiles at them, but he often cries when he is dropped off at child care. In addition, Mason seems to easily tire of the rattles he is given and often cries for attention. Henry and Gale pick Mason up and give him a bottle to comfort him. If that doesn't work they put him in a swing, and he eventually falls asleep. The room is small and the crawlers are constantly on the move, so Henry and Gale like to keep the non-mobile infants up off the floor. There are only a few toys around the classroom, because the babies put them in their mouths. Henry and Gale don't plan specific activities for the infants; they have their hands full keeping the infants safe and don't have time even to read to them much.

Henry has noticed that Mason doesn't vocalize the way the other infants do. He rarely coos or babbles; instead he communicates by fussing and crying. Henry uses a pacifier to limit Mason's fussing and to keep the classroom quieter. Last month Henry spoke to Mason's mom about his delayed language skills. She took him to see his pediatrician and was reassured that there were no medical reasons for Mason's lack of language.

Cynthia has been talking to her mom recently about Mason's child care experience. Cynthia really likes visiting with Henry and Gale when she picks Mason up every day, but she is worried about how Mason is doing. When she compares him to a friend's baby about the same age, he seems to be behind.

Cynthia's mom is also worried about her grandson. She wants to help find another child care setting that will be better suited to Mason's needs. She sees an ad in the paper by a family child care provider who has a current opening for an infant less than 12 months of age. After talking with the provider, Lucy, Cynthia's mother learns that she has been doing family child care for 8 years and has just completed her AAS degree in early childhood education. She believes that she learned a great deal from the classes and that they helped her improve the quality of the program she has for young children. Cynthia's mom is impressed with her conversation with Lucy and tells Cynthia about the opportunity for Mason.

Cynthia calls Lucy on the weekend and takes Mason over to visit her home after work on Monday. Lucy cares for two girls and a boy, ranging in age from 15 months to 4 years. Cynthia is amazed at the play area for the children. In one corner of the kitchen there is a child-sized table and chairs where two children are squeezing and pounding green playdough. In the adjacent family room are low shelves holding plastic tubs filled with sturdy toys and blocks for building, a small bookshelf in a cozy corner filled with board books and other types of books, and a small play kitchen with toy dishes and food in another corner. The children seem happy and engaged in play. The toys around on the floor are all free of potentially "chokable" parts. In another area, there are larger pillows and toys to crawl over and through. The backyard has a large grassy area, climbing structure, and riding toys.

After a warm greeting and brief tour of her home, Lucy shows Cynthia a portfolio to look over and a parent handbook to take with her about her child care home. Lucy invites her to have a seat and look at the materials. Lucy talks to Mason and shows him around the home. As they tour the rooms, they stop to touch some of the toys in the bins. Lucy introduces him to the other children and reads a story to two of them while holding Mason on her lap. Cynthia examines the portfolio containing print evidence of Lucy's education, her child care policies, and photographs showing children involved in various activities while in Lucy's care, including field trips to the zoo and a recent local festival. Cynthia is quite impressed with the variety of activities, the happy faces of the children, and the educational background shown in the portfolio. She also likes the explanation of Lucy's approach to guiding children rather than punishing them.

When Lucy finishes reading to the children, Cynthia talks with her about Mason's current child care situation and her concerns for Mason. Lucy suggests that a more stimulating environment could be what is needed to help Mason's development. She mentions that she takes the children to story hour at the library twice a week and checks out books they like to read. She takes them to the indoor park located a few blocks away several times a week when the weather isn't warm enough for them to play in her backyard. The two women talk some more, and then Cynthia and Lucy say good-bye.

Cynthia really likes her visit with Lucy, and tells Yashar and her mom about it. After these discussions, she decides to move Mason to Lucy's family child care home and gives notice to the Critter House Child Care Center the next day. On Mason's first day at Lucy's family child care home, he is a little unsure initially because of the unfamiliar setting. He cries when his mom leaves, but a child gives him a stuffed bunny to hold and he is soon distracted. Lucy calls Cynthia within the first half hour to reassure her that Mason quickly stopped crying after she left. She says that Mason is enjoying the stuffed animals and the other children seem to be quite taken with him. The rest of the day goes smoothly, with the children helping Mason adjust to his new surroundings.

A few months go by and Cynthia notices Mason's response to Lucy's family child care home setting. He holds his arms out to be picked up by Lucy when he is dropped off in the morning, giving her a big smile. He moves around the ample child care space in her house with ease, and enjoys spending time with the activities, the other children, and Lucy. He especially loves getting out of the house when they go to the indoor park and library. Lucy and the children talk to Mason often and he responds with vocalizations. Mason's mom, dad, and grandmother, inspired by Lucy's practices, talk and read to Mason often to help with his language skills. All areas of his development seem to have improved in just a few short months. His eyes are bright and focused, his fussing and crying are greatly reduced, and it almost seems to Cynthia as if he has awakened from a kind of malaise or "holding pattern" that he seemed to be in while in his previous care setting. Cynthia thinks about how important the quality of a child care setting is to the children's well-being and how glad she is that her mother made the effort to help find Lucy's child care home for Mason.

## QUESTIONS

1. In what ways do you think Mason's experiences were different in the Critter House Child Care Center from his experiences in Lucy's family child care home? How do you think such differences influenced Mason's development? DAP 1D, 1E(2), 2D, 2E(1,4), 3D(2); Code I-1.5

2. What are the major differences in how the two child care settings respond to Mason's individual needs? DAP 3A(1); Code I-1.3

3. How might the child care providers' training and qualifications in early childhood education be a factor in their beliefs and goals about their caregiving roles? Code I-1.1, I-1.2

4. What does Lucy do to help Mason and his mom feel welcome and trusting of her home when they first visit and again on the first day Mason attends her program?

5. What might she do to support the cultural diversity of Mason's family in her child care setting? DAP 2B(1), 5A, 5B; Code I-1.4, I-1.12

# CASE

# 3

# Helping Jack Be Mobile (Toddlers)

## JACK'S FIRST DAY IN FAMILY CHILD CARE

Ava owns a family child care business in her home. Her own high school daughter enjoys helping Ava when she is not in school. Currently Ava cares for five children, ages 7, 6, 4, 3½, and 15 months, and it is now the first day for new 15-month-old Jack. Today Jack enters the foyer in the arms of his mom, Emily. Emily lives with another woman, Darla, and Darla's 10-year-old daughter. Darla also works full time and is involved in Jack's upbringing. Jack has a big smile on his face as he points to the round light fixture in the entryway. "Ball, ball," he exclaims. His mom replies, "That's a light. It looks like a ball, doesn't it?" After Ava greets Emily and Jack, Jack's mom sits on the bench, takes Jack's coat off, and Ava hangs it up on a hook. She shows Emily where to put Jack's diaper bag too, and introduces the other children who are playing in the living room area. The older children are in school this morning. Emily then places Jack on the rug near the shape sorter. "You have the square blue one, Jack," Emily says, as Jack picks up a shape and tries to place it in one of the holes of the sorter. "Does it fit in that hole?"

Jack sits contently in one spot as he explores the toy and imitates his mom's words, "Bu un!" (blue one).

In a few minutes Ava comes over and sits beside Jack. She talks to both Jack and Emily while they use the shape sorter. "My toddlers always seem to love playing with this shape sorter," Ava says. "Here Jack, try this square hole for your piece."

Jack follows Ava's suggestion of which hole in the sorter to try, as he imitates her words, too. "Sare ho" (square hole), he shouts in delight.

Fifteen-month-old Sophia crawls over to the group, picks up the round shape, and tries to put it in the sorter. Jack watches her intently, picks up the star and square shapes, and bangs them together. Sophia crawls away with the round shape in her hand as Jack says, "Ball, ball!" Jack reaches out toward Sophia.

Ava tells Jack, "Sophia has taken the round shape—it is round like a ball, Jack. Sophia has crawled away with it." When Jack turns back to the shape sorter, Ava offers Jack a different shape to try and suggests, "Here's a triangle shape, Jack."

Emily has not left Jack in child care before. Ava asks Emily, "I'm just wondering how Jack does when you leave him at other places, and how you want to handle the separation process here?"

Emily says, "Jack may cry when I leave, but I don't think he will do so for very long. I'd like to stay with him for two hours on this first day, and about a half hour on the second day. Then I need to start working the following day but will stay for about 10 minutes."

"Do you have any suggestions for how I might help Jack during the transition?" Ava asks.

Emily thinks for a minute and suggests, "It usually helps if someone reads a book to Jack as I leave."

"Great, I'll try that. If you can bring Jack in the morning before 8:30 it will be the easiest time for me to read to him. I have only Sophia at that time."

## QUESTIONS

1. What might the advantages and disadvantages be of Jack's mother gradually leaving him at child care for longer and longer periods of time over several days? DAP 5D; Code I-1.3, 1.4
2. What information about Jack is Ava gathering through observation as she interacts with his mom and him?
3. What do these observations tell you about Jack's temperament, interaction style with other adults and children, and language skills?
4. What can Ava learn about Jack from talking with his mom and watching the two interact?
5. What aspects of Jacks development are being nurtured as he explores and works with the shape sorter? DAP 2E(1)
6. Should Ava have tried to get the round shape back from Sophia? Do you think Sophia was wrong to take the shape from the area next to Jack? Code I-1.3

## USING ASSESSMENT TO OBSERVE JACK

A week has passed since 15-month-old Jack began coming to Ava's child care home. Ava has been getting to know Jack by informally observing, interacting, and talking with Emily and him. Ava believes that Jack is an easy-going, happy toddler in her program. His separation from his mother went well. He easily verbalizes by using two-word sentences and by initiating his own words and imitating adult language. Jack is interested in other children and doesn't act aggressively in response to their advances.

He is content to sit in one spot, eliciting attention from others by smiling or talking so that he gets what he needs without having to move. He can crawl, but appears to have little inclination either to crawl much or to try to walk. Emily is delighted in his verbal, cognitive, social, and **fine motor skills**, but is concerned that Jack's gross motor development might be delayed. She mentions this to Ava and asks her what she thinks, and if anything should be done to help Jack. Ava responds that she is also wondering about this. "I have a child development textbook and a developmental chart I can share with you, but these just indicate the ages children, *on average*, develop specific skills. The range of typical development at specific ages is very broad, however. I think at this point I need to make some more focused observations."

Ava wants some objective observations before she talks to Jack's mom about his gross motor skills. She takes a small pad of paper out of her pocket whenever she sees Jack moving about throughout the morning during activity time. She sits off to the side to jot down notes and writes anecdotes concerning his gross motor abilities. Ava writes an anecdote about Jack struggling to pull himself up with the help of a low table as he clumsily steps on the unsnapped leg of his overalls. She writes another anecdote in which Jack begins to crawl, gets the overall fabric caught under his knees, and sits up. He then points to the ball nearby, smiles, and says, "Ba! Ba!" and the 3½-year-old boy rolls the ball to him.

Ava then decides to take a closer look at what Jack does during a 30-minute period. Her 14-year-old daughter, Mandy, likes to assist with the children after school. Ava arranges with Mandy to help the children so that Ava can use the **time sample method** to note what Jack does at 5-minute intervals. For the entire half hour of sampling, Jack sits on the carpet in the living room near the shelves. He manipulates the toys nearby, points to one he likes that is out of his reach, smiles and verbalizes, and then one of the other children or Mandy brings the toy to him.

## QUESTIONS

1. In what ways are Ava's various assessments appropriate for monitoring Jack's development? DAP 4A, 4D, 4F
2. What information do these two anecdotes tell the teacher about Jack's gross motor development and temperament?
3. What conclusions do you believe Ava reached from what you know of her observations? DAP 4A
4. What would you do to help Jack with his gross motor development?
5. Why might crawling be important for Jack's overall development?

## CONFERENCING WITH EMILY, JACK'S MOTHER

Ava decides to set up a time with Emily to share her observations of Jack and ask some questions. She approaches Emily when Emily picks Jack up one day after work. "I'd like to talk with you when you have some time about Jack's wonderful adjustment to my child care program and the concerns we both have had about his mobility."

Emily is happy to have a chance to visit with Ava to talk about Jack. Ava also suggests that if Emily would like to include her partner, Darla, in the conference, perhaps they could work this out by using the speakerphone feature of a cell phone, or by visiting Ava together after the other children have left for the day. Ava and her partner decide to visit at the end of the following day and they let Ava know that they will have Darla's 10-year-old daughter with them.

The next afternoon, Ava welcomes both women and expresses pleasure that Darla has come to the conference with Emily. Ava notices that Darla's daughter Stacie has also come, and she asks

Stacie, "Would you mind sharing a small prepared snack with Jack in the kitchen while we talk in the living room?"

Stacie agrees and Ava guides the parents into the living room area where they all have a seat. To begin the conference, Ava describes Jack's many positive experiences in child care and indicates how much she enjoys caring for him. All agree that his verbal skills are advanced for his age and that he engages adults and children around him in a positive manner. Ava then discusses her informal observations and the results of the anecdotal records and time sampling regarding the mobility issue. She supplies the family with paper copies of her observations. Ava says, "Jack is making only a few attempts to crawl, and when he makes little progress, he uses other methods to get what he wants. Older children often give him books and toys he asks to see. I do this for him as well, but I am starting to think perhaps I should not do this so often."

Ava asks Emily and Darla about Jack's experiences at home. Darla reports, "Stacie loves to carry him around, give him baths, and play with him."

"Jack's family physician was concerned about Jack's mobility delay and wanted to run some tests on him," Emily adds, "But Darla and I really can't afford that. We hope that Jack is simply just a little slower than other children in his physical development and will walk when he is ready."

Ava then tells Emily and Darla that she wonders if there are some roadblocks for Jack that they aren't aware of. "Can you think of anything in the observations or your own experience that might discourage Jack from crawling?"

They think briefly about Ava's observations and the current discussion. Emily says, "I can see that perhaps our family has been too helpful to Jack, but I know he will be awfully unhappy if we stop helping him."

Then Darla says, "Jack has mastered unsnapping the legs on his one-piece overalls, and they hang from his shoulders like a cape. I think maybe Jack's clothes often get in his way. It might help if we replace his overalls with some pull-up pants that don't unsnap."

Emily covers her mouth in surprise and says, "I never thought of that!"

Ava kindly replies, "It is easy to overlook the forest for the trees. I agree with your conclusions. Let's see if pull-up pants help Jack's mobility and why don't we all try to help Jack a little less often, and wait longer before we help him, to encourage his motivation to crawl?" She asks, "Do you think this might be a good plan, and can you think of anything else?"

Ava writes out the plan in an outline form on a paper tablet, placing a piece of carbon paper under the top sheet so that there is one copy for the family and one for her. She checks to see if Emily and Darla are both comfortable with the plan as it is written. They agree to the plan, and Ava asks them to keep thinking and observing Jack at home. They agree and Ava suggests they compare notes via e-mail over the next few weeks. She then thanks them for coming. As they are packing up Jack and his things, Ava talks to Jack and finds a few more complementary things to say about him as Emily and Darla depart.

## QUESTIONS

1. What were the benefits of asking Emily if she would like to include Darla in the conference with Ava? DAP 5A, 5B, 5E, 5F; Code I-2.2, 2.3, 2.4

2. What were the benefits of Ava asking Emily and Darla if they think there is anything in the observations or their own experience that might discourage Jack from crawling? DAP 5E, 5F

3. Ava asked Emily and Darla to work at home with Jack on the strategies she has planned to use in child care. How is this effective in helping Jack's development? DAP 5A

4. What information would you ask from Emily to help you better understand Jack's development? DAP 5E

5. What additional suggestions might you have for Emily to help with Jack's motor development?
6. Do you feel the need to know whether Emily and Darla are lesbians or just very good friends? Why?
7. Why did Ava include lots of positive information and opinions regarding Jack during the conference with his family? DAP 5E; Code I-2.8

## IMPLEMENTING THE PLAN

Ava learned valuable information about Jack's development during the conference she had with his family. Now she develops a plan of action to work on helping Jack become more mobile. First she asks her daughter and the other children in her child care program to say "in a minute" and let Ava respond to Jack's requests for help in obtaining things that he can't reach. Ava explains the reason for this. "Jack needs some encouragement to use his own ability to crawl to get what he wants." She will make him wait a little longer than he wants to get things, and she will also verbally encourage his use of crawling to get them for himself.

Emily purchases and dresses Jack in pull-up pants without snaps. This makes it easier for Jack to crawl, pull himself up on furniture, and take steps. Emily, Darla, and Stacie also work on acknowledging Jack's requests but taking a longer time to actually help him get what he wants, meanwhile encouraging him to crawl to get it himself. Stacie decides she will often demonstrate crawling for Jack as well. Ava suggested that they try to get Jack interested in the toys by holding them up and excitedly saying something like "Come over here, Jack! Look at this puzzle. Can you find the place where the ball goes?" At times Jack is encouraged to move to get toys that are placed just out of reach. His favorite toys are placed on low tables or chairs and he is encouraged to crawl over to them, stand, and take a few steps to reach them.

Ava and Emily report weekly to each other on Jack's progress. Within a few weeks Jack is making tremendous gains in crawling to get the toys he wants, and he pulls himself up to reach books on the low table or couch. Everyone is pleased that their efforts are paying off and several of the other children in Jack's new child care home compliment Jack often each time they see him achieve a new mobility milestone.

## QUESTIONS

1. How does Ava encourage the children and families in her care to consider and contribute to each other's well-being and learning? DAP 1B; Code I-2.9
2. In what ways does Ava provide a responsive environment for Jack to develop his gross motor skills? DAP 2E(1)
3. Why do you think Ava asked the other children to respond verbally to Jack's requests but to let her handle them?
4. What other suggestions do you recommend for Ava and Emily to use to help Jack?
5. In what way was observation useful in planning activities and methods of interacting with Jack? DAP 4C
6. What do the supportive comments of the other children indicate about the characteristics of Ava's child care home? DAP 1A, 1B 1E(1)

# CASE

# 4  Edward and Keon Invent a Game (Toddlers)

Bettina sets up an activity on the art table to encourage toddlers to explore papers of similar colors but with different textures. As children pick up different papers out of the trays, Bettina helps them find descriptive words such as smooth, bumpy, slippery, and sticky. Children can then seek out a sticky place on a big piece of paper to put their small piece of paper. Bettina plans to put this group project up on a low place of the wall so that children can continue to feel the textures and link them to the words she has introduced.

After sitting at this activity for a few minutes, 20-month-old Keon looks over to see 15-month-old Edward crouch down behind a big curved foam block and then pop up. Bettina looks on as Keon jumps from his chair with a huge smile on his face, rushing over to where Edward has once more disappeared behind the block. Keon stands in silent expectation that Edward will reappear and squeals in delight when he does. This sequence of disappearance and reappearance continues for about 3 minutes to the delight of both children. Then Keon decides to return to the texture project.

As Keon approaches the art table, Bettina welcomes him by pulling out a chair for him, saying, "Here is a place for you Keon." Once he is settled, she comments that "I saw you playing a game with Edward. It looked like you were having fun!" Keon looks up at her, smiling. Using her own hand, she moves it below the table and then pops it up, saying "Edward went down and then he popped up!" Keon crouches down in his chair when she says "down" and stretches his body up as she says "up." Then he is ready to focus on the textured papers again.

## QUESTIONS

1. Bettina encouraged children to select where they would put their textured papers rather than directing the placement so that the project would look "neat." In what ways is this an effective teaching strategy to enhance development and learning? DAP 2E(1,2)
2. Bettina's teaching approach allows Keon to leave the table rather than requiring him to stay until all the children were done. In what ways did this promote Keon's learning? DAP 1B, 2F(1,2); Code I-1.3, I-1.5
3. How did Bettina support the learning that was initiated by Edward? How did Keon respond to this support? What additional benefits to Keon might come from Bettina's teaching strategy? DAP 3D(2)
4. Based on this observation of Keon and Edward, describe another activity that could be offered to these children.

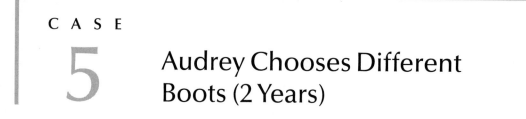

# 5 Audrey Chooses Different Boots (2 Years)

Children in the classroom for 2 year olds are getting ready to go outside. It rained the night before and there are puddles in the play yard. The lead teacher, Yolanda, has decided that the children need to wear boots when they go out to play so that they can walk in the puddles without getting their feet wet. The classroom intern, Helen, begins putting boots on a small group of children. She sits on the floor with Joey and as she puts on the boots that she has selected for him, she sings, "Joey's wearing red boots, red boots, red boots, Joey's wearing red boots so he can go outside." She repeats the same procedure for Joshua, Maria, and Katya. Each child is eager to sing the song and easily participates in getting their feet into the boots and tucking in their pant legs.

When it is 2½-year-old Audrey's turn, she is busy putting a baby doll to bed and does not respond to Helen when she asks her to come over to get her boots on. Helen tells Audrey to make sure the baby is safe and warm in the bed and then come put on some boots. In the meantime, Helen puts boots on another child, singing the same song. Now Helen starts singing to Audrey and Audrey comes over to her to get ready to go outside. Just as she did with the other children, Helen selects a pair of yellow boots for Audrey, but when she starts to put them on, Audrey shouts "No!" while kicking her feet.

"We need to put boots on so your feet won't get wet!" states Helen firmly.

"No! No!" Audrey is now screaming and kicking making it impossible to slip the boots on.

Helen starts to sing "Audrey's wearing yellow boots . . .," but Audrey shouts "No yellow boots! No yellow boots!"

Helen restates the rule that everyone is wearing boots today because of the puddles but Audrey only cries harder.

Teacher Yolanda comes over and squats down by Audrey. "Audrey, Helen trying to put boots on your feet and you are screaming 'No yellow boots!' Are you saying that you do not want these?" asks Yolanda, holding up the yellow boots.

"No," says Audrey, calming down. "I want the red ones with the blue stripe."

"Oh, you want the red ones, not the yellow ones. You were very frustrated when we didn't know what you wanted. You can just tell us what your plan is with a gentle voice. You do not need to scream. When you tell us the problem without screaming it is much easier to help you," says Yolanda, using the gentle, calm voice that she is encouraging Audrey to use.

Audrey runs over to the boot box and picks out the red pair with the blue stripe and brings them back to Helen. "Now sing about my red boots with a blue stripe," requests Audrey with a smile.

Audrey helps Helen tuck her pant legs into the red boots with the blue stripe while singing the song, laughing as she tries to squeeze all those words into the tune. "Now you are all ready to go outside with your red boots on," says Helen. "I didn't know that you wanted these red boots but I am glad you told me so that we could work together."

## QUESTIONS

1. Often rules help make the classroom day run more smoothly. Yolanda chose to use respectful listening to engage cooperation with the "boot rule" rather than focusing on obedience. In what ways does this strategy create a caring community of learners and support the growth of Audrey's self-regulation abilities? DAP 1C(4), 1E(1); Code P-1.7
2. What strategies did Helen use to gain cooperation from the children? Were they effective? Why or why not? DAP 1C(1)
3. What strategy did Yolanda use to gain Audrey's cooperation when she was refusing to put boots on? Was this strategy effective? Why or why not? How was it different from what Helen did? DAP 1C(1,3), 2F(2)
4. How do the interactions with the teachers support Audrey's social and emotional growth?
5. Continuing to think about supporting social and emotional growth, what strategies could be used if Audrey repeatedly found reasons to refuse to put on boots when asked? What if she insisted on boots that another child was wearing?

# 6   Nurturing Connections in Rafael's New World (2 Years)

## RAFAEL'S FIRST DAY

Shontelle greets 2-year-old Rafael and his mother Rosa as they enter the toddler classroom at around 9:00 A.M. Rafael and his mother are originally from El Salvador and moved from Modesto to Redding, California about a month ago to live near her sister and her family. Rosa will be working mornings, 8:00 A.M. to noon, Monday through Friday, for one of the wireless phone companies in the area. She is delighted that Redding School District has a child care program, Turtle Bay Child Care Center, at the elementary school close to her apartment. She does not begin work for 2 weeks and is glad that she can be available in the classroom to assist Rafael as he adjusts to the child care program. She is hoping that this program will be a good choice for Rafael, a place where he can learn and play, and at the same time learn English and prepare for his elementary school years.

From their prior phone conversation, Shontelle knows that for Rosa and her son, Spanish is the first language. She smiles and greets them in Spanish with simple greeting phrases she knows. Her assistant, Jorge, can speak both English and Spanish fluently. He speaks with both Rafael and Rosa and shows them to Rafael's new cubby to hang up their jackets. Then Jorge shows them around the classroom.

As they walk, they see several pictures on the walls that include children and their families that appear to be of various ethnic backgrounds, including Latino children. As Rosa looks closely at the pictures, Jorge comments that these are photographs of the children and their families who are a part of the toddler program. Rosa scans the large areas with foam surfaces for crawling, walking, and climbing. She and Rafael watch several children hold and carry foam shapes as Jorge shows them the large foam block area nearby. As they walk further, Rosa looks over at the carpeted picture book reading area. They watch an assistant teacher read and talk about a story with three other children. There is also a housekeeping area with a set of multicultural dolls, a small bed, a high chair, and several other props. Jorge tells Rosa how much he appreciates her willingness to participate with Rafael during his first week or two at child care and how this will enhance his adjustment into the classroom setting.

As they talk, Rosa asks about the ages of the other children in the classroom. Jorge tells her there are about 12 toddlers in this classroom with five teachers, Shontelle, Jorge, part-time teaching assistants Lisa and Martina, and intern Sara. He also points out the general schedule that is posted on the wall. It includes self-selected playtime, hand washing, snack time, outdoor time, a large group time for songs, finger-plays, and games, and a small group story time. He mentions that for children and parents who arrive before 8:00 A.M., a breakfast is available. Rosa tells him that she will try bringing Rafael to child care before 8:00 A.M. and see if he can adjust to an early morning routine. Jorge tells her that he encourages parents to participate in center activities any time their schedule allows them to do so.

In between greetings with other children and families, Shontelle watches Rafael hold his mother's hand and wrap his other arm around her leg as he turns and holds his face and body close to the front of her body. Every other minute, Rafael turns his face and looks toward Jorge, then buries his face again. When they stop by the sand table Jorge introduces Rafael and Rosa to student intern Sara, a preservice teaching intern, who is seated on one side of the table. Sara greets them and invites Rafael and his mother to feel the sand. When Rafael turns his head toward Sara, Rosa takes his hand and they touch the sand together. After several minutes, Rafael releases her hand and stands facing the sand table while moving his hands through the sand. Rafael watches as Sara pushes the sand into a mound. Then he pushes sand toward the mound. Shontelle observes Rafael's involvement and smiles. Later, Sara points out the small cup containers that can be used to scoop and pour. Jorge checks in with Rafael and Rosa frequently and encourages both of them in their involvement.

Rafael loves to touch, pat, and push the sand. As he and his mother continue to do this, several other toddlers join him. Jorge sees their enjoyment as they push sand toward the middle and look at each other. As Rafael continues his play, Rosa realizes that she is no longer sitting beside him as she did earlier, but is now sitting a couple of feet behind him,

Rafael seems delighted to try new activities. After spending 10 minutes at the sand activity, Rosa sees him look over at the foam block area and point with his left arm and hand. As he takes some steps toward this area, his mother follows him. They walk over to several foam shapes. Martina holds out a triangle shape for him to grasp. He grabs it and holds it close to his body and smiles. Martina talks to him about his shape and moves his hand back and forth over the foam texture. She shows him a circle shape, and he shouts, "Pae-ota" (pelota, meaning ball) as he looks at the foam. Martina replies in Spanish, "It looks like a ball and let's see how it feels." Together they stroke the texture and move around the edges of the circle as she talks about the round circle shape. Rosa watches as Rafael continues his involvement and other toddlers also touch and hold the foam shapes.

After riding in a wagon, walking around the play yard, and scooping sand into containers during outdoor time, Rafael sits on his mother's lap for large group time. Several other parents, who are able to return to the center about 30 minutes before the end of the program, are invited to sit with their children and sing songs in a short circle time. Shontelle welcomes everyone with her "Hello Everyone" song. Then she introduces Rafael and Rosa to the others. Jorge speaks Spanish to them and others in the group who are also Spanish speakers. Jorge then leads the "Hello Everyone" song in English and Spanish. Next Jorge spends several minutes asking Rosa if there is anything she would like to share about Rafael's family. Jorge translates her words and tells the group that Rafael enjoys playing with his three cousins. A few minutes later, as teachers say their good-byes to the toddlers and their parents, Shontelle introduces Rosa and Rafael to another family, Enriche, Sofia, and their son Agustin. As Shontelle and her staff talk over future curriculum ideas and plans with several other parents, she observes the two families as they enjoy conversing in Spanish and laughing over the next 15 minutes. As they watch their children gaze at each other and smile, Enriche suggests that Rosa and Rafael join him, Sophia, and Agustin for an afternoon at Turtle Bay Park. They then wave "good-bye" to the staff as they depart.

## QUESTIONS

1. In what ways do Shontelle and her staff include and support Rafael and Rosa in this new classroom experience? DAP 1A, 1B, 1E(1), 2B(1), 2J(2,3), 5C; Code I-1.10, I-1.11, P-1.2, P-2.5
2. What are the benefits for Rafael and Rosa as Shontelle speaks simple Spanish phrases? Consider how Rosa would feel about her initial classroom experiences without a staff member who speaks Spanish? How would this limit the experience for her and Rafael? DAP 1A, 1B; Code I-1.10, I-1.11, P-2.5
3. What possible resources would you consider if no one on your staff could speak the primary language of a child and family? Code I-1.11, P-2.5

4.  Name two curriculum goals for the toddlers you can deduce from this section of the case study. DAP 3A(1)
5.  How can English-speaking children benefit from the bilingual contribution Jorge offers as he speaks in Spanish and English in the classroom? How does this contribution impact staff, parents, and the program in the community? Code I-4.2
6.  Consider the impact of Rosa and Rafael meeting Enriche, Sofia, and their son and describe how this relationship may nurture Rafael's development and involvement in a variety of ways. Describe how this relationship may support Rosa's role as a parent. Code I-2.9
7.  Imagine that you are a parent from another cultural background and you are in an unfamiliar town or city, speaking a language that only a minority of people shared. What are some of the feelings you would experience as you entered a new program for your child? What are some of the feelings your child would experience?
8.  How would you describe Shontelle's role in the classroom on this day?
9.  In what ways would you connect or follow up with Rosa and Rafael during the first days and weeks of their involvement in your classroom? DAP 1E(1), 5B, 5C, 5E, 5F; Code I-2.6

## RAFAEL'S SECOND DAY

Rafael and Rosa return the next morning. They are greeted at the door by both Shontelle (in English) and Jorge (in Spanish) and Jorge invites them to join him for breakfast. They sit with Martina who is speaking in English with Amarissa and her 2-year-old daughter Angelina as they eat their snack together. Jorge greets each person by name in Spanish and passes Rosa and Rafael pieces of soft, ripe pear with a cracker to eat and enjoy as they continue to talk about what they did to get ready for school this morning. As they converse, Rosa and Amarissa talk about their families and things they like to do, watching both Rafael and Angelina as they converse. Rosa is delighted to be making some new connections for both her son and herself.

As they finish their snack, Jorge invites them to place their napkins and plates onto a center tray and sets it on a cart that is later rolled into the kitchen area. Jorge then suggests that they walk outside. Rafael looks ahead, holding Rosa's hand as they walk along with Angelina and Amarissa. "Mira, Mira!" ("Look, Look!") exclaims Amarissa to Angelina as she points to an outside table full of water and then smiles at Rafael and Rosa. Today the outdoor sensory table is filled with water and small, floating, animal-shaped sponges. Sara, who is sitting nearby, greets them and invites them to touch and squeeze the shapes and sponge the nearby child-size plastic chairs and table. Rafael releases his hand from his mother and picks up a sponge and smiles at Sara. As he watches her, Sara dips another sponge in the water, squeezes it, and moves the sponge over the table. Rafael dips his sponge and repeats the same actions while laughing.

Two other toddlers, Michael and Emma, walk over to the activity as Rafael holds his sponge and watches them. Sara greets them and offers them each a sponge to help clean furniture. Jorge continues to converse in Spanish to Rafael and Angelina and their mothers while Sara converses in English with Michael and Emma. Jorge likes to speak to very young children in their native language as much as possible as they are acquiring fluency in their first language heard from their parents. Jorge also knows that toddlers like Rafael and Angelina will feel more comfortable in this classroom if a familiar language is used there. He is careful to also include Michael and Emma in their conversations, using English and translating as needed between the two languages to help the four children get to know each other.

Shontelle keeps an eye on Rafael as he becomes involved. Later Jorge walks up to Rosa and talks to her about the activity in Spanish. Jorge encourages her to sit at a nearby table and watch Rafael. When she does, Rafael continues sponging off furniture along with Angelina, Emma, and Michael. Then he looks at Rosa and continues to sponge. He looks at her a number of times as he continues his play. Jorge and Shontelle approach her together and suggest that in the days that follow, she can sit a little further away from him each day as Rafael's comfort increases in the classroom, and, move in and out of the room as he becomes more relaxed without her close by.

## QUESTIONS

1. What areas of development are encouraged and supported for Rafael during breakfast? How does this activity support Rosa? DAP 1A, 1B, 2I(2); Code I-2.5, 2.9
2. Describe the developmental skills exercised by the sponge activity. Which of these skills is Rafael involved with during his play? DAP 2E(1), 3F
3. What kinds of feelings and concerns do you think Rosa has while she is watching Rafael?
4. How would you begin a conversation with Rosa at a later time to increase both your own and her understanding of how to help Rafael adjust to the classroom?
5. Suggest two ways you could extend this activity to continue to encourage Rafael's interest and involvement. DAP 2F(2-4)
6. Suggest an activity that you could facilitate the following day that would continue to encourage Rafael's social and emotional development. What would the activity setup look like and what would you do and/or say to Rafael to encourage his involvement, as well as his social and emotional skills?

# 7 The Library Construction Project (2 Years; First Grade)

## A PROJECT EMERGES FOR THE MEADOW ROOM

It is the beginning of spring term at Glenview School, a private school for children ages 18 months through 12 years. The school uses the **project approach** to integrate learning in the classrooms. On Monday, as children and parents walk from the parking lot to the school's entrance, they pass the familiar public library building located just around the corner from the school. One side of the building is fenced off with a new chain-linked fence. Parents of children in Dalia's Meadow class, ages 30 to 40 months, relay their children's questions about the library to her. Dalia talks to her children at breakfast time about the library they passed on their way to school today. Quite a few of the children answer excitedly, and indeed have many questions. Maggie is especially animated when she is talking about the "diggers" and asks, "Can we tsee? Pwease, we go tsee digguth?"

Dalia is making plans for a walking trip to view the construction area in a few days. She will need to get permission slips signed and parent volunteers to help her assistant and her to keep the children safe during the trip.

The following Friday, after eating their morning snack, the whole class walks over to see the part of the building that is fenced off and the large equipment working in the area. Maggie stands very close to the fence and intently watches the digging equipment. She points to a backhoe that is digging, exclaiming, "Wook! Digging big hoh!" Dalia acknowledges Maggie's statement and tells the other children nearby to watch the backhoe digging.

Upon returning to school, Dalia gathers the children on the rug and talks with them about what they saw and what they think might be happening. She decides to use the Library Construction Project to study vehicles that help with construction, since several children in her group talk quite enthusiastically about the trucks they see.

Dalia reads picture books about construction equipment to the children and talks about her past experience of watching apartments being built down the street from her house. She sends a letter home to parents letting them know about the new Library Construction Project. She describes the project approach, indicates how the study of digging equipment has emerged, and asks for input on their children's interests about construction. She mentions in her letter that when a topic for a project is initiated by the teacher it is especially important to build common background knowledge within the group before the study begins. Many parents talk to her about their children's excitement about the topic and some bring books to share in class. To help build a sense of class unity about the project, Dalia sets up construction-building situations with trucks and blocks, both in the sensory table with small digging trucks and outside in the sandbox with construction vehicles. The children eagerly use the play equipment to imitate what they saw at the construction site and in the books Dalia has read to them.

After a week or so, and several field trips to visit the library construction site, Dalia uses a tape-recorder to record what children say about the vehicles. She records language samples while they play with digging equipment and talk about stories being read to them about construction. One time Maggie remarks, "My twuck has big whees!" Jim counters, "My hah bih soop (scoop)!" While reading stories questions come up such as "What does this truck do? How does the driver make it work?" Dalia uses the information from her ongoing assessment she has recorded to create a **curriculum web** that she will share with the children at circle time.

During the next week Dalia talks with the children at lunch time. She shows them the curriculum web she made using pictures to illustrate what she believes the children have learned about construction vehicles and what questions she has heard them ask. What parts do the trucks have (wheels, windows, scoops, etc.)? What is the job of each vehicle? What does the driver do?

To document what the children are learning with the Library Construction Project, Dalia takes pictures using the classroom digital camera, prints them, and gradually adds to a picture book she is making with the children to record the Library Construction Project's progress over the next month. Children tell her what they remember about the events in the pictures, and Dalia writes their words below each picture. They regularly "read" the book to review the progression of what happens with the Library Construction Project. Maggie frequently asks Dalia to read the part about the "digguth," and they talk about what the machinery does to help with the construction project. Maggie's father reports that Maggie is now playing with her older brother's toy trucks, although she had little interest in them until now. Maggie's father thanks Dalia for her support of Maggie with this project and asks how he can continue her interest at home. Dalia lends Maggie's family one of Maggie's favorite books they have been reading in class. She suggests that Maggie might like to observe another construction site Dalia has noticed near her home.

When the library addition is complete, the class invites parents, other classrooms, and the library staff to come to an open house one afternoon in the first-grade classroom, since the first grade has also been studying the Library Construction Project. The visitors examine the Meadow Class book and listen to Dalia's tapes of their conversations about the construction. The first graders also share the project books that show what they have learned, and the older children introduce the visitors to some models of the trucks and construction site that they made with clay.

Children continue to request playing with the construction toys in Dalia's classroom and often want to read stories about construction vehicles. Dalia reflects on the Library Construction Project and to what extent her learning goals have been achieved before moving on to another project.

## QUESTIONS

1. How does Dalia encourage self-discovery and an emergent curriculum with her children? DAP 2F(1,2,3); Code I-1.5
2. How does Dalia build on children's previous knowledge and help them to move forward with new concepts and skills? DAP 3C(2)
3. In what ways does Dalia involve families in the new project? What value do you see to this approach? DAP 5F; Code I-2.3
4. In what way is the Library Construction Project meaningful for the Meadow Room children at Glenview School? DAP 2F(3), 3D(2)
5. How do the teachers stimulate curiosity and learning with this project? DAP 2F(2), 2F(4)
6. What was the purpose of the open house at the end of the Library Construction Project? DAP 5C; Code I-2.8, 2.9
7. What was the purpose of Dalia's assessment of the Library Construction Project at its completion? How would you use the information from reflections to modify your teaching practices? DAP 4C, 4D; Code I-1.7

## A PROJECT EMERGES FOR THE FIRST GRADE

On the first day back from spring break the children in Ruby Tyree's first-grade class are also very interested in the new addition to the library that is being built around the corner from their school. Six-year-old Kuan-yin is especially excited to tell Ms. Tyree about his walk to school. "Guess what I saw, Ms. Tyree," Kuan-yin exclaims. "Lots of workers at the library. They're building something on the library I think. We could go and see!" he suggests. Ruby is surprised to see this enthusiasm in Kuan-yin because he has been fairly quiet most of the school year. She can't remember when she has seen him so excited.

Later that day, Ruby takes her class over to see what is happening. Kuan-yin asks, "How do the workers know what to do?" He notices workers walking around the construction site with clipboards, talking to each other. They have very large books open and are pointing to places on the paper as they talk. Kuan-yin remarks, "I think they are the bosses. They tell the construction workers what to do."

Upon the class's return to school, the children are very excited about what they have seen and want to talk about it some more. Ruby talks to them about doing a project on the library's new addition. She gathers the group on the carpet and guides them through a process of helping her make a curriculum web of what they already know about construction and what they would like to learn about it (see Figure 7.1). Kuan-yin talks about the construction workers and wants to know more about what they need to do to build the library's new addition. Ruby and the class decide they are most interested in studying the different jobs people do in the construction project. The class decides to document what they are learning by making a video. Together they compose an article for the "Family Newsletter" describing the class plans for the Library Construction Project and asking parents for their input and assistance.

Ruby helps the children gain information for their project by setting out all of the building materials she can find and she purchases a large bag of gray clay to aid in the children's involvement in the project. She talks to the library personnel about her class's interests in the construction. The children's librarian invites the class to come for a story time. She reads stories about construction workers and helps the children check out books from the library on the subject. Ruby invites a foreman from the construction site to visit the class and talk about her job and those of the other workers and the foreman agrees. A parent who is a contractor also visits the class, bringing with him several old hardhats and an old book of blueprints.

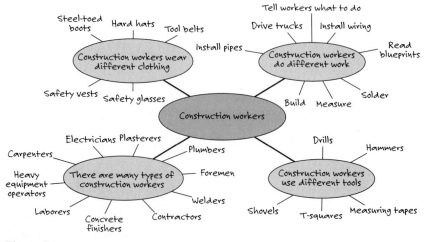

**Figure 7.1**

In addition, the children make frequent trips to the construction site. They use the classroom digital camera and camcorder to record the progress of the project. This will aid their later written documentation of what the workers are doing as they build the library's new addition. Kuan-yin continues to be excited about this and participates in his seat work with great enthusiasm. Ruby feels very gratified that he has found something that thoroughly engages him in the **learning processes**.

Ruby uses ongoing observations and work samples to document the children's development and learning and to plan many focused activities related to construction workers in various areas of the curriculum. For example, she sets up a math center with the old construction hats, blueprints, and measuring materials to explore. For literacy skills the children write in their journals about the new information they are learning. They use "guess & go" invented spelling, drawings, and photographs to illustrate their ideas. For geography she has the children make a two-dimensional "blueprint" of their playground structures. Kuan-yin is very involved in the class activities; he spends a lot of time writing in his journal and drawing pictures to go with his descriptions of the construction workers' jobs. On several occasions he announces that he would like to be a foreman some day so he can be the boss.

The teachers videotape the workers at the construction site, the class visitors, stories that are being read, and the class activities. When the class finishes with the project, they invite parents, the early preschooler classroom, the library staff, and several construction workers to a lunchtime celebration party to see the video, the clay models, the book of drawings and writing, and other documentation of what they have learned. Later, Ruby reviews the Library Construction Project and assesses how well her learning goals have been achieved.

## QUESTIONS

1. Why do you think Kuan-yin became so interested in his "seat work" during this project?
2. How was the Library Construction Project similar and different for the first-graders in comparison to the younger children? DAP 2C
3. The staff at Glenview School value the project approach and involve each others' classes when they share what they have learned. How does this practice help to build cooperative relationships among co-workers? How do the children benefit? Code I-3A.1, I-3A.2
4. In what ways does the project approach strengthen the sense of being part of a learning community for children in this classroom? DAP 1C(1)
5. How did the current project build relationships with the community?
6. If the school were to approach project learning by using the same project topic across age levels, all at the same time, with teachers in particular classrooms adjusting the project to meet the developmental needs of their children, how might this change the children's experiences?

# CASE

# 8

# Observing Stephen's Aggression (3 Years)

In the past, 3-year-old Stephen frequently resorted to hitting other children playing near him when a disagreement occurred about a toy or another child rejected his idea. The lead teacher, Anthony, and his assistant teacher, Miriam, have been working with Stephen to teach him ways to cope with conflict without hurting other children, and they have noticed a decline in his physical aggression.

However, today Anthony becomes particularly concerned when he sees Stephen hitting a child who was already crying about another incident. This new situation seemed to be an escalation of his old aggressive behavior. Anthony and Miriam decide they need to carefully observe this new frightening situation in order to determine the best way to stop it. Why would Stephen want to leave his play situation and hit a crying child?

Anthony and Miriam plan to stay especially alert to Stephen's behavior at the first sign of tears in the classroom so that they can see the entire sequence of events. The next day a child begins to cry in the classroom. Anthony observed what happened to this child. Three-year-old Betty bumped the edge of the table as she walked by and started to cry. Stephen is playing with the blocks. He raises his head and looks at Betty. Stephen quickly jumps up and runs over to where Betty is standing. Miriam has been **shadowing** Stephen and she moves quickly to follow him. He arrives to where Betty is crying, stands in front of her, and attempts to gently wrap his arms around her with a relaxed, concerned look on his face. Betty stiffens her back and pushes Stephen away from her, crying "Noooooo!" Stephen immediately squints his eyes and tightens his mouth. His body tenses and he raises his right hand, looking as if he is about to hit Betty. Miriam is close enough to grab Stephen's upraised arm and prevent him from hitting Betty.

Anthony moves quickly to where Miriam and the children are. While Miriam squats down and puts a comforting arm around a crying Betty, Anthony kneels down by Stephen putting a firm, restraining arm around him and moves him away from Betty. Anthony remains calm as he speaks to Stephen.

"Miriam and I can't let you hurt other children, Stephen. Betty is safe now, but she looks very frightened. See how she is crying? She thought you were about to hit her. Were you, Stephen?" Stephen looks down, and doesn't answer Anthony's question. "Did you see that Betty was crying when she bumped herself on the table?" Anthony asks. Stephen nods his head vigorously up and down. A look of hope crosses his face, and his body is still very tense but he is not trying to strike out. Anthony continues, "I saw you come over to Betty when you heard her crying. What did you want to say to Betty?"

Stephen's body is relaxing and he looks at Anthony as he is talking. "Hugs," he states clearly. "Did you want to give Betty a hug when she was crying?" Stephen nods, still looking into Anthony's face. "Let's ask Betty if she wants a hug," Anthony suggests, and Stephen shifts his gaze to Betty who is sitting on Miriam's lap on the floor. "Want hugs, Betty?" cajoles Stephen. Betty tenses when Stephen talks to her and pushes herself back into Miriam's lap, watching Stephen closely. "No," she says quietly. Stephen tenses his body at this response. "I think Betty is a little scared right now," explains Anthony. "You wanted to hug her and make her feel better but she said 'No!' It made you very angry when she said 'No!'" Stephen nods his head. "But sometimes people don't want hugs. We have to ask first and if they say no, then we have to listen." Stephen looks at Anthony and then over at Betty. "When you were angry and started to hit her, Betty became frightened, so we need to think of another way to help her feel better. Betty says no hugs. What else could you do to help her feel better?" Stephen gets very quiet for a minute and then with an excited expression on his face, he says "ice pack!"

"Good idea, Stephen. Why don't you ask Betty if she wants an ice pack to put on her bump?" Stephen moves close to Betty and says, "Ice pack? You want ice pack for your owie?" Betty continues to sit in Miriam's lap but she smiles and says, "Yes, for my owie," pointing to her hip where she had bumped it on the table. Anthony asks Betty if she wants to come with them when he and Stephen go to get the ice pack. She takes one of Anthony's hands and Stephen takes the other and they go to get an ice pack. Stephen hands it to Betty. After a moment they are both finished with the ice pack. "Shall we ask Betty if she is all better now?" suggests Anthony. "All better now?" asks Stephen. Betty nods her head "yes." Squatting down between the two children, Anthony says, "Stephen, you really wanted to help Betty feel better when she bumped herself on the table but she didn't want a hug, did she?" "Nooo!" says Stephen. "Did she like it when she thought you might hit her?" "Noooo!" says Stephen. "What did she want?" "An ice pack!" says Stephen triumphantly. Anthony replies, "Right! When someone is crying, you can ask them, 'What will make you feel better?' You can talk to them or you can go get a teacher to help you. Then everybody feels better and nobody gets angry or hurt."

## QUESTIONS

1. What new information did Anthony gather by looking at the beginning, as well as at the end part, of the problem behavior? DAP 2B(2)
2. How did this new information impact the way in which Anthony and Miriam responded to the situation with Betty and Stephen? DAP 1C(1,2,3,4); Code I-1.5, P-1.5

3. If Anthony had not observed Stephen's intent and had punished him for his aggression, what learning opportunities would be lost?

4. Why do you think Betty did not want hugs from Stephen? How was Betty feeling about accepting help from Stephen at the end of this process?

5. On which of Stephen's interests and strengths was Anthony building when he asked Stephen to think of a way to help Betty feel better. How did he scaffold this learning for Stephen? DAP 2G(1,2)

6. What strategies were used to make sure that Betty felt safe in this process? DAP 1E(1)

7. What were the benefits for Stephen of Miriam's being quick and stopping him from hitting Betty? What were the benefits for the other children in the class? DAP 1C(1,2), 1E(1); Code I-1.4, I-1.5

# 9

# "I'm Sorry" (3 Years)

ofia Santiago enjoys staying for about 10 minutes with her 3-year-old daughter Jovita when she brings her to the child care classroom each day. This morning she and Jovita are using wooden blocks to build a tower. Nearby 3-year-old Dakota is also creating a structure with some blocks. Both children are involved in their own play with no interaction between them until Jovita walks toward the block shelf seeking another block. As she approaches Dakota and his structure, which is right in front of the block shelves, he sits up and shouts "No!" swatting Jovita on the leg. Sofia is very surprised by this attack on her daughter and immediately goes to her. As she holds her child, she looks at Dakota and says, "You need to apologize right now! Say you're sorry." Dakota responds by shouting, "My boks!" and turning back to his own structure.

Taj Washington, the lead teacher, comes over and squats down next to Jovita to show his concern as she is comforted by her mother. Then he asks Dakota if he knows why Jovita is crying. Again Dakota responds with a gruff, "My boks. No Jovita boks." When Taj turns to Jovita to ask why she is crying, her mother responds, "She was just going to get another block and he hit her, right on the leg!"

"Oh," says Taj. "You were both using the blocks to build. Is that right, Jovita?" She nods. "Dakota, were you worried that Jovita was going to take too many blocks and you wouldn't have any?"

"My boks. My tower up to sky!" asserts Dakota, stretching his arms over his head.

"Yes, these are the blocks you are using," confirms Taj pointing to the blocks immediately next to Dakota. "Where are some blocks that Jovita can use?"

Dakota turns to look at the shelved blocks. "Der," he says pointing to the far end of the shelf. "My boks! Ah my boks!" he asserts, pointing to the rest of the blocks.

"There are enough blocks for both of you to use," Taj assures both Dakota and Jovita, who is now standing next to him as he sits on the floor by the block shelf. "Dakota, you can show Jovita where the blocks are that she can use. You do not need to hit her. Hitting her makes her cry because it hurts. Do you see that Jovita has tears on her face?" he asks with a concerned voice, pointing to her face. Dakota looks from the blocks to Jovita's face. "When you hit her, it made her very sad and scared." Taj puts an arm gently around Jovita, saying, "I am so sorry that Jovita got hurt. It makes me sad when anyone in our class gets hurt. We need to keep everyone safe in our room. If you talk to Jovita and tell her where more blocks are, then you don't need to worry that she will take the blocks you are using. Then everyone is safe and no one gets hurt." Taj pauses and then asks, "What can we do to make Jovita feel better?"

After a moment of silent staring at the floor, Dakota asks, "You OK now?" as he looks directly at Jovita.

She nods, rubbing her leg. "All better now!" she says.

"Here one," he offers, handing her a block from the shelf before going back to his building.

"I am glad you are feeling better now, Jovita, and Dakota, thank you for offering her a block so you can both build," says Taj.

Sofia looks at her watch and realizes it is time for her to go. She and Jovita walk to the door for their good-bye hug and kiss. "Good-bye, Sweet Pea. I love you a bunch!" "I love you a big bunch!!" giggles Jovita as she waves to her mother vanishing at the door.

That morning when Taj is checking e-mail during his office work time, he finds a message from Sofia:

Hi Taj

I just wanted to check in with you about a concern I had. On my way to work, I was thinking about the incident this morning when Dakota hit Jovita. I realized that you never made Dakota apologize. Manners are very important to me and I was hoping that Jovita would be learning about making apologies in your class. Do you ever make children apologize? Jovita really loves coming to your class every morning and talks a lot about all her friends. I just don't understand about the apologies.

Thanks, Sofia

Taj promptly replies to this e-mail:

Hi Sofia

I am so glad that you mentioned this concern to me. Manners and helping children learn social skills that allow them to relate well to others are also very important to me but you are right, I do not require the young children in the class to apologize if they are not ready. My goal is to help children develop the ability to *genuinely* feel sorry when one of their friends is hurt or an accident happens and in order to be genuine when they say "I'm sorry" children first need to develop some foundation skills. We do a lot of work on those skills so that they will be ready and able to say "I'm sorry" and really mean it.

Again thanks for bringing up this issue. I know it is an important one for you and I would like to talk with you more about how we can reach this shared goal. Do you think you would have some time this afternoon when you pick up Jovita? Or we could set up another time if that is more convenient.

Thanks, Taj

That afternoon, Sofia enters the room with a smile and watches Jovita who is busy putting a puzzle together with Dakota. Taj, smiling, walks over to her and says, "Hi, Sofia. Did you have a chance to look at the e-mail I sent you?"

"Oh, yes. Thank you. I would like to talk to you some more about it though. Do you still have some time now? I can't stay too long but I did have some more questions."

While Taj checks in with his assistant teacher to tell her that he will be talking with Sofia for a few minutes, Sofia kneels down by her daughter to give her a hug. "Hi Sweet Pea! You look really busy with that puzzle. You can play a little while longer. I am going to talk to Taj for just a little bit, OK?" Jovita nods and goes back to the puzzle.

Taj and Sophia step into an adjoining office and Taj offers her a chair. On his desk is a painting that Jovita created earlier in the day and Taj shares it with her mother. "I know you don't have much time but before we get started, I just wanted to show you what Jovita did today. She started with just one color . . . this blue. But then she asked for the red and this green and this purple. She was so excited to have so many colors on her paper. She really wanted to show it to you and I told her that she could take it home this afternoon." Taj explains this with an animation that reflects the joy he takes in Jovita's excitement about her work. He hands Sophia the painting.

"Thanks!" says Sophia, smiling as she looks at the painting. "We have a special place in the house where we put these pictures so everyone can see them." After she looks at the picture a moment, Sophia says, "But I really wanted to check in with you about the apology business. What did you mean when you said in your e-mail that children need to have some foundation skills before they are ready to say 'I'm sorry'? Jovita already knows how to say 'I'm sorry' when I ask her to. What else does she need to know?"

"Well, I guess we are talking about two different skills," Taj reflects. "There is the skill of pronouncing the words 'I'm sorry,' which most of the children in our class can do, and then there is the skill of actually feeling the emotions involved in being sorry. At our Parent Night last month, we discussed how the children in this group are all working on the big task of learning to correctly identify feelings and emotions in themselves and in others."

"I remember that," Sophia responds quickly. "That's when you were talking about labeling how kids are feeling . . . if they're sad or happy or angry."

"Right," confirms Taj. "We work at connecting the correct labels to the emotions that children are feeling and also to the expressions that they are seeing on the faces of others. Since being sorry is an emotion just like being angry or being happy, we need to be just as careful to label it correctly. Young children sometimes strike out intentionally in anger or fear and are not feeling at all remorseful about what they did. I think that happened today. Dakota did not look like he was feeling 'sorry.' He seemed to be angry and perhaps fearful that his territory was being invaded so I did not want to put an incorrect label on those feelings by requiring him to state that he was sorry. Since these 3-year-old children in the class are still trying to correctly identify all those strong emotions that are exploding inside of them, it can be confusing if we label what they are feeling with different terms. That is, if we label a child's feelings one time as 'angry' and then another time when he feels the same way, we label it 'sorry.' This can really hamper the process of learning to identify and manage their emotions. Also, if a child is consistently required to say 'I'm sorry' even if she or he is not sorry, then that child will often decide that the phrase is a magic escape from responsibility for his or her actions. That is, 'I can do what I want as long as I say I'm sorry afterward. I don't actually have to *feel* sorry. I just have to *say* sorry.'"

"Well, that part makes sense to me. There is a little boy down the street who does that. I don't want Jovita to be like that," Sophia confides. "But I do want her to learn to say 'I'm sorry' and I want her to mean it! How is she going to learn if she doesn't have to practice it at times when she should say it?"

"Oh, I really agree with you about how important it is for children to learn to be genuine in their apologies," says Taj. "We use a variety of strategies to help children learn the social skills that they need in order to truly feel responsible for their actions and to feel sorry when a wrong is committed rather than just saying words that are not connected to genuine feelings. This morning I wanted Dakota to see that his actions made Jovita sad and scared and I had him look at her sad face and tears. He did not appear to be feeling sorry at that moment for his actions and I can't control what he is feeling, but I can ask him to take some responsibility for his actions. So I had him think about what he could do to help her feel better. He chose to check in with her and offer a block to use. In other circumstances, a child might get an ice pack for comfort, help wash off a wound, or repair a damaged toy."

"I am glad they are learning responsibility but what about the being sorry part? How are they going to learn to say 'I'm sorry' if no one is saying the words?" Sophia ponders.

"Oh, we work on that part, too!" Taj smiles. "I'm glad you brought it up. Again thinking about what happened today, I knew that Dakota was not feeling sorry but I wanted him to see that I was feeling sorry, so I modeled that behavior for him by saying how sorry it made me feel when Jovita got hurt. I used those important words and tried to make my face really show how sad I was feeling. Children can learn a tremendous amount by watching our actions! Jovita has learned a lot from you about being gentle with the other children.

"I also wanted to mention that I tried to make sure that the children were not only identifying Jovita's scared and sad feelings, but also Dakota's worried feelings. I want the children to know that when they are feeling worried there are positive strategies they can use, such as showing where there are more blocks so that everyone will be safer. Dakota feels safer because the threat to his block collection is taken away and Jovita will be safer because Dakota knows a different way to defend the blocks than with a swat on the leg."

"But Jovita wasn't going to take his blocks. She just wanted one and there were lots. He didn't have to worry," Sophia suggests.

"You know that and I know that, but Dakota didn't know that," says Taj. "It is all part of the skills that the children are working on: being able to label other people's emotions as well as their own and being able to use that knowledge to predict the actions of others. These are skills that children need to have before they can become empathetic and take the other child's point of view. As these skills grow, the children become more successful in managing their feelings in positive ways and their own feelings are not so overwhelming to them. With these foundational skills, children do start showing cues that they are feeling sad or remorseful when something happens to someone else. When this occurs, I try to be there to identify that feeling for them, too, so that the label 'sorry' gets connected to the proper inner feeling."

"So if they look like they are feeling sorry, then you ask them to say sorry?" Sophia questions with a twinkle in her eye.

"Right!" Taj chuckles. "If a child looks as though he or she is feeling sorry about another child getting hurt, I might say 'Looks like you are feeling very sorry that Susie got hurt' or I might say 'Do you want to tell Susie that you are sorry she got hurt?' and leave it up to the child to say 'I'm sorry' or not. I would also ask the responsibility question, 'What can you do to help Susie feel better?'"

"Oh my goodness," exclaims Sophia, looking at her watch. "I need to get going but I am really glad we had a chance to talk. You gave me lots to think about! Now that I know that we are working on the same goal, I'm feeling better about this. It is a little more complicated than I thought, but when you put all those pieces together it starts to make sense."

"Well, I am certainly glad that you asked all of those questions. It really helps me think about what I need to do to help children develop all the skills they need," Taj says as they walk back into the room. "Just let me know if you have any more questions about the subject of apologies and feelings. Do you think other parents would be interested in having a discussion on the topic?" Sofia is nodding her head as her daughter grabs her around the knees for a hug. "I'll check with a few more parents and then perhaps set up a time," he says, laughing with Sofia and Jovita at the exuberant greeting. "Are you ready to go home with your mother, Jovita?" Taj says as he squats down to give Jovita a good-bye hug. "Look! Your mother has the picture you painted with all the colors. Show her all the colors you put on it."

Jovita and Sophia gather up all of her belongings and head for the door. "Good-bye, I'll see you tomorrow," Taj says in farewell. "And let me know, Sophia, if you have any more questions."

## QUESTIONS

1. Why does Taj feel that children need to learn to identify feelings (their own and those of others) before they can be socially responsible to each other? Why is it important to take into account the feelings of all participants in a dispute, not just those of the injured party? DAP 1C(4), 2F(6), 2G(3), 3C(3)

2. What are possible unintended outcomes if children are required to say they are sorry even if they are not? What are the underlying messages that children might learn from such teaching?

3. Describe the cues that indicate how both children were feeling after Taj helped them deal with their problem? How did this process help build a "caring community of learners"? DAP 1B, 1E(1)

4. Taj is very careful to use each of the children's names when talking to them. What role does using names play in creating a "caring community of learners"?

5. Describe the different ways that Taj used to communicate with this parent. Were these successful? Why or why not? What other methods could be used? DAP 5A, B, D

6. Sofia expressed concern about how apologies were handled at school. How successful was Taj in balancing the concern of the parent with his own concern for appropriate practice in the classroom? Why is this balance important? DAP 5D; Code I-2.4, I-2.7, P-2.2

# CASE
# 10
# Learning to Climb (3–5 Years)

In the school outdoor play yard is a large play structure with various platforms, bridges, bars, and a slide. Alicia (3 years old) and Kevin (3 years old) are sitting together under one of the 3-foot-high platforms putting rocks in a pail. Adrian (4 years old), Helene (5 years old), and Julia (5 years old) are standing on the platform at one end of the "monkey bars." Julia stretches out and grabs the first bar with both hands and swings her body free of the platform. After hanging for a few seconds she focuses on the next bar and swings her body again, grabbing the next bar with her right hand while still holding on to the last bar with her left. In this position, she hangs for a few more seconds and then drops down to the pea gravel below. With a smile, she announces, "I can do two bars!"

Adrian moves to the edge of the platform, saying "I can, too!" When he puts his arms up, his eyes open wide as he feels his body leaning into space and he quickly steps from the edge putting his arms down. "I want a turn. I can do it," he laments. "Help me, Nadine!" Nadine, the lead teacher in this group, steps close to where the children are standing on the platform. "Adrian, did you want to hang onto the bars like Julia did?" Adrian nods, "Yeah, I can do it."

"What do you think you need to do first?" asks Nadine. Adrian begins to stretch out one hand tentatively before he pulls back, saying "Help me!"

"Is it a little scary to reach for the bar? Does it feel as though you might fall down?" asks Nadine. "Yeah," agrees Adrian. Julia has come up behind Adrian. Nadine suggests, "Let's ask Julia what she did when she reached for the bar." Julia stands next to Adrian and with a serious voice she says, "See, I stand right here and go like this." Nadine notices that Julia braces herself by placing one hand against an upright post of the structure as she leans toward the bar with the other hand. "Adrian, did you see that Julia puts one hand on this post so that she won't feel as though she is falling when she reaches for the bar? Do you want to try that too?"

"Yeah," says Adrian, "it's my turn." He watches Julia who has swung out to the second bar again and then drops. Adrian begins to grab the bar with both hands and then pulls back. "Remember to put one hand on the post," advises Nadine. Adrian puts one hand on the post but is still very tentative as he begins to lean toward the bar. "Hold me! I'm falling!" he cries. Nadine calmly says, "I will stand right here next to you while you try to touch the bar. Let's see if your arm is long enough to reach it. You hold on to the post with this arm and stretch this other arm out. You don't have to grab it. Let's just see if your arms are long enough to reach. I will be right here and I will not let you fall."

Adrian holds tightly to the post and stretches toward the bar. At first, his fingers barely touch; then he loosens his grip on the post a little and his arm stretches far enough to grasp the bars. "Look!" exclaims Nadine, "Your arms are long enough to reach! You can grab the bar!"

"Yeah, I can do it! I have long arms and I can reach. I'm a monkey with long arms!"

"I'm a monkey, too!" says Helene who has been watching Adrian work on this challenge. "I can swing like a monkey. It's my turn."

"Yeah we're monkeys, aren't we?" laughs Adrian and he steps back so that Helene can grab the bar. She swings out to the second bar and drops down, just as Julia did. The two girls run together over to the sand box. Nadine keeps an eye on the entire playground as she continues to stand by the platform and monitor Adrian. He repeatedly practices grabbing for the bar with one hand while stabilizing himself with the other.

Kevin and Alicia come over to the monkey bars with their bucket of pebbles and watch Adrian as he grabs for the bar with two hands. They start to climb up and Adrian retreats back to the safety of the platform. Kevin moves toward the edge, holding up his arms. Nadine watches him and when he starts waving his arms up and down in frustration, she asks him what he wants to do. "I want to swing!" Kevin declares. "You want to hang from the bar and swing?" Nadine clarifies. "Yes! I can't!" Kevin wails. His feet are about 6 inches from the edge and his arms are stretching in the direction of the bars but missing them by about a foot.

"You need to have long arms to reach this high bar," advises Nadine. "Julia and Helene reached this bar before they swung out. Every day you are growing, but your arms still aren't quite long enough right now. Let's find a bar that you can reach. Let's go find one for you, Kevin." With a furrowed brow, Kevin watches Nadine move from the monkey bars over to a set of stationary bars. The first set is 2½ feet tall. "Can you hang from this bar, Kevin?"

Reluctantly, Kevin comes down to the bars, followed by Alicia. He stands next to the bar, which comes to his shoulders. "I'm too big!" exclaims Kevin. "Yes," agrees Nadine. "You need a taller bar. Will this one work?" She points to the 3½ foot bar. Kevin rushes over to the new bar and reaches up to grab the bar that is a few inches above his head. He picks up his feet and hangs from the bar with a smile of achievement on his face. "Look, Alicia. I did it!" Alicia comes over and stretches up her arms, too, to grab the bar. Kevin moves over to make room for her and they both laugh as they hang like monkeys. "Two little children, hanging on the bars. One named Kevin, one named Alicia. Hooray for Kevin, hooray for Alicia. Two little children, hanging on the bars!" sings Nadine.

## QUESTIONS

1. Nadine was supervising a group of children of varying ages, skills, and temperaments. How did her observations of these children impact her expectations of them on the climbing structure? DAP 2B(2); CODE I-1.3

2. What strategies did Nadine use to help each child develop his or own potential? DAP 2F(4), 2G(1,3)

3. Did Nadine use praise or encouragement as one of these strategies? What impact did it have on the children? DAP 2F(7)

4. In what ways did Nadine encourage children to support each other's growth? DAP 1A, 1B

CASE

# 11

# Natural Settings: "Does It Tickle?" (3–5 Years)

Twenty 3- to 5-year-old children from Kathy McMurphy's class at a community child care center emerge from the building onto the play yard. The play yard is about 50 by 75 feet in size and is used by three classrooms of 20 children each, but at this time Kathy's room is the only group on the play yard. As Kathy looks around, she sees that the children are gathered in four separate areas. There are six children in the sandbox, three children by the raised bed garden space, and three children walking along a shrub-lined pathway next to a wood chipped area. There, six children are maneuvering through an **obstacle course** made out of some of the playground's **loose parts**.

Kathy walks over to the group on the path. The three girls are intently looking through the low shrubs that line a pathway. "I found one!" Brenda screams and the other two girls immediately scurry to her side to see what is in her hand. Kathy asks what she found. "It's a ladybug!" Brenda announces with delight. "I want one!" demands Caitlyn. "Where did you find this ladybug, Brenda?" Kathy asks. "Over here," answers Brenda, pointing to the bush next to her. "OK," says Kathy. "Maybe you could look for one there, too, Caitlyn." Caitlyn and Lin carefully start pulling back leaves to see if they can spot their own ladybugs. Brenda stands and watches the insect crawl over her hand, gently turning her wrist as the ladybug gets to the edge so that she can keep it in sight. As it crawls between her fingers, Brenda starts to giggle. "Does it tickle?" asks Kathy. "Yes," laughs Brenda, "It has teeny, tiny feets, and they tickle me." "Can you see the feet?" asks Kathy. "How many feet do you think it has?" "Oh, lots and lots of teeny, tiny feets," Brenda asserts. "Can we count them?" asks Kathy. "No, they're too teeny, tiny," answers Brenda.

"Oh, do you remember that we have some little bug boxes with magnifying lenses on them so we can see teeny, tiny things?" asks Kathy. "Do you think we should find one of those bug boxes so we could make the ladybug feet bigger? Then maybe we could count them." "Yeah, great idea!" exclaims Brenda.

On her way to the porch to search for bug boxes, Kathy quickly asks her associate teacher, Daniel, who is with children by the raised bed gardens, to keep an eye on the obstacle course until she gets back. While their teacher is gone, Brenda helps Lin and Caitlyn in their search for some more ladybugs. When Kathy gets back all three girls have bugs they are inspecting in carefully cupped hands. In anticipation of more bugs, Kathy has brought three small clear plastic boxes with removable lids that contain magnifying lenses so that each girl can have one. Lin and Brenda each carefully place their ladybugs in one of the little boxes and snap the lid on. Caitlyn chooses to let the ladybug crawl up and down her arm.

"Now, can we count the legs?" asks Kathy. Brenda and Lin stare intently into the little boxes. Brenda points with her finger as she counts, "One, two, three, four, five, six! There are six teeny, tiny feets. How come it has so many feets?"

"Why do you think it has so many feet?" asks Kathy. "Maybe it can run really, really fast!" suggests Brenda. "It needs six feet . . . I mean legs, so it can be an insect," announces Caitlyn. "Insects have six legs like in our book!" As Caitlyn is looking down at the ladybug crawling on her arm, it flies off. "Oh, it's gone. Up in the air!" she complains. "Did it jump off?" asks Lin. "No it went way up in the air. It has wings and it flies," explains Caitlyn. "Mine doesn't have wings," says Lin as she studies her ladybug in the clear bug box. "It just has spots."

"They have spots and wings," asserts Caitlyn. "Where? I can't see them!" exclaims Lin. Kathy leans over and suggests that she look very carefully to see whether the ladybug will show its wings hiding under the spots. While these girls are engrossed in their ladybug studies, Kathy checks in on the six children who are exploring the obstacle course, so that Daniel can focus again on the garden area. This morning, she created this obstacle course from loose parts: a few pieces of climbing equipment, six tires, some boards, and a slide. She watches the children as they climb up and over one of the A-frame climbers, then stretch out their legs to mount the second one. They walk across a board that is placed between two of the tires before spreading their legs to balance on the outside of the remaining tires, which create a path to the slide. After slipping gleefully down the slide, each child rushes back to the climbing frames to start the process again.

As one child walks across the tires, she stops and jumps down on the grass. With the help of two of the other children, she puts one tire on top of another and then adds one more, making a tower three tires tall next to the climbing frame. The next time the children go through the obstacle course they climb up and over the frame, then carefully mount the 2-foot-tall tire tower before leaping off onto the grass with a great "Ta da!" They are thoroughly enjoying their addition to the activity. Kathy walks over to check this new tire tower and shares with the children her observation that they stacked the tires very carefully on top of each other so they don't wobble, making it safe for children to play on it. She also checks to make sure the walking boards are still safely attached by their cleats to the tires and that the A-frames are still in a safe position while they create a physical challenge.

While Kathy is working with the children on the obstacle course, Daniel is talking to a few of the children about making plans to plant seeds. In their classroom, they have been talking about seeds and have put radish seeds and sunflower seeds in a clear container with wet paper towels to see what would happen. They have been looking at some pictures from the seed catalogues and trying to match seeds to the plants into which they will grow. From all the seeds that they have been looking at, they will choose five kinds to plant in their section of the garden. To help them decide, they are a making a graph on which children can draw or paste a picture of the plants they would like to grow.

"Before we can plant seeds," Daniel tells them, "we need to make sure the ground is ready. Let's see if the compost is ready to put in the garden." He lets them look in the compost bin that has been closed up over the winter. "What is in there?" Daniel asks. The children answer:

"It's dark in there!"

"It smells yuckie."

"There are white things in there."

"I see a worm!"

The previous fall, three pumpkins had been put in the compost bin and some of the seeds have sprouted in the dark environment. Daniel carefully puts on a rubber glove and reaches into the compost bin to remove a white sprout about three inches long. "What do you think this is?" he asks. "It's a worm," one child exclaims. "Do you remember how worms wiggled in your hand when we held them before?" Daniel asks. "Do you think this can wiggle?" The children stare intently at the sprout waiting for the long whitish stem to start wiggling. "No!" asserts Melanie. "It can't wiggle. It's a seed. It's growing. My mom has seeds at my house. They're growing, too. With roots. Down in the ground."

"The sunflower has a root, too!" remembers Liam, thinking about the sunflower that is growing in the classroom. Daniel and the children continue to explore the pumpkin sprout trying to figure out why it is white. They decide to leave some of the white sprouts in the compost bin and plant some of them in a pot. They put the pot in the sun and will wait to see what will happen. The children are very busy with this project and Daniel decides to postpone work on getting the garden soil ready for planting until the afternoon.

One end of the garden area is planted with perennial herbs, such as mint, rosemary, and creeping thyme. Kathy notices that several children are running over to the herb garden and then back to the sand box. She walks over to see what they are doing. When she gets there she sees that Aletta and Alejandro are picking rosemary leaves, putting them to their noses for a sniff, and then placing them in a bucket that they take back to the sandbox. On the way, they scoop up some of the fresh grass clippings that were left from mowing the lawn that morning. Kathy asks them what they are making.

"We're making a cake. It's Chang's birthday, so we need a cake," Aletta tells her. "What kind of cake are you making?" Kathy asks. "Oh, it's a chocolate cake. See, we need to mix it up in this bucket," Alejandro explains as he puts sand in and then adds some water from the hand pump that is mounted on the edge of the sandbox. "Yeah, we mix it in here," Aletta adds, as she puts more dry sand in and stirs it with a wooden spoon. "Then we push it down. You have to push down really hard or it won't make a cake. And then we dump it out! See it makes a cake," Alejandro says triumphantly as they all look at the bucket-shaped sand formation that slid out of the bucket.

"Now we need the frosting," Aletta declares as she and Alejandro start sprinkling the grass clippings on the "cake." They reach down into their bucket and take out the rosemary leaves. "These are special. They smell really good. You want to smell them?" Alejandro holds some out to Kathy to smell. "Ummm. They do smell good," Kathy agrees. Aletta searches for some little sticks and collects about six of them. "Hey, Chang! I have candles for your birthday cake. How many are you?" she asks. "I'm five. It's my birthday and I'm five!" asserts Chang, moving over to where they are creating the birthday cake. Aletta carefully pushes sticks into the decorated "cake," counting "one, two, three, four, five" with each push. She has one stick left over. She looks at it, trying to decide what to do with it and then pushes it in with the rest. "Now we have to sing," Alejandro directs. He starts singing, "Happy birthday to you" and the other children in the sand box join in. Beaming at his "birthday cake," Chang blows out the "candles."

After about an hour outdoors, Kathy walks to the porch to get the cow bell and rings it five times, which is the signal for 5 minutes until it is time for the class to come inside. After ringing it she checks in with the girls who were studying ladybugs. Two of them have moved up onto the porch and are drawing pictures of their bugs still in their bug boxes with materials that are kept on a shelf there. Kathy asks them where they can put the bugs to keep them safe while everyone is inside. They decide to let them go under the mint plants "because they smell so good and ladybugs like it there." As Kathy rings the final bell, the children quickly finish what they are doing and run inside.

## QUESTIONS

1. How is the children's learning enhanced by exposure to the outdoor environment? DAP 1D, 2E(1,2,3,4)
2. How would this learning be impacted if the outdoor environment consisted only of metal climbing structures on a rubber mat?
3. How have the teachers used this outdoor environment to develop skills in physical, social and emotional, cognitive, and language areas of development? DAP 3D(1,2)
4. Is this outdoor environment flexible enough to meet the needs of a wide age range of children?
5. What is the value of having materials such as tires and boards that children can move and create things with in the outdoor environment? What issues need to be considered to make the environment safe but challenging? DAP 2F(4,5)
6. How do Kathy and Daniel connect the learning that takes place in the classroom with the learning that occurs outside? What is the benefit of making these connections? DAP 2F(6)
7. Why did Daniel change his plan when the group he was working with discovered the pumpkin sprouts? Was this an effective teaching strategy? Why? DAP 2F(3), 3C(2)
8. How do Kathy and Daniel encourage and support the children to extend their learning on their own? DAP 2F(1)

# C A S E

# 12

# The ABC Train (3–5 Years)

Rebecca has been working part-time in a faith-based preschool program in a small midwestern town for 3 years. The program has a pre-academic focus, with teachers implementing activities related to letters, numbers, and science in their daily curriculum. Rebecca began a 2-year degree program in early childhood education at the local community college in the fall and is taking two classes each term. She is excited to be enrolled in her first curriculum class this spring term and hopes to learn a lot of new activities to use with the preschool children she teaches.

Kenji Kagawa has taught early childhood education classes at the local community college since the program began 15 years ago. He is teaching the introductory curriculum class spring term, which covers the curriculum areas of mathematics, language and literacy, and science. Kenji presents information on current research and practice for each curriculum area. Next the students write an activity plan, practice the activity with their classmates, and then implement the activity with 3- to 5-year-old children in one of the classrooms in the laboratory school.

The first curriculum area covered in the class is early literacy. Kenji is especially interested in this area because he has attended workshops at state conferences and read recent journal articles about how early literacy is correlated with later school achievement. He has thought about the topic and talked with colleagues about the present focus on early literacy. Kenji enjoys working with students on developing and implementing literacy activities that are developmentally appropriate for children of this young age.

Rebecca is quite interested in the early literacy curriculum area because she recalls the difficulty she had learning to read as a young child. She remembers how in first and second grade she avoided reading out loud in class because she didn't know all the words. She would like to help 3- to 5-year-old children get a good start in reading before going to kindergarten so they don't have the same problems she had.

Today in the curriculum class, the students break into small groups of four or five and decide on a literacy activity the group will do with the children in 2 weeks. They have used curriculum books, Web sites, and other resources to develop an activity plan and to share their ideas with each other in the group. From all these ideas, the group chooses one plan to implement with the children or combines several plans to create a group plan.

Rebecca's group discusses the literacy plans each student has brought to class. Vanessa is very eager to try her activity with the children and suggests that the group use it. Most of the group members agree this plan would be ideal for literacy development, but Rebecca has some reservations about it. She states, "I'm concerned that not all the children are ready for this activity. I observed 3-year-old Mika at the beginning of the term in the classroom in which we will be implementing our literacy activity. I noticed that Mika didn't seem very interested in letters and consistently recognized only the first letter in her name."

Vanessa responds, "Well, all the children need to know their letters, so this would be a good way to get Mika on board!"

The rest of the group agrees with Vanessa. They choose her plan to implement next week with the children and ask Kenji to approve the plan. Kenji reads the following activity plan.

## ACTIVITY PLAN

**Curriculum Area:** Literacy
**Age Level:** Preschool
**Reference:** Internet site

## Activity: ABC Train

1. **Rationale:** The preschool children are interested in letters, and many know the letters in their name. If children know letters of the alphabet they will be more successful in school. Not all of the children in the class know all 26 letters. This activity will help the children learn more letters.

2. **Goal:** To promote early literacy development through recognition of upper-case letters.

3. **Objective:** As a result of this activity, the children will name all the upper-case letters in the correct order and then glue them together to make an alphabet train.

4. **Materials/Equipment/Supplies:**
   - Construction paper—-various colors
   - Glue sticks
   - Crayons

5. **Procedure:**
   a. **Setup:** Cut out squares of various colors of construction paper. Write upper-case letters on each square. Leave some squares blank for the engine. Place squares and glue sticks in the center of the table that is set up for six children. Display a model ABC train to show the children how it is made.
   b. **Motivation:** At circle time, introduce the activity by reciting the ABC song with the children. Tell them they will be making their own ABC train at the art table after circle time that has all the letters in the ABC song on it.
   c. **Teaching:** Show the sample train to the children and give each child a blank square and a set of 26 alphabet squares. Have each child make a face on the blank square and glue the lettered squares together in the correct order. Ask the children what the letters are as they glue them down.
   d. **Closing:** Sing the ABC song when they are finished, having them point to each letter as they sing. Display the trains on the bulletin board for everyone to see.

6. **Followup Activity:** Do another alphabet activity, such as matching upper-case letters to lower-case letters that are glued to two sides of a plastic egg.

Kenji sits down with the group and reads the plan. He begins by saying that "You have nicely incorporated the classroom theme of transportation into your plan. I see you noticed that many preschool children are already interested in recognizing letters in their name. That might be a good reason to focus on letter recognition for your literacy activity. Do you remember the areas we talked about that help promote early literacy development?"

Rebecca responds, "Yes, we talked about a lot of other areas that help with reading. I remember that alphabetic knowledge, print knowledge, and oral language skills are really important."

"I liked what you said about shared reading and dialogic reading," Bob adds. "I already read stories to the children; I just have to change how I do it to include more questioning and discussion while I read."

"Right," Kenji replies. "There are lots of ways to provide language and literacy experiences for young children besides letters. I'd like to encourage you to think about early literacy activities in a broader sense. Letters are important for reading but, as you know, experiences need to be meaningful for children. Many can recite the ABCs, but the letters don't have much meaning for them. Children often start learning letters in their names because they are important letters in their lives. They then learn letters that are familiar to them, such as ones they see in their environment, particularly in words that have meaning for them."

"Like 'stop' or 'exit,' right?" asks Bob.

"Yes, and a few of the older preschool children are even spelling simple words such as 'cat,' 'hat,' and 'mat' because they have heard them many times in stories this year," continues Kenji. "The children are each at different stages in learning their letters, and in order to help in this area of literacy, an activity should be flexible enough to meet most of them where they are in alphabetic skills."

Kenji also tells the group that the use of a model ABC train implies that there is only one correct way to do this activity. He tells the students that the use of models tends to limit children's creativity and frustrate children who can't make their work look like the model. Instead, he suggests the students talk to the children individually about making their own unique train from the squares of construction paper and letters as they manipulate them.

"I'll give you two choices with the activity you'd like to implement with the children next week. If you really like the one Vanessa planned, you may modify it so it is more appropriate for the different developmental levels of all the children in the class, or you may use a different one that addresses another literacy area of the curriculum, such as shared reading or oral language. Perhaps you can take pieces from several of your plans and put them together into a terrific activity!"

Kenji moves on to another group in the class that is discussing what he has said. "I hadn't really thought about letters that way," Vanessa says. "It makes sense to consider different levels of the children. I know not all of them are ready for the whole alphabet yet. Do you want to scratch this plan and do someone else's?"

"No," replied Bob. "I like the idea. Let's think about how to modify it."

The students discuss the plan for awhile longer and come up with the idea of using shared reading as their "motivation" since Bob wants to try modifying his reading techniques with the children and change the ABC train to be more developmentally appropriate.

After the students have modified their plan, Kenji gives them suggestions and approves the plan. The next week students practice their planned literacy activities by presenting them to the rest of the curriculum class. After each activity is discussed in class and suggestions are given by Kenji and the students, the groups are ready to conduct their activities with the children. Rebecca, Venessa, and Bob decide on a final plan as follows.

## ACTIVITY PLAN

**Curriculum Area:** Literacy
**Age Level:** Preschool
**Reference:** Internet site

## Activity: ABC Train

1. **Rationale:** The preschool children are interested in letters, and many know the letters in their name. Becoming better acquainted with the letters of the alphabet is an important component of literacy. Not all the children in the class know all 26 letters. This activity will help children become more familiar with letters.

2. **Goal:** To promote early literacy development through experience with upper-case letters.

3.  **Objective:** As a result of this activity, the children will manipulate upper-case letters and include them on an alphabet train picture they have made.

4.  **Materials/Equipment/Supplies:**
    *   20 pieces of construction paper, 11 inch by 17 inch—white for the base sheet
    *   Construction paper—various colors, cut into 2-inch squares, about seven per child
    *   Alphabet letters made from various textured papers, such as sand paper, felt, and cellophane
    *   Three glue sticks for children to share
    *   Eight fine-tipped markers

5.  **Procedure:**
    a.  **Setup:** Cut out squares of various colors of construction paper. Cut out upper-case letters from different types of paper and felt. Place squares, letters, glue sticks, and markers in the center of a table that has a large sheet of construction paper placed in front of each chair.
    b.  **Motivation:** At circle time, introduce the activity by doing a shared reading of the book *Trains.* Talk about the title, author, and what the story might be about before reading it. Ask the children to describe their experiences with trains. While reading the story, talk about how trains are put together, one car after another, and stop to ask what they think might happen next. After the story talk about what happened in the story and what they liked best.

         Pass around a sample of letters cut from different textures and talk about how they will be making their own train pictures at the art table after circle time using letters like these on the cars of their train. They can select which letters they want to use and make their pictures just the way they'd like.
    c.  **Teaching:** Have each child sit at one of the places in front of a large piece of paper. Point out the squares and letters to make a train. Encourage the children to pick up and feel the letters, naming the letters and sounds as they touch them. They can glue squares and letters on their paper to make a train. Some may spell their name or other words if they like. Assist children only as needed.
    d.  **Closing:** After the children are finished have them describe their picture and what letters they chose to put on it. Talk about how each train looks different. Display the trains on the bulletin board for everyone to see.

6.  **Followup Activity:** Do another letter recognition activity, such as following a laminated paper lily pad path that has letters displayed on each lily pad and labeling the letters as they go.

The next week Rebecca and her group come prepared to implement the ABC Train activity. Bob begins by doing a shared reading of a story about trains, and then the children go to the tables to make their ABC Trains. Rebecca works at a table at which Mika and three other children are seated. She wants to pay close attention to Mika while she makes her train so she can see how Mika responds to this literacy activity.

The children choose several colored squares of paper and glue them on their large white piece of construction paper. Some need assistance with separating the colored squares and some need assistance in applying the glue. Rebecca suggests they might like to use the markers to draw parts on their train such as the engine or some connections between the cars.

"We have only three glue sticks, so we will need to share and ask our friends for a turn when they are finished," Rebecca remarks.

"While some of you are drawing, the rest can be gluing letters on the cars of your train. Have you noticed how the letters are made from different materials and feel differently?" she asks the group.

Mika picks up an M that is made from sandpaper and rubs her index finger over and over it.

"It's rough, it's rough!" she exclaims. "I want to glue the M on the yellow car."

Rebecca assists Mika in getting the cap off of the glue stick and then asks, "What other letter would you like, Mika?"

"I want an M," says Mika. She hunts through the letters and finds one made of felt. "It's my M." Again she rubs her finger over and over it and glues it next to the sandpaper M on the yellow train.

"They are mine!" she tells those at the table.

Rebecca remarks, "Yes, your name begins with a M. You have two M's on the yellow train car. Shall we find the rest of the letters in your name for the other cars?"

Mika shakes her head saying, "No, I'm done."

Rebecca writes Mika's name on the white paper with a pencil below the train and talks with her about her picture. Rebecca comments on specific characteristics of each picture as the children show their work to her. Some have letters that spell out the child's name, one spells the words "dog" and "cat," four have random letters glued in a line that looks like a train, one has a drawing of a train and some letters written on it but no letters glued on, and five have letters randomly placed on the paper. Two papers have some or almost all of the letters of the alphabet glued on in order, left to right and top down, although a number of the letters are glued on backward. The use of the markers and the cut out "cars" shows even greater diversity. Rebecca notices that the sandpaper letters don't stick very well to the paper using the glue sticks. She had intended to put the pictures on the bulletin board, but the sandpaper letters tend to fall off them. Perhaps they should have used school glue instead of glue sticks for this activity. She puts the pictures on a counter to dry instead.

After conducting the activities, the college students return to their classroom and each is asked to write a reflection paper on how he or she thinks the activity went, its successes, and how the plan could be changed the next time it is implemented. Rebecca thinks about Mika and the other children she observed doing the activity and sits down to write her reflection.

## QUESTIONS

1. In what ways does Kenji encourage the students to implement a developmentally appropriate literacy activity?
2. How does the second activity plan allow for the different developmental needs and interests of the children? DAP 2C, 2D, 2G(3), 2I(1); Code I-1.3
3. What do you think of having a model of the ABC Train to use in showing the children how to make the train?
4. Under what circumstances would it be appropriate to limit the number of art materials as was done with the gluesticks in this activity? What learning purpose might this serve?
5. How did Rebecca encourage Mika's literacy development while she made her ABC Train? What else could Rebecca have done? DAP 2F2, 2G2
6. What parts of this literacy activity do you think were successful and what suggestions do you have for improvement?
7. Why was it helpful for Rebecca to have observed the classroom and a specific child prior to planning this literacy activity? DAP 2B(2); Code I-1.7

# How a Child-Centered Environment Nurtures Maya, a Child with Down Syndrome (3–5 Years)

## UNDERSTANDING MAYA AND RECALLING EARLIER CHALLENGES

Maya laughs with a broad smile as she embraces her teacher, Akiko, and enters her classroom in an integrated preschool and child care program at Opal Creek Creative Learning Center. "Umm he, umm he (I'm here, I'm here)!" she exclaims as she looks at Akiko, smiles, and moves her tongue past her lips and back and forth. Maya, who is 5 years old, holds the teacher's hands, one in each of her palms, as she shifts her weight from side to side. "Good morning, Maya. You have big smiles to share with us this morning," Akiko replies as she gazes at Maya and then at her parents, Beth and Miguel. Beth hands Maya the caterpillar book they borrowed overnight and says to Maya, "Here's the book to return to Akiko." Maya grasps it with both palms and fingers on each side of the cover and holds it up to show Akiko. Akiko points to the bookcase in the library across the room and says, "Do you think you can place it back on the library shelf?" Just as Akiko says this, Maya exclaims, "I ee id oe ere (I see it over there)" as she quickly steps from side to side to maintain her balance. She approaches the bookshelf and using both hands, returns the book into the empty space. She then quickly picks up another picture book and pulls herself up onto the couch cushion. The library bookmobile came by yesterday and there are a number of fresh library books on the shelves, chosen by the children.

Maya flips through pages pushing her whole hand against the right page until it flips to the next picture. As she does this, she laughs and talks about what she sees in the pictures. As she continues, several other children exchange smiles and giggles with her as Maya pats the bear in the forest scene and exclaims, "He a be (here's a bear)." Kelton sits next to her holding his book, and touches the bear's claws. "Bih kaws (big claws)," he says as he looks on. Lakitia and Eli join in the conversation as they share what they find in the pages of the picture books they are "reading."

Maya and all of the other 14 children, seven girls and eight boys, begin each morning with a self-directed activity hour as they explore several centers such as the library with adjoining listening and writing areas, **dramatic play**, unit blocks, painting, sand and water table, and natural artifacts with magnifying glasses in a discovery area. In addition to Maya, who has **Down syndrome**, there are several other children with special needs in the class. At the age of 5 years, Maya is approaching a developmental age of 3 years.

As Maya participates, she often looks up at a specific child in her area and gives that child objects as she smiles. At times she looks across the room and smiles at individual children as they play. Two other part-time teaching assistants help Akiko attend to Maya's ongoing needs and encourage Maya's involvement. Along with **speech** and **physical therapists**, an **early interventionist**,

Tandi, works with Maya for an hour each week in the classroom and collaborates with Akiko and her staff.

As Akiko, Beth, and Miguel watch, they smile. Beth recalls that as a family over the past year, they have been experiencing this delightful arrival each morning with a borrowed book. She watches her daughter enjoy her special fondness for books with a sense of playful joy and appreciation within each moment. Maya's parents are especially happy they have these delightful experiences with her at Opal Creek in Akiko's classroom. Maya will leave Opal Creek in 3 months and will be attending full-day kindergarten in the fall. They are most grateful for the arrangements and efforts made by Tandi, whose collaborative participation and support for their child are important factors in Maya's classroom progress.

This is especially true as Beth considers Tandi's critical observation of Maya's continuous wandering around the classroom furnishings and activities at her former child care center, Early Years Learning Center. A tear comes to Beth's eye as she recalls these past memories. A little more than a year ago—

---

*Beth listens as Tandi describes Maya's involvement in any planned activity at the Early Years Learning Center as minimal, although she shares her smiles and fun-loving self with many of the children in the classroom. She agrees with Tandi that Maya's teacher, Catherine, appears focused on Maya's challenges as she describes her mumbled speech, her lack of both fine and gross motor muscle strength and control, and her lack of attention and focus on daily academic activities, such as recognizing and working with colors, letters, and numbers. Exasperated, Catherine exclaimed to Beth and Miguel one day, "When Maya moves around the classroom spontaneously smiling at children and giving them hugs, she is being noncompliant and disruptive. She also often wanders away from the group during both indoor and outdoor times and lies down on the floor, whining and mumbling in protest against rejoining the small and large group activities. There is simply very little this child can do and little I can do to help this child!" Tandi, Beth, and Miguel realize that this teacher views Maya as noncompliant and disruptive, and doesn't understand or accept the limitations of her congenital disability.*

*Beth remembers that during this time Tandi is also frustrated as she observes how little attention and encouragement Maya is receiving in this classroom. Both Beth and Miguel express their relief when Tandi agrees to a meeting to discuss Maya's experience with Catherine and to review her goals and objectives. At the meeting, Tandi reviews Maya's **Individualized Family Service Plan (IFSP)** and focuses on one of Maya's early objectives: to participate in small group activities. Tandi points out that the initial expectation is for Maya to participate in one activity with encouragement and then later this objective will be revised to increase her participation to include two or more activities. As the discussion begins, Catherine clearly states that she does not have the experience, time, or energy to work with a child who has this type of disability. In spite of her blatant honesty and the fact that Maya's parents are also concerned about Maya's adjustment in this classroom, Catherine's words sting as her attitude of resentment toward Maya permeates the discussion. Within minutes, everyone agrees that a new classroom program needs to be found for Maya to make progress on the objectives in her IFSP.*

*After the teacher leaves, Tandi describes another classroom program at Opal Creek Creative Learning Center, where a variety of children with mild to severe special needs are encouraged to participate in a mainstream setting along with children who are developing more typically. Beth recalls how Tandi said, "In this classroom each individual child is special and an important member of the classroom community." Toward the end of their discussion, Beth and Miguel agree to consider Opal Creek and Tandi offers to arrange for a visit, observation, and discussion with the classroom teacher.*

*Beth remembers their experience observing the new classroom and meeting with Akiko that remarkable day. Akiko even invites them all to bring Maya to sit next to her at the playdough table. Akiko hands Maya a piece of playdough and suggests that Maya roll one end while Tandi holds the other end. As Maya and Tandi become involved with pressing, rolling, and molding the playdough into different shapes, Akiko gives Beth and Miguel a tour and talks about the schedule for a typical day. It is evident from their discussion that children's playfulness, social engagement, and involvement in a variety of active learning activities are valued as the staff takes into account the needs and interests of each child. Beth and Miguel discuss with Akiko how this classroom could be a better placement option, given Maya's social and playful disposition, her challenges for focused involvement, and her need to progress in her physical, cognitive, language, and literacy skills. Beth and Miguel quickly conclude that this classroom is likely to be a place where Maya can be more successful. They decide to give this classroom a try and make arrangements to enroll their daughter.*

Just as Beth wipes her tear away, her memories fade as she sees her daughter walk toward her in the greeting area. Maya holds her hands and arms out and gives her mom a hug. "Oo aye, mom," she says. "Thanks, Maya, you have fun and I'll be back after story time."

## QUESTIONS

1. How can Akiko utilize Maya's positive social characteristics, skills, and interests to assist her with social classroom routines such as greeting, clean-up, snack time, departure, or other similar routines or transitions? DAP 1B, 1C, 2B(1), 2G(1-3), 2J(4); Code I-1.3, 1.8, P-1.2
2. How can Akiko further encourage Maya's interest in books in future curriculum activities? DAP 2J(4), 3D(2); Code I-1.3, 1.8
3. On what basis did Maya's former preschool teacher, Catherine, conclude that Maya could do very little at school? If you were Beth or Miguel, how would you feel and react to Catherine's comments about Maya? If you were Tandi, how would you feel and react? Code P-1.2, P-1.3, P-1.7
4. How do you think Catherine's perception of Maya might have affected her behavior toward Maya? To whom or to what do you think her former teacher attributed the cause of Maya's challenges? How did this have an impact on Catherine's ability to work with Maya? Code I-1.3, I-1.5, I-1.8, P-1.3
5. How might Catherine's approach with Maya also have impacted the other classroom children? DAP 1A, C(4), E(1,2); Code P-1.1
6. In what ways do you think differences in curriculum in the two classrooms may have affected Maya's behaviors in each? DAP 3C(3)

## CURRICULUM THAT HELPS MAYA PROGRESS

As with all of the 15 children in her classroom, Akiko includes Maya's current specific needs, interests, goals, and objectives as she plans and offers the daily schedule of various developmentally appropriate curriculum activities. Akiko also considers Maya's adjustment to the classroom environment. Based on her early observations, she has noticed that Maya, on occasion, may run and hide if something unexpected happens, such as a fire drill or another child displaying a tantrum. As she and her assistants discuss this behavior with Beth and Miguel, they create a plan to make a small photograph album of Maya's favorite pictures of familiar people, such as family members, her home, a pet, and a couple of favored objects from Maya's room. Beth and Miguel plan to create the album with Maya's participation. Maya could then keep it in her cubby at school. When Maya has difficulty coping with an unpredictable event, Akiko and her assistants can then use the photograph album as a way to reassure Maya that she is safe. Akiko and her assistants believe that this is a critical area to discuss and explore so that they can encourage Maya to feel more secure about her new classroom experience.

Typically, each day begins with the less structured, self-directed activity hour that allows Maya to choose from a number of activity options. These activities allow her to freely express her joy and enthusiasm, especially as she greets other children. Once Maya initiates her delightful greeting, children often greet her and others in return. The overall effect of these positive interactions encourages their social involvement, which also nurtures each child's self-esteem and joy in their social play together.

As Akiko watches Maya smile, give hugs, and hand other children materials and objects they may need in their play, she realizes how much Maya contributes through her social interactions, skills, and interests. Her qualities of playfulness and joy help to inspire an overall social and emotional climate that appears to enhance everyone's involvement in, and enjoyment of the day's learning activities.

At the same time, Akiko recognizes Maya's challenges in several major areas for skill development, such as her fine and gross motor muscle control, **eye–hand coordination**, **speech articulation**, and **cognitive processing skills** for language and speech. She also knows that children with Down syndrome take longer to process directions. She provides all the children with 5-, 3-, and 1-minute reminders before transitions from one activity to another.

Each day, Akiko includes specific materials, tools, and equipment that attract Maya's interest and beginning skill level to help her make progress. Presently, the dramatic play area is set up as a restaurant with a kitchen and eating area. Akiko knows that Maya will be attracted to this kind of activity. Along with cooking pans and containers, Akiko includes plastic measuring cups and tongs to place different foods and meal portions onto plastic plates and bowls to serve and enjoy together at the dining table. The use of the tongs to pick up and place a variety of items will help to strengthen and develop hand, finger, and arm muscles and coordination. Tongs and other tools that grab may also be used in other activities. At the same time, Maya will enjoy the social engagement as she plays with the other children. As Akiko and others talk to Maya about the food and what others wish to eat, she is surrounded with conversational **expressive language**. Akiko also plans to watch and encourage the children to measure and compare a variety of foods. As the children place and take orders, they will be encouraged to utilize markers and pads to draw or write as they take orders for their peer's food selections.

Akiko and her assistants also interact with Maya in strategic ways to encourage her progress in other areas. For example, they know that Maya loves to connect with other children but may not become as involved in activities that focus on motor, cognitive, and language skills. As Akiko observes Maya at the playdough table, she notes that Maya often looks up at children at her table and those in other areas around the room as she lets her ball of playdough rest. Akiko and her assistants help direct her attention back to touching, rolling, squeezing, and pressing the playdough in a variety of ways. Their guidance often helps Maya become more focused on the activity at hand. For Maya and all of the children, Akiko has labels of printed words in English with a small photograph of each item posted on many of the furnishings and materials in the classroom, including chair, table, books, blocks, playdough, kitchen, oven, stove, refrigerator, and mirror.

Akiko is pleased that Tandi, along with a **speech therapist** and a **physical** and **occupational therapist**, are able to work with Maya each week as they participate in free choice activities and a later activity time as well. Akiko also collaborates with Tandi and the other therapists to enhance the kinds of activities and interactions she can include to maximize learning opportunities for Maya. Akiko observes Maya's behaviors frequently to stay informed about her progress on specific skills, as well as her involvement in each of the activities throughout the day. Akiko and her assistants meet daily to discuss their observations of all of the children, including how they can further guide Maya in making progress.

Over the past year, Akiko has observed that Maya generally understands the concept of a schedule and the major activities that occur at different points in the day. As she participates in free-choice activities, for example, she may talk about going outdoors when it occurs next on the schedule (after clean-up). Maya has benefited from more closely monitored guidance with tasks for clean-up. Since she enjoys mimicking the actions of her peers, she is likely to do specific clean-up tasks that they are also doing.

Akiko involves Maya in a special way in the clean-up process. She prompts Maya to help her begin clean-up tasks after the second clean-up time reminder at 3 minutes. Akiko gives her a quart bucket to hold on a nearby table as Akiko shows her six prepared sponges to place in the bucket. As Maya places them in the bucket, Akiko gives the 1-minute reminder. Finally, Akiko begins the clean-up song.

"It's time to put things back, put things back where they go, then wash, wash, wash tables 'til they glow'." As Akiko holds the bucket of sponges by Maya's side, they walk around the activity areas while Akiko's assistants and children begin to return items and materials to their shelf or bin locations. As children finish putting items away, Akiko and Maya talk about who can be offered a sponge to wipe their table. After Maya passes out five of the sponges, she often takes the last sponge and joins others as they wipe tables. Akiko has been pleased with Maya's positive response to clean-up time and her enthusiasm for helping to collect and pass out sponges. She is also delighted at how well the children participate in clean-up tasks and their enthusiastic responses toward Maya as she passes them sponges.

During outdoor time, Akiko features a special physical activity each week to encourage gross motor control, strength, coordination, and balance. All of these aspects of physical development are important for preschoolers, but especially for children like Maya. Akiko knows how important it is to have activities and games that are noncompetitive and fun. These activities work best to encourage children who have major challenges in their physical development. This week, Akiko has set up an obstacle course that begins with blowing air through straws at small, light cars, blowing them across a small table. Next the children crawl through a 15-foot tunnel, walk across a low balance beam, and climb over a set of bars. They often enjoy repeating the process several times. Akiko has included specific tasks that help Maya develop her skills at each point in the course. Control of her facial, mouth, and tongue muscles is important for Maya as she expresses herself by articulating her words. The blowing activity is fun for her, as she blows many times to push the car to the other side. Akiko has noticed that as Maya engages in specific physical tasks embedded in a variety of daily activities, she will repeat actions in an effort to reach her goal until she succeeds. This persistence is a wonderful strength. Maya progresses through the sequence and accepts a little assistance while climbing. During outdoor time, Maya also chooses to ride in wagons, scoop and sculpt with sand, sit with others on the tire swing, participate in adventures in the row boat, and slip down the slide while she is engaged in outdoor play.

Maya's experience with hand washing and snack time work well for her. Passing food, napkins, cups, and plates, using tongs, and pouring juice from small pitchers give Maya and the other children regular exercise in the use of fine motor skills.

Maya also enjoys large group activities, especially singing simple songs and finger plays. Akiko or an assistant often sits near her so that she can be closer to the finger play motions. A favorite for Maya is "Head, Shoulders, Knees, and Toes." Maya and the other children love music along with simple movement routines. These can be as simple as walking, crawling, or jumping in a circle to chants, songs, or recorded music. If large visuals are used for short stories, Maya is more involved with these stories. Akiko has noticed Maya's love for looking at books and has observed that her engagement is more optimal during a small story time segment of no longer than 15 minutes. For this reason, Akiko or other assistants extend her interest in books in the library during the self-directed activity time by reading favorite books to her. During small group time, Akiko assigns four or five children to one of the teaching staff at a specific table with an arranged small group activity. Each table activity is designed for the developmental needs and interests of the children assigned there.

Today Maya's table is covered with newsprint. Each child picks out an animal sponge shape from a paper bag. There are three colors of paint set out in shallow bowls on the table, each with three paint brushes in it. Akiko explains that the activity today is to use the paint brushes to paint the top side of the sponge. The children may use as many colors as they wish. Akiko urges the children to try to remember to put the brushes into the same color paint bowls that they came out of when moving from one to another color of paint or when it is time to get more of the same color of paint. After the children load their sponge with color, they will then press the sponge, paint side down, onto the paper surface to make a print of the sponge animal shape. Maya is brushing blue onto a bear shape. As she does this she brushes the color onto the sponge several times, then dips her brush in the red and brushes the red paint onto the sponge next to and on top of the blue. She continues doing this for several minutes. When she sees Michael, who is sitting next to her, dipping his brush into the yellow, she does the same and places her next brush strokes all over the few bare spots left on the sponge. After this, she continues to paint the sponge, but then sees Michael press his sponge onto the paper surface. Maya smiles as he lifts the sponge and shouts, "A dog, it's a dog!" Then Maya replies, "A doh, a doh (a dog, a dog)." Akiko replies, "You see a dog" and encourages Maya to try out her sponge as she says, "You can try yours too." Akiko helps Maya turn her sponge over and press it onto a clean spot on the paper surface with both hands, then lifts her sponge as she watches the image emerge. She shouts, "A beh, a beh (a bear, a bear)" as she looks at Michael who replies, "A bear."

Other discoveries are shared around the table. Akiko holds out the bag again for children to choose sponge shapes and they proceed to brush colors on their shapes. Later as they look at their animal prints, they talk about where these animals might live. Maya looks at Jaime as he talks about his dog, Fiddler. As she smiles, Akiko asks all of the children where they think a bear might live? Some of them say the zoo and another child suggests a forest. It is clear to Akiko that a small group painting experience involving several tasks—choosing a shape, dipping a paint brush into a selected color, painting the sponge with one to three colors, then pressing the color-filled sponge onto the paper surface—is a successful process for Maya as she demonstrates her enjoyment and involvement throughout these tasks.

After they make their prints, Maya and other children use their brushes to add more color onto various areas of their printed shapes. Maya freely adds brush strokes of different colors around the body of the bear print at various locations and looks at Michael several times as he brushes around his dog print.

Akiko observes and reflects on the improvements Maya has accomplished based on the time and quality of her involvement with a variety of classroom activities. She finishes writing her notes about Maya's involvement with picture books, dramatic play, clean-up, the obstacle course, large group activities, and the sponge painting activity. Akiko is delighted that Maya has had the opportunity to grow and learn from these experiences and hopes she will continue to have these opportunities when she attends kindergarten.

Later that day, Akiko joins Beth, Miguel, Tandi, and Maya's therapists for a transition to kindergarten meeting with the special education staff at Mt. Taft Elementary School. Akiko has prepared a special brochure featuring Maya. It includes her picture and sections featuring her strengths, interests, current skills, goals, and objectives, and the kinds of assistance she has benefited from the most. The brochure offers an accurate introduction to the important features and aspects of Maya's experiences in the preschool classroom. Providing copies of the brochure for everyone participating in the meeting and additional ones for anyone working with Maya in the fall, may help her new teachers and therapists obtain a better idea of her previous experiences, strengths, and needs.

The group arrives at Mt. Taft Elementary School and is greeted by both an early childhood special education teacher and Maya's future kindergarten teacher. After introductions, they proceed to a conference room and begin to discuss Maya's transition and adjustment to the kindergarten classroom experience. In addition to the brochure Akiko gives in her report, she presents and discusses Maya's classroom portfolio, describing specific weekly classroom observations along with samples and pictures of her work. Akiko ends her report by informing the group of the important role a **child-centered** classroom environment plays in Maya's life. Akiko expresses her belief that Maya will continue to learn and develop best in a classroom that features developmentally appropriate practices.

Akiko then listens as Tandi and the other therapists each provides a report about Maya's progress and current level of skills, and her need for specific types of classroom assistance and **accommodations** to help maximize her development and learning potential. Beth and Miguel also attend and state how their daughter has thrived in her current classroom and that they hope she will continue to progress with the appropriate staff system and accommodations at Mt. Taft Elementary School. They also indicate that they will expect to continue to provide appropriate home activities to support staff efforts at school. At one point they mention how helpful Maya's photograph album is, especially when Maya begins in a new classroom or she experiences unfamiliar, new events. Beth and Miguel also add that they hope they can visit often with teachers and staff about Maya's needs. The special education staff and the kindergarten teacher welcome Beth and Miguel at the end of the meeting and suggest a time that Maya, Beth, and Miguel can visit over the summer to become better acquainted and to discuss how they can provide services collaboratively to maximize Maya's positive adjustment as she begins her public school education.

The next day, Akiko asks Beth and Miguel how they felt about the **transition meeting**. As they respond, she recalls their hopeful smiles and sense of gratitude for the professional support of those that came and advocated for Maya's needs and interests. Beth and Miguel also express their feelings of relief and joy that this critical meeting seemed very successful. Beth admits though that their sense of hope can easily falter as they consider the work ahead to help Maya meet her potential in all of her developmental areas. Miguel adds that some days are better than others. They are hopeful that they can be involved partners in Maya's education with these special professionals that care for her well-being. As they continue their discussion, they share favorite memories of Maya's experiences in Akiko's classroom. Akiko tells Maya's parents how gratified she is to have had the opportunity to teach and learn from Maya and work collaboratively with both Beth and Miguel. As Akiko talks with them she thinks about how much she will miss Maya in the fall, but reassures herself that because of Maya's accomplishments and continuing support, she will be ready for her next steps in kindergarten. She is hopeful that the teachers there will also be ready for Maya to accomplish new goals and objectives in her efforts to grow and learn.

As Akiko says good-bye to Maya and her parents the following week, Akiko gives Maya a picture book about going to kindergarten. The pictures are large and feature different **learning centers** in the kindergarten classroom, the tables and chairs, the books, the dramatic play area, and other features. The book also describes what the children and teacher do in the classroom and shows pictures of the school bus, crosswalks, the playground, and the library. After Akiko shows the book to Maya, she hands it to her, saying, "This is for you, Maya." Maya beams and gives Akiko a big hug, saying, "Ank oo, teaer Ako (thank you, teacher Akiko)."

## QUESTIONS

1. What strengths or assets does Maya display as she engages in classroom activities? How do these strengths assist her as she works on challenging tasks?
2. Which specific developmental skills support Maya's progress as she engages in the animal sponge activity? The outdoor obstacle course? Dramatic play? Clean-up and snack time?
3. What final preschool activities could help Maya depart from her preschool peers and her teacher in a meaningful way? Describe two activities. DAP 1B; Code I-1.12
4. What initial kindergarten activities could help Maya adjust to the kindergarten classroom experience. Describe two activities. DAP 2J(4), 3D(2); Code I-1.12
5. Based on your understanding of Maya's interests, developmental needs, skills, and strengths, what aspects of the physical classroom environment (furniture, equipment, materials, and arrangement) would you consider using to ensure her involvement and success? Describe them. DAP 1D, 1E, 2B, 2J(4)

# 14 From Home to Preschool (3–5 Years)

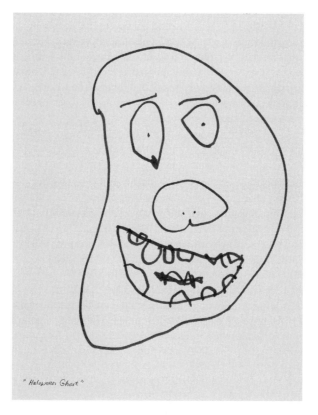

" Halloween Ghost "

## THE INITIAL HOME VISIT

Francisca is conducting home visits to all of the children and their families enrolled in her preschool class-room this year. It is 2 weeks before the first day of class and a little over a week before the Open House event as Francisca approaches the home of Todd and Mary Porter and their 4-year-old daughter, Katie. When Francisca called to make arrangements for this visit, Todd described recent family changes. Todd is

Katie's father and Mary became her stepmother when she married Todd 6 months ago. Todd quit his job a month ago and is looking for a new one. Mary works as a nurse at the local hospital. As Francisca knocks on the door, she hears Katie's shouts, "She's here! My teacher's here! I'll open the door."

When the door quickly opens, Francisca smiles and introduces herself to Katie and her parents. As Francisca enters, she observes that Katie jumps and shouts repeatedly, "Let's go to my room!" While Francisca talks with her parents, Katie runs from room to room and comes back to her parents and asks, "Can she go to my room now?" As Francisca steps into Katie's room she mentally notes the abundance of dolls, puzzles, books, crayons, wall posters, and a number of other toys either on shelves or piled into a large rubber tub.

Francisca watches and listens as Katie shows and talks about her toys. When Katie finishes talking about each item, she tosses it across the room onto her bed and then runs to several points in the room before picking up the next item to show Francisca. Then Francisca pulls out a book from her shoulder bag and shows Katie pictures of what the classroom looks like, such as the cubby and special activity areas, children playing in the classroom, and the different learning centers. When they finish, Francisca suggests that they show the book to Katie's parents.

As they look at the photographs together with Katie's parents, Katie and Francisca talk about school. While they discuss the photographs and school routines and activities, Francisca asks about Katie's favorite activities with their family and special interests of her parents. Mary and Todd mention how they enjoy cooking dinner with Katie and taking walks together at a park nearby. Then Francisca asks Todd and Mary if she can take a family picture to display on Katie's cubby at school. They are delighted and pose for a shot as they sit on the fireplace hearth. Later Francisca provides the family with an information sheet about herself and asks them to fill out and return a packet of enrollment papers that includes a list of questions about Katie's health, daily routines, and behavior patterns. She also invites the three of them to visit and explore the preschool classroom at a scheduled Open House for all children and their families during the following week.

## QUESTIONS

1. In what ways does Francisca's home visit with the Porter family reflect developmentally appropriate practices? DAP 5B; Code I-1.2 to1.5, I-1.12, P-1.4, P-1.7, P-2.2, P-2.6
2. In what ways can Katie and other children in Francisca's classroom benefit from home visitations? How can parents benefit? How can Francisca and her staff benefit? Code P-1.7, P-2.6
3. Identify three challenges that may discourage a teacher's efforts to visit children and their families? What strategies could a teacher use to overcome these difficulties for home visitation? Describe what the teacher might do or say to overcome each of the three challenges.
4. Discuss how Francisca, Katie, and Katie's parents can each benefit from this initial visit. Code I-1.12
5. What kinds of behaviors did Katie display during Francisca's visit? What possible clues about Katie's home environment and her social, emotional, language, and physical development could Francisca describe based on her observations at this initial visit? How can she use this information as she prepares for the Open House? Code P-1.2
6. List the kinds of information that you think is important for Francisca, in her role as a teacher, to collect about Katie and her parents during this first visit and from the enrollment papers.

## PLANS FOR THE INITIAL CLASSROOM VISIT AT OPEN HOUSE

Francisca has finished her home visits with the enrolled of the children and their families. She reviews her notes and enrollment information completed by each family and identifies their most significant needs and interests. She has also collected photographs of all of the children and their families. As she prepares for the Open House, she includes her assisting staff, Amy and Dewan, and an intern, Lora, in a discussion about the characteristics and cultural contexts of the children and their families. Together, they identify goals that they believe will benefit all children and their families: to welcome each child and family to the classroom and to help them become familiar with the classroom environment and the overall program. Francisca asks for ideas and suggestions from the staff as they make their plans. They discuss how they will set up and prepare the classroom environment for this event using a simple layout of accessible furniture, equipment, and materials. The classroom layout with decorations is designed and evaluated to determine if it will be welcoming to each child and his or her family. Adjustments and changes are then made for improvement.

Referring to the notes she made after each home visit, Francisca summarizes the main points of the conversations she had with the families. As she talks about each of her visits, she recalls her visit with Katie and her parents. Francisca and her staff include a discussion of how they can build on Katie's conversational language and social skills at school. They also discuss how important it is for the staff to spend time greeting each child and his or her parents during the Open House. As Francisca and her staff arrange the classroom, they identify centers and activity areas that will encourage the interests of Katie and a number of the other children.

## QUESTIONS

1. In what specific ways would you arrange the classroom's learning environment to best encourage Katie's interests and skills for the Open House?

2. As you consider the room arrangement you proposed for Katie, imagine that you have another child, Nathan (you have observed in your home visit), who talks and interacts less with you than with his parents and who also stands or walks by toys and activities without focus or engagement. Suggest ways that you can encourage Nathan's interaction with you and his engagement with activities and materials. DAP 2B(1-3) How can you modify the arrangement of the learning environment? DAP 1D What can the staff and Nathan's parent(s) do or say to encourage his involvement? DAP 2B(1-3); Code P-1.7; P-2.2

3. If you were greeting Katie and her parents at the Open House, what would you say and/or do?

4. If you were to offer a special activity or feature a learning center at the Open House that would nurture Katie's skills at home, what would you recommend?

5. Describe how you would set up the classroom for this event. How would it look as children and parents entered the classroom?

6. How would you facilitate a special activity or learning center for the Open House? What would you do and/or say?

## THE OPEN HOUSE, TUESDAY, 6:30–7:30 P.M.

Francisca and Amy are waiting at the door as Katie, Mary, and Todd walk into the classroom. Francisca talks with each one, introduces Amy, and shows them Katie's cubby area for things such as sweaters and jackets. She points to Katie's family photograph mounted on her cubby area. Katie looks at it and smiles. "That's me and mom and dad" she says as she touches each person in the photograph with her index finger. Mary and Todd smile as Francisca comments that Katie can see this picture when she comes to school each day. When Katie takes off her sweater, Todd points to a hook. Francisca says, "Oh, yes, thank you Todd," and then shows Katie the hook for her jacket and her name tag above it. Francisca points out her own name tag that hangs around her neck and then helps Katie find hers on a nearby table. She then tells her parents that they have nametags on top of the cubbies to wear whenever they come to school. Mary and Todd put on their nametags.

Then Francisca shows Katie and her parents around the classroom and introduces them to an intern, Lora, who is facilitating a playdough activity at one table and teaching assistant Dewan, who is encouraging participation at the dramatic play area with the housekeeping furniture and props. Katie and her parents watch other children as they play in the housekeeping area. After several minutes, Francisca suggests that Katie go ahead and join the other children who are placing plates at the table, taking plastic food items out of the refrigerator, or stirring items in pans on top of the stove. Dewan welcomes Katie and her parents and invites them to help the other children with the "special party celebration."

After about 5 minutes Francisca observes Katie as she tugs on her dad's sleeve and says, "Let's go over there" as she points to the playdough activity. Francisca hears Katie and suggests that they walk over. As they approach, Lora greets them and shows them a large hunk of red playdough in the middle of the circular table. Lora invites Katie, Mary, and Todd to sit down at the table and pull off a piece. As Katie rolls her piece back and forth, Lora, Mary, and Todd also roll their pieces back and forth. The program goals for this activity are to (1) encourage the children to become familiar with the physical properties of materials, (2) exercise their control of fine muscle movements, (3) engage in creative work, (4) practice **expressive and receptive language** skills, and (5) get to know the other children and build social skills in the process. In addition, the staff knows that relationships between children and adults and those between peers are important and should be facilitated by interactions between children and staff and the activities they offer each day.

Lora notices that after several minutes of rolling, Katie presses, pulls, and pats her piece into a vertical shape. She picks it up, holds it, and looks across the room toward the dramatic play area. Suddenly, she walks over to the refrigerator in the dramatic play area, opens it, and places her shape on a shelf inside.

As both Lora and Francisca observe Katie, they notice that Katie is talking with the other children in the kitchen area. Francisca continues to watch Katie as Dewan prompts her to tell what she put in the refrigerator. Then Katie opens the refrigerator and holds her shape for everyone to see. "It's a cake," she says excitedly. "Hmmmm, yum," replies Dewan. "Yummy in my tummy," shouts 3-year-old Emma as she stirs the pot on the stove.

At this point, Dewan says to Katie, "Lora would like to see the cake that you made." Katie looks over at Lora who is smiling at her. Then Francisca walks over to look at Katie's cake and talk about its features as they walk back to the playdough area. As they arrive, Katie holds it out as she shows Lora and the other children her "cake." Lora suggests that Katie tell them about her cake. Francisca watches with Katie's parents as Katie talks about the cake she made. As she talks, children look at Katie and her "cake." Then, Jacob, Michael, and Alina each talk about cakes they had on their birthdays. Francisca, Lora, and Katie's parents watch as the other children at the playdough table talk together as they shape their dough pieces into a variety of cakes.

Moments later, Francisca asks Dewan if he would like to consider having his dramatic play group walk over to the playdough area to see the cakes that have been created. Dewan welcomes the idea since his group has been preparing for a special celebration that most of them have identified as a birthday. Dewan's group walks over to the playdough group and together they talk about cakes and birthdays.

After 5 minutes, Francisca signals the children indicating that they have 5 more minutes to play before they need to clean up. Dewan leads his group back to the dramatic play area. Francisca walks over to each group of children around the room to make sure that all of the children have heard the 5-minute signal.

Because many of the children have not had experience with such transitions before, Francisca also provides a 2-minute signal to make sure that all of the children have heard her. When Francisca shakes a Bolivian rattle and calls out "Time for clean-up," her staff begins to sing a clean-up song. Then each staff member suggests ways in which the nearby children and their parents can help. When all the toys are cleaned up in the area, each staff member tells the children and their parents to find a place for their child to sit on the big circle, marked by a permanent circle of paint on the carpet. Francisca sings a welcome song, naming each child in the song, and then invites everyone to join in to sing it again. She talks briefly about each of the activity areas and then asks children what they did. When it is her turn, Katie mentions the cake she made in the playdough area. Others talk about the kitchen things in the dramatic play area, the picture books, the blocks, and the classroom fish, among others. Francisca talks to them about additional things the children will be doing at school and then points to a large poster showing the schedule through pictures with a capitalized one-word description next to each. She briefly describes the routines represented by each of these pictures.

Francisca then directs groups of several children and their parents toward specific tables with cups of juice and crackers to share. As they sit at their tables, Francisca and each staff member sit down and encourage conversations by asking open-ended questions while everyone eats together. Francisca observes that Katie and her parents are talking with others and sharing experiences. Then the staff member at each table tells the children, as they finish eating, where to take their plates and cups and directs them to some **manipulatives** set out on one table or to the library area to look at the books until the other children have finished their snack. Francisca gives another 5-minute signal when she thinks most of the children are going to be done eating in that span of time. When the 5 minutes are up, she calls everyone over to the large circle area again for a story.

Francisca knows that this is an excellent moment to model for the parents how to read books to their children at home, and she uses all of the recommended techniques as she involves the children in the process in fun ways. When the story is finished, she reminds everyone when the first day of class will be held and asks them to turn in the enrollment forms if they haven't already done so. Then she asks them to join hands in a large circle to sing the good-bye song. After the song staff members talk individually with the children and their parents as they place nametags in cubbies and pick up the chart in handout form with pictures and single words describing the daily classroom activity schedule. Francisca encourages Katie's parents and others to place the schedule at their child's eye level on their refrigerator.

## QUESTIONS

1. What did the staff do or say to make Katie feel welcome, secure, and comfortable at the open house? What suggestions would you include to enhance these feelings at this type of event? DAP 1D, 1E; Code P-1.2

2. Specify the ways in which the staff made her parents feel welcome at this event. What suggestions would you include to enhance her parents' experience of feeling welcome? DAP 5C; Code I-2.2-2.5

3. List and describe the specific steps you would take to create a "caring community of learners" in your classroom. DAP 1

4. List and describe the developmental skills young children can gain through unstructured, child-centered activities such as playdough and dramatic play. DAP 2F

5. In what ways do you think Francisca and her staff met their goals for the Open House event? DAP 3D(1,2)

6. Should Francisca encourage children at the playdough and dramatic play areas to share materials and playtime together? Describe how this could be facilitated. DAP 1A, 1B

7. What would be two benefits of giving children the opportunity to play with manipulatives or look at books if they finished eating their snack before the other children?

8. What are some examples of topics a teacher can talk about with children during snack time? What are some effective ways to begin these conversations?

9. How can Francisca stimulate conversation between parents? Why is it important for parents to have opportunities to talk with each other? Code I-2.9

## PREPARING FOR THE FIRST DAY AT SCHOOL

Francisca has several days to prepare for the first day of school. Most children and their parents were able to attend the Open House. She is now reviewing the enrollment papers Katie's parents and other parents turned in. One of the survey questions asks if the parents have any concerns about their child's behavior. Katie's parents write that their daughter picks up items such as blocks, a doll, or crayons for 1 or 2 minutes, then discards them and picks up something else. They are concerned about her lack of attention or involvement in any one activity. Francisca calls Todd and Mary and discusses this concern further. Mary tells her that Katie does spend more time with activities when they are also involved, such as talking with her during the activity.

Francisca includes this information with her knowledge about other needs and concerns expressed by other parents in this classroom. She also recalls what she has observed about individual children, such as Katie, at the Open House and during the initial home visit. Francisca plans her activities to provide the teaching staff and children with opportunities to interact at each activity location in the classroom. Activities are designed to be child-centered and unstructured with opportunities for three or more children at each activity area in the classroom. For the first week of school, Francisca plans to have half of the children come to school on the first two days, the other half on the next two days, and all the children to come on the last day of the week.

## QUESTIONS

1. Based upon Francisca's initial interactions with Katie so far, her informal observations of Katie's behavior and developmental skills, and her knowledge of Todd and Mary's concerns, suggest what actions you would take right away to benefit Katie and develop her interests, needs, and skills. DAP 2B(1-2), 2E; Code I-1.2, P-1.7, P-2.6

2. Describe ways in which Francisca can monitor Katie's (and other children's) interests, developmental progress, and needs on a frequent or daily basis and include this information for curriculum planning decisions. DAP 3C(1,2,3), 4A

3. How can Francisca's plan to have half of the children come to school on the first two days and the other half on the next two days benefit Katie and the other children? Are there any limitations? What suggestions or modifications would you make?

4. Given what you know about Katie, what activities would you suggest for her first day(s) in the classroom? What activities would you suggest for all of the children?

## THE FIRST DAY OF SCHOOL

On the first day, Katie arrives at the classroom door with her father Todd. Katie smiles at Francisca as she is greeted. Francisca observes that Katie takes off her sweater and places it on her cubby hook and pulls her nametag over her head. She jumps in place several times. Then Amy shows Katie and Todd the activities. Francisca continues to watch as Katie scoops sand into a cup and tells Dewan she is making a pancake. She continues making pancakes as her father watches. Francisca wonders if Todd is unsure when to say good-bye to Katie.

A few minutes later, Francisca asks Todd if she could talk with him by Katie's cubby while Katie continues to play at the sand table. Francisca takes this opportunity to ask Todd what he thinks about Katie's involvement at the Open House. Francisca briefly shares her own observations about Katie's positive involvement that evening. She then tells Todd that she is observing Katie's positive involvement now and that he could take a break and, if he wishes, join them later for circle time. Todd walks over to Katie and tells her he is going to leave and come back to join her when everyone sings songs at circle time. She looks toward him as he walks away, but turns back toward her pancakes as Dewan asks her what kinds of fruit would taste good on top? Katie continues her play and conversation with Dewan and some nearby children.

## QUESTIONS

1.  If Francisca asked you to facilitate the sand table activity, describe how you would set it up for three or more children, 3 to 5 years of age. DAP 2E, 3D(1-2)
2.  What would you do and/or say to Katie and the other children participating in this activity? DAP 2B(1), 2F(1-5)
3.  What would you do and/or say if Katie began to cry as her father walked away? Identify benefits Katie will experience if her father stays in the classroom during the first day of school. What limitations may exist for this course of action? DAP 5D, E; Code I-1.4, I-1.5

# 15 Problem Solving and the Blocks (3–5 Years)

## ROBERT AND THE GARAGE

Robert and Emma are building with small blocks on the carpeted floor. Four-year-old Robert begins stacking the blocks so that a three-sided, hollow column is formed. Five-year-old Emma watches how he places the blocks and begins to build a similar structure about 2 feet away. She stacks blocks 3 units high and begins to add small plastic dinosaurs around the top. She talks to the animals as she arranges them. "Hop up here little T-rex."

While she is engaged in her activity, Robert begins to drive small cars around his building. "Hurry!" he says. "The dinosaurs are coming!" He crashes one car into the side of the building and it falls. He laughs, as does Jason, age 3 years, who has been sitting and watching him play with the cars. Robert begins to build a long low room that is open on one side. He looks around and finds a thin 4-inch board that he places over the top to make a roof. "This is a garage. All my cars can hide in here so the dinosaurs won't find 'em." Once, the "garage" is constructed, he lies on his stomach and starts parking his small cars inside it.

Jason has continued to watch Robert as he has worked, smiling and laughing as Robert prepares to hide from the dinosaurs. Jason grabs two cars out of the basket and starts to park them in Robert's garage. "No!" shouts Robert. "You can't put your cars in my garage. You hafta' find your own place!" and tosses Jason's cars out of the garage. Jason's smiles turn to tears. "I can, too! There's room for me!" he says while attempting to push Robert out of the way.

Miranda, the lead teacher, has been watching the children confront problems, make choices, and carry out their plans in the block area. When Jason starts to push Robert, she decides to intervene. She signals to her nearby intern, Chen, to accompany her. She kneels down on the floor next to Jason and asks Jason to stop pushing. When the children are safe, she sits with them, gently touching each child, with Chen sitting nearby. Calmly Miranda asks the two boys what the problem is. Jason says loudly, "Robert won't let me put my cars in there," and he points to Robert's garage. Miranda replies, "You sound angry about that." Then Miranda turns to Robert and asks, "Robert, what did you want?"

"He can't put his cars in here" says Robert, with a frown. Miranda responds, "You don't want to share your block structure with Jason?"

"It's just for me," responds Robert.

"Jason sounds very disappointed that he can't play in the garage with you, Robert. I think he saw that you were having so much fun with the garage and cars, he wanted to play with you. It made him sad and disappointed that you said 'No,'" says Miranda with an arm around each child. "Yeah! I wanted to hide my cars in there." Jason's voice is quieter now but he is still frowning.

"So we have a problem" says Miranda. "Robert built a garage for cars and does not want Jason to put his cars in it. Jason really wants to put his cars in it. What can we do so you can both be happy?"

"He can put his cars over there," says Robert, pointing to a spot on the shelf several feet away.

"No!" says Jason.

Miranda has been working with the children on problem-solving skills for several months. She continues, "Jason, can you think of a solution so that both you and Robert can be happy?"

"Robert could help me build a little garage for my cars," Jason suggests hopefully, "but there aren't many blocks left."

Emma has been listening to the discussion and suggests that Jason could put his cars in her dinosaur castle. Robert looks at Emma and then at Jason.

"You have to ask me nicely first," Robert tells Jason with certainty. Emma shrugs her shoulders and turns back to her play. "That was very nice of you, Emma," says Chen.

Miranda smiles at Emma and then asks Robert, "Oh, did that make you angry when he just put his cars in your garage without asking?"

"Yes," says Robert with his head down. Robert's voice is still firm but the anger is gone. "Jason, you have to ask first. Then you can put your cars in my garage."

"Can I put my cars in the garage, Robert?" asks Jason, quickly moving out of the circle of Miranda's arm to stand in front of Robert.

"OK" says Robert and both boys lie down on their stomachs, laughing as they rush to drive cars into the garage before the dinosaurs come. Emma makes dinosaur noises and warns the two boys that her dinosaurs are getting hungry, waving her T-rex in their direction before settling back to her play on the floor.

Fifteen minutes later Robert and Jason are finished with their block play. Miranda seeks the boys out. "I saw you playing with cars in the garage that you made. You were both laughing and staying safe from the dinosaurs." Both boys looked at each other and smiled. "You figured out how to solve the problem that you had. Do you remember what you did?"

"What?" says Jason.

"Do you remember that you were disappointed when Robert would not let you put cars in the garage?"

"Yeahhh!" says Jason with eyes wide. "He said 'No' and I wanted to do it." He pauses and ponders, "What's disappointed?"

"Disappointed means that you expected that you would be welcome to put your cars in Robert's garage, but then you found out that you weren't welcome to do that. So you felt disappointed," Miranda tells him. "However, it made Robert angry when you just started to put your cars in. What did you do?"

"I *asked* him if I could put my cars in!" announces Jason with a beaming smile.

"Did that work?"

"Yeahhh!" say both boys together.

"When you talk to each other, you can work out your problems! You both worked hard on problem solving today," concluded Miranda.

## QUESTIONS

1. What opportunities to build social skills would be lost if Miranda simply told Robert he must share and that if he did not, all of the blocks would be put away? DAP 1B, C(1), 2F(2), 3C(2); Code I-1.5
2. What observations would indicate to Miranda whether these children were ready to work this problem out by themselves or if they needed some specific guidance in the problem-solving steps? DAP 2B(2), 2F(5), 2G(1)
3. The problem-solving process works better when children feel safe and calm. Why is this? How did Miranda establish a sense of safety and calm for these children? DAP 1E(1,2)

4. Why did Miranda seek out the children after the problem was solved? DAP 2F(6)
5. What specific social problem-solving strategies did Miranda use to help Robert and Jason resolve their problem?
6. What emotions might Robert and Jason have been experiencing that led to their argument?

## KNOCKING DOWN THE BLOCKS

Four-year-old Tiffany stacks colored cardboard blocks. She places two green blocks one way and two blue blocks perpendicular to the green ones. She repeats this pattern until the stack is as tall as she is. She stands back to admire her building. Gabriel, who has just finished painting a picture, dashes over to knock it down, then laughs and runs away. Tiffany runs after him, with tears in her eyes, shouting at Gabriel to stop! Before Tiffany can start hitting Gabriel, Chen intervenes. Sitting down so he can see each child, he asks Tiffany what happened.

"Gabriel knocked down my building!" Tiffany announces, hands on hips.

"Gabriel, did you knock down Tiffany's tall building?" Chen asks.

"Yes!" laughs Gabriel, clapping his hands together.

"Do you like to watch the blocks fall down?"

"Yes!" repeats Gabriel with glee.

"You are looking very happy, Gabriel, but let's look at Tiffany's face. Is she laughing?" Gabriel looks, stops laughing, and shakes his head. Focusing on Tiffany, Chen asks, "Did that make you happy when Gabriel knocked down the blocks, Tiffany?"

"No, I am very angry!" says Tiffany.

Chen continues: "She says she is very angry. Her face looks very angry. She did not want you to knock down the blocks. Gabriel, you like knocking down blocks, but Tiffany worked hard on this building and she did not want it knocked down. If you want to knock down blocks, you need to knock down your own towers, not somebody else's tower. What can we do to help Tiffany feel better again?"

Gabriel looks away, not speaking. "Is it hard to think of ways to help Tiffany feel better?" Chen asks.

"Yeah," Gabriel says quietly, looking at Chen's face.

"Maybe we should ask Tiffany what she wants us to do to help her feel better," suggests Chen in a calm, supportive voice.

Gabriel sighs, steps closer to Tiffany, and asks, "Can I help?"

Looking at Tiffany, Chen extends Gabriel's words: "Can Gabriel help you make your tower again? Would that make you feel better?"

"Gabriel knocked it down!" Tiffany states very firmly.

"Yes, and that made you very angry. But now Gabriel is asking if he can help you build it again. What do you want us to do?" restates Chen.

Gabriel is trying to pull away, but Chen reminds him that when he knocks a tower down he needs to help build it back up again.

"Gabriel doesn't know how to put the blocks. You can give me the blocks and I will put them on because I know where they go." Tiffany is relaxing and starting to place the first green blocks down.

"Now what do you need?" asks Chen.

"Blue!" says Tiffany, and Chen hands Gabriel a blue block.

"You can give the blue block to Tiffany," directs Chen, and Gabriel does. After two more blocks, one blue and one green, Gabriel begins to listen for Tiffany's request without waiting for Chen to hand him the block. As Chen moves back, Gabriel streamlines the process by bringing the fallen blocks over in stacks so that he can quickly hand Tiffany the color that she needs.

When the tower is complete, Chen returns and checks with Tiffany to see if the tower is as she wants it to be. It is, and Chen thanks Gabriel for his help. "Thanks, Gabriel!" Tiffany says brightly, looking at Gabriel and then at her tower. Gabriel leaves the area and becomes involved in the dramatic play area. Tiffany continues to use the colored blocks, constructing smaller towers at the base of her original blue and green one.

## QUESTIONS

1. Why did Chen choose to involve these children in the lengthy process of problem solving rather than choosing to require Gabriel to quickly say "I'm sorry" to Tiffany and making him sit for 5 minutes on a time-out bench for punishment? DAP 1B, 1C(2,3,4), 2G(2); Code P-1.1

2. Do you think Tiffany felt she was in a "caring community of learners?" What would indicate her feelings? Did Gabriel feel this way? What would indicate his feelings? DAP 1A; CODE 1.3

3. Problem solving is more effective when each person is included in the process. How did Chen make sure that both Gabriel and Tiffany had a role?

4. How did Chen keep the children focused on the problem of the broken tower? Why did Chen feel this was necessary?

5. Chen chose not to require Gabriel to say "I am sorry." He did ask Gabriel to help Tiffany feel better. Why do you think he made that decision? DAP 1C(1,3), 2G(1); Code P-1.2

6. Miranda was pleased to see Chen trying to facilitate problem solving with the children. Later when they had a chance to talk, what do you think Miranda had to say about the steps Chen used to facilitate problem solving between Tiffany and Gabriel? Did Chen leave out any of the steps? What would you have done differently, if anything? Are there any other steps you think might improve the outcomes for Tiffany and Gabriel?

# 16 Elena's Fears and How She Learns from New Experiences (3–5 Years)

## FAMILIAR EXPERIENCES WITH ANIMALS

Jolene, her assistant teacher Nita, and her early childhood senior intern Ramon Simon plan to prepare and offer a variety of activities about animals over the next several weeks in their childcare classroom, Puddle Play Discovery Center, located near a rural community that borders a large city.

During the first week of April, Jolene, Nita, and Ramon introduce a curriculum with an emphasis on animals that begins by focusing on stuffed animals and pets that the 3- to 5-year-old children have at home. Nita is able to visit each of the children and their families and take pictures of each child with either a favorite stuffed animal or a live pet. When Nita brings the pictures into the classroom and sets them on a table, the children look at them enthusiastically. She helps each child to label his or her own picture with the animal's name and to place it on a bulletin board titled "My Favorite Animal Pals." Children talk more about their animal pals informally during the daily activities and in more focused discussions about animals during small and large group times.

During a family potluck the same week, parents ask Jolene if pet animals can visit the classroom, especially during large group discussions. After they eat, Jolene invites the children and their parents to join her, Nita, and Ramon in a large group time by the animal bulletin board. They sing several songs and then talk about the children's classroom activities during the past several days that were related to animals. Jolene invites each child and parent to point out their animal pal on the bulletin board and say anything they wish about it. Some children mention the names of their stuffed animals or pets, others talk about where their pals like to "hang-out," and several children share funny stories about their animal pals.

After the children and their parents share this information about their animal pals, Jolene suggests that the group discuss possible short day trips they could plan for the purpose of learning more about animals. One child asks, "Can we go to the Animal Petting Fair?" Some children smile while others show their delight with a stream of soft giggles. Another child suggests that she and her mom can show everyone the llamas. Her mother adds that she can assist in the arrangements with the fair's management, since she helps out at the fair's exhibits, which are held each year in the spring and summer months at the county fairgrounds. Individual children and parents spontaneously raise their hands and speak favorably about this possibility. Jolene, Nita, and Ramon are excited about this opportunity since they have seen the wide variety of animals there. Nearby university faculty, staff, and students from several departments, including Animal Sciences, Veterinary Medicine, and Entomology, bring a variety of animals each year for their displays. Three parents say they can take time off from work to help on the morning of this field trip and Jolene writes down their names.

Jolene suggests that the class visit the Animal Petting Fair on Wednesday in 3 weeks. Before everyone leaves, Jolene organizes a schedule for several of the parents to bring in their family pet to share at large group time. The schedule also includes times for those children who don't have live pets to bring in one favorite stuffed animal to share at large group time.

After the potluck, Jolene, Nita, and Ramon express their delight about the enthusiasm with which families and children told stories about their animals. In the days that follow they observe how their discussions with children about pets and stuffed animals expands to animals owned by relatives, neighbors, and/or friends, as well as those seen on TV. Then spontaneously, children and parents bring in updated pictures of their stuffed animals or pets, as well as pictures of their friend's and relative's pets. Ramon decides to send home used wildlife magazines and to ask the children and their parents to cut out their favorite animal pictures to share with the class. The variety of pictures displayed on the bulletin board increases rapidly. Children, parents, and teachers seem excited about the activity. In the following days space on the bulletin board near the photographs of pets and stuffed animals is used to post the magazine animal pictures. Soon it becomes necessary to expand the bulletin board beyond the frame and onto the surrounding walls. Jolene and Nita add a variety of songs, stories, and special displays around the classroom that feature a variety of different animals.

Each day the children and some of the parents study the bulletin board. On one of these occasions Ramon notices that 4-year-old Elena forms her fingers into cylinders and raises them to her eyes as if she is looking through binoculars. As she scans the bulletin board with her "binoculars" over her eyes, she frequently closes the front ends tightly with her pinky fingers. Then for other views, she opens her pinky fingers as she gazes through the opening.

On the next day when she does this, Elena says to Ramon, "I c'n see the 'at and the dawh' and oh—that's my dawh, Dimpuhs (Dimples)." As she says this her pinky fingers are open. Then, closing her pinky fingers, she says, "Oh," with a long breath and then whispers, "I 'an't see the spiduh." Ramon scans the pictures with his "binoculars" over his eyes with his pinky fingers open and says, "I can see some different animals." Elena watches as he names several of them including the sheep, rabbit, and a rat and then she tells Ramon to look at Dimples. "He's not s'ary," she says. Ramon asks her, "How does Dimples make you feel?" Elena replies, "He ma'es me feel 'ood. I li'e to hol' 'im and look at boohs." Elena then moves her binoculars toward the goat and announces, "I see another dawh." They continue to identify their discoveries. Then Ramon says, "I see a rooster and a spider," but as he does, Elena shakes her head and says, "You 'an't see it (referring to the spider), don't loo' at it. It will s'are us and zhump at us. It can 'ite you!" Then in a quiet voice she whimpers, "I don' want to do this anymore" and she quickly walks away toward the dramatic play area and joins several children as they "bake muffins."

Ramon decides to observe Elena's behavior near the animal display in the coming days to better understand her creative strategy for blocking out the spider. He wonders if perhaps there is a way to help Elena become more comfortable with the spider and any other animals she fears.

After school, Ramon thinks about how the curriculum activities are evolving from the children's enthusiasm for the animals. As the day for the trip to the Animal Petting Fair nears, he also considers how individual children, including Elena, might respond to the experience. Having been to these animal exhibits before, he knows that there are some sounds, smells, and sights that may seem unfamiliar to some children. He recognizes how challenging it can be to predict which children may experience surprise or fear about a particular aspect of the experience.

At their usual conference time after school, Ramon discusses his experiences with Jolene. He talks about his playful experience with Elena and how he is intrigued with Elena's use of her "binoculars" as she scans the bulletin board display. Ramon mentions that he thinks that Elena may have some fear of spiders that may prevent her from exploring the characteristics of these animals. At this point Jolene asks him what evidence he has to support his conclusions. They discuss his informal observations and Ramon concludes that he needs to examine Elena's behavior more thoroughly in the coming days. He talks with Jolene about spending more time observing Elena over the next several days.

## QUESTIONS

1. What were some of the benefits of the involvement of children and families in the evening potluck? DAP 5A-D; Code I-1.2-5, 2.2-5
2. How did the involvement of the children and families in the growing bulletin board display of animals contribute to both children's learning and the classroom community? DAP 5A-D; Code I-2.3
3. What kinds of things do you think the children may learn from the focus on animals?
4. Think of several ways Ramon can support Elena when she uses her strategy to avoid pictures of spiders. Is Ramon effective in his response to her? Specify how you would respond or interact with her based on her behavior. DAP 2 B(1-3), 2F(5)
5. Elena looks at the goat and calls it a dog; what does this tell you about her cognitive development? If you were Ramon, how would you respond to Elena? DAP 2B(2), 2F(2)
6. Suppose that when Elena's mom comes to pick her up, Ramon describes Elena's behavior with the animal pictures and her mom replies, "at home she becomes very agitated and scared when she sees a spider. I notice that when she doesn't want to see something that bothers her, she holds her "binoculars" up to her eyes with her pinky fingers covering the opening. I wish my daughter wouldn't be so silly about this." How would you reply to Elena's mom? DAP 2A, 5D, 5E
7. Suggest an activity that might help Elena identify and express her feelings in a comforting situation. Could this activity also relate to the needs of other children in this classroom? Describe how it could appeal to the general needs of preschool children 3 to 5 years of age. DAP 2B, 2C, 2D; Code I-1.2-4
8. To ensure the Animal Petting Fair trip will be a positive experience for Elena, what could Ramon do to support Elena and her mom in their preparation for this event? DAP 5; Code I-2.4

## OBSERVING ELENA

Ramon observes Elena the next day by recording several anecdotal records of her behavior when she is near or at the bulletin board display. After he writes a couple of records, he quickly determines that the behavior he informally observed recently is very consistent with his written record. In fact, she appears to be repeating the binocular episode several times each day. He is interested in finding out if there are any variations in these episodes and how long she spends looking at cats and dogs and looking at other animals. As he observes the third day, he writes that Elena spends approximately 30 seconds looking at either a dog or a cat and 15 seconds looking at other animal pictures posted nearby. The second time she does this on the same day, she spends about 20 seconds looking at either a dog or a cat and 20 seconds looking at other animal pictures. This pattern continues into the next day except that Elena also visits the display a third time and looks through her "binoculars" for about a minute at a variety of animals in various locations next to the spider. Then she closes her binocular openings with her pinkies and points her binoculars in the direction of the spider and holds this pose for 20 seconds. Ramon notices that her pinkies are very slowly moving to reveal tiny crack openings in her binoculars. Ramon observes a similar pattern for 2 more days and then discusses his findings with Jolene after school.

Ramon tells Jolene that over the past week, Elena is looking at new animals on the display more often and for longer periods of time. He also tells Jolene that it appears that Elena is beginning to peek at the spider through small openings in her hands (her "binoculars") for longer periods of time. They discuss these findings and both agree that it is important for Elena to have opportunities to continue her exploration of animals. Ramon then suggests that he will share his findings with Elena's mom soon. As he says this he gets an idea about how he can help Elena and all of the children better prepare for their upcoming visit to the Animal Petting Fair. He tells Jolene he hopes to take large pictures of key exhibit areas and share them with the children the day before the field trip. Jolene is very enthusiastic about Ramon's idea and hopes it will be very successful. She comments on his special efforts to meet the individual needs of children and suggests that he arrange a display area on a table near the bulletin board that features realistic plastic snakes, lizards, spiders, and insects for children to examine, touch, and feel.

Early that evening, Ramon thinks about Elena's mom, Renee, a single parent who works at the post office each day. He calls Renee, describes his recent observations, and asks her what she has observed recently of Elena's behavior. Renee mentions that Elena is talking about a variety of animals she looks at on the bulletin board and about the pets of several of her classmates. Ramon suggests a book of baby animal pictures with a simple text that he will place in her cubby for them to borrow and enjoy together.

Then Ramon talks to her about how he is developing an idea to create a special activity with photographs taken at the petting zoo to help children prepare for their visit there. Renee states that this is a good idea and wonders if he will include a picture of a spider, since Elena seems to be alarmed and frightened when she encounters one. Renee thinks it is a good idea for him to include a spider in his group of pictures.

## QUESTIONS

1. Why doesn't Jolene tell Ramon to stop worrying about Elena's behavior and just tell her that spiders aren't going to hurt her?
2. Why did Ramon decide to call Elena's mother and discuss his plans with her? DAP 5B, 5E; Code I-2.2, I-2.4
3. What effect do you think Elena's spending more time looking at the variety of animals on the bulletin board might have on her feelings?
4. How would you support Elena's interests in your curriculum at school and at home? What additional activities would you recommend? DAP 2B(2), 2C, 2F(1)

## THE PETTING FAIR PREVIEW

Over the weekend, Ramon checks out the classroom's digital camera and visits the Animal Petting Fair. He hopes to take several key pictures of each of the main sights the children soon will be visiting on their field trip. He takes a picture of the entrance and then sectioned areas identified for the llama, sheep and lambs, goats, rabbits, cows, chickens and rooster, pheasants, emu, frogs, lizards, spiders, and insects. He also takes a picture of the adjoining park where they will have lunch. Ramon decides to use only one picture of each area, since he doesn't want to ruin the sense of mystery and discovery the children may feel when they explore the Animal Petting Fair. He downloads his photographs to the Puddle Play office computer and is able to print large pictures of each scene on heavy cardstock to show to the children during a large group discussion.

The day before the field trip, Ramon tells Elena that he would like her to help him look over the photographs of the petting zoo. Elena smiles and seems eager to help. Ramon describes each photograph briefly and then asks her questions focused on capturing specific details and characteristics in the picture. Elena enjoys talking about what she sees. Sometimes she uses her binoculars to peer through her fingers. Other times she simply looks at the photographs. Before the spider photograph is revealed, Ramon says he is going to get his binoculars out and Elena does the same. As the snake photograph is revealed, Elena adjusts her "binoculars" from very small openings to larger ones. Ramon also does this. He describes the photograph and asks questions as he did with the other pictures as they discuss the snake picture further while holding their "binoculars" up. They proceed in the same fashion with the spider picture and then the final two pictures. When Ramon asks her later how she liked the pictures, Elena announces that the spider has little eyes and it can use its body to move around. As she says this, Ramon repeats her words, and smiles as she talks more about how the spider is resting on the tree branch. Ramon is thrilled that Elena can describe these characteristics and look at the spider as more than just a scary creature.

Later that morning, Elena stares at the sand and rock display in the discovery area that holds about five different rubber and plastic snakes, lizards, spiders, and bugs. At first she stands and stares at them as two other children pick up and examine a variety of snakes and spiders. As they do this, Ramon kneels by Elena and the display, holds his "binoculars" up to his eyes, and touches his pinky fingers on a garter snake and then on a brown spider. Elena watches him and holds her hand to her mouth and giggles each time Ramon touches a spider. Then Ramon says, "My 'binoculars' are getting tired, can you hold my 'binoculars' up to your eyes?" She nods and holds "his binoculars." As they move around the display area she sees several snakes, spiders, a caterpillar, and a fly. As the "binoculars" touch a spider, Elena shouts "Eek!" and then giggles. They continue to do this about a dozen times. Next Ramon picks up a spider with one hand and looks at it through his "binoculars" as he holds them with his other hand. He asks Elena if she wants to look at the spider through her "binoculars." She does and also touches it with her pinky fingers. Soon Elena is picking up a variety of spiders, bugs, snakes, and lizards and examining them with her "binoculars."

That afternoon Ramon presents the card stock photographs to the children with similar comments and questions. The children discuss characteristics of each animal picture. Ramon feels more assured that these children are prepared for the Petting Fair experience. He also feels a sense of accomplishment about his observations, his interpretation of Elena's behavior, his discovery area display, and his production and presentation of zoo pictures that support an informative and meaningful discussion before their trip. Jolene shares her enthusiasm with him about the success of his photograph project and the discussions with the children that have evolved from his focused observations.

The next day, the field trip is enjoyed by all. Children, parents, and teachers often engage in conversations about what they see and raise new questions about the animals. One of the parents takes notes on what the children say at each area while Ramon takes pictures of the animals with the children standing nearby. Ramon anticipates sharing these pictures and the children's comments with families and others in a new bulletin board display in the classroom.

## QUESTIONS

1. Describe what you believe Elena gained from her experiences with the photographs and discovery area display. What do you imagine her experience is like on the day of the field trip?
2. What do you think Elena's experience would have been if there had not been any examination of her behavior with the "binoculars," follow-up observations, and staff discussions and reflection?
3. Describe what Ramon gains from his experience collecting and then sharing the photographs with Elena and all of the children. Describe what you predict his experience is like on the day of the field trip.
4. Imagine that there is a group of large spiders in a glass compartment on display at this event and your class has a child who now approaches this area of the petting zoo and becomes very frightened. As the child's teacher, how would you react in this situation? How would you offer your support? If the child's parent accompanied this child on the field trip, would your reaction be the same or different? Describe how. DAP 2B(3); Code I-1.4
5. How would you use the pictures that Ramon is taking and the notes of what the children are saying at each of the exhibit areas after the field trip is over? If the children's comments were recorded on a small recording device, how might you use them? DAP 2F(1,2,3,4,5,6); Code I-1.3
6. How can a teacher utilize the experiences the children gain in this field trip for curriculum planning over the days and weeks that follow? DAP 3C, 3D

# 17 Brent and Cory Need Extra Help (3–5 Years)

## MEAN TALK

Two new boys have entered Cassandra's child care classroom this week, Cory and Brent Johnson, who are 4-year-old fraternal twins. Cassandra is the lead teacher for a group consisting of 20 3- to 5-year-old children and an assistant teacher. Her classroom is part of a large child care center located in a small city. Cory and Brent are not getting along with the other children. Both boys play only with each other and have a habit of saying unrealistic but threatening things to anyone who displeases them, including Cassandra. They both say threatening things such as "I'm going to kill you. I'll bomb your house. I'll beat you up and crush your head!" They are often uncooperative and disruptive to the classroom routines. Cassandra has been keeping observational notes of their behaviors for 5 days. They refuse to cooperate during large group times, disrupting every day. The boys seem to intensify each other's misbehaviors: when one begins such behavior, the other usually joins in.

When the twins first began using "mean talk" with the other children, Cassandra pointed out to Cory and Brent, and to all of the other children, that it is okay to pretend, but that it can be hurtful to other children's feelings when they hear such "mean talk" even though "we all know that it is just pretending." However, she wasn't certain that either of the brothers actually viewed their talk as pretending. They said it like they meant it.

Now things are getting worse. Brent is lashing out and hitting other children with very little warning or provocation. Fortunately, Cory is not joining in. Cassandra always responds to violence in the classroom by comforting the hurt child first. Then as a consequence she takes the aggressor aside and sits with him or her in a quiet area of the room, explaining why the behavior was hurtful and not okay. She asks the child why he or she behaved that way and what he or she could have done differently to express their feelings or get what was desired. She does this with Brent each time he hits another child, but he refuses to talk and she has to hold onto him to keep him sitting with her for the 3 minutes or so she usually keeps a child involved in this "talking with the teacher" consequence of physical aggression. Each time Brent hurts another child, Cassandra makes a note in a very small spiral notebook she keeps hanging from a beaded string around her neck. She writes down the date, the time, the hurt child's name, the apparent cause or preceding situation, and the type of aggression. When time allows later in her day, she enters brief anecdotal records based on her notes and memories of what she has observed that day. and any related thoughts that occur during these reflections.

When Brent continues to hit other children, Cassandra assigns her assistant teacher to "shadow" him, staying nearby and trying to stop his hitting before it happens. Cassandra shares with the assistant teacher her observations about what happens just before he hits another child. It happens most often when another child gets in Brent's way while he is playing and when he wants something the other child is playing with. Unfortunately, the assistant teacher is unable to adequately focus on Brent and react quickly enough to prevent the aggressive acts.

Cassandra compiles her observations and meets with the center director, Mrs. Ortiz. Cassandra asks Mrs. Ortiz if she thinks it would be a good idea to ask the brothers' parents if they can move Cory to another classroom to separate the brothers. She believes this will prevent them from reinforcing each other's defiant behavior and help each of them adjust to the behavioral expectations of the center and classroom. Mrs. Ortiz agrees and Cassandra contacts Mr. and Mrs. Johnson by telephone that evening to arrange a meeting "to discuss Cory and Brent's adjustment to school." Mrs. Johnson answers the phone and pins down Cassandra on what she wants to talk with them about, asking, "Are the boys getting into trouble again?" Cassandra says, "There has been some difficulty with their adjustment to the classroom." Mrs. Johnson says, "I'm afraid those boys are always getting into trouble, but boys will be boys!" Cassandra asks if she could meet with Mrs. Johnson and/or Mr. Johnson to discuss their boys' adjustment to the center. Mrs. Johnson says that she is too busy and asks if they can just talk about it now on the phone. Cassandra briefly describes the boys' behaviors, mentions her observations that the boys seem to reinforce each other's aggressive words and behaviors, and suggests the idea of moving Cory into a neighboring classroom the same size, and with the same number and ages of children, as the classroom both boys are in now. Cassandra explains how she thinks that will help each of them.

Mrs. Johnson expresses surprise at the idea but has no objections. Cassandra asks Mrs. Johnson if she would like some time to think about the move and discuss it with Mr. Johnson, but Mrs. Johnson tells her to go ahead with the plan right away. Cassandra tells Mrs. Johnson about the way the boys talk meanly to the other children and adults, and asks her if the boys have been exposed to such talk somehow, perhaps from a friend or relative. Mrs. Johnson says no and that she needs to go clean up the dinner dishes, ending the conversation.

The following day Cassandra reports the conversation and decision to Mrs. Ortiz and Mrs. Ortiz agrees to the move and decides on the classroom into which Cory will be moved. She explains to the teacher in the new classroom that the reason for the move is to separate the two brothers, being careful to avoid negatively coloring the new teacher's view of Cory as much as possible. They decide the move will happen on Monday of the following week, so that the brothers can be told about the move ahead of time and will have 3 school days to adjust to the idea. Cassandra calls Mrs. Johnson again to tell her which classroom Cory will move into and when the move will happen. Cassandra asks Mrs. Johnson to talk with the brothers about the move several times before that Monday. That afternoon after naps and during **self-selected activities** time, Cassandra asks the brothers to accompany her into Mrs. Ortiz' office, and once there, allows them to play with some playdough at a small table while she explains to them the plan to move Cory into a different room and the reasons for the move. Cassandra describes the room and how similar the routines are in the two classrooms, and provides the name of the teacher, Stephanie. Mrs. Ortiz sits and observes. The boys get terribly angry at the news and start telling Cassandra that they will bomb her house and kill her dog and other cruel things, similar to what they have been saying every day in the classroom. Mrs. Ortiz is dismayed. Cassandra tells the boys that she understands that they are very angry with her, but that their mother has agreed that Cory will be moved into the neighboring classroom. She then leaves the office with Mrs. Ortiz watching the boys pound the playdough until they have calmed down enough to return to the classroom just before the school day ends.

## QUESTIONS

1. Could Cassandra have established a "caring community of learners" without solving the problem presented by the twins' behaviors? DAP 1E(1) What alternatives might be available to her?
2. How would you have handled "mean talk" in the classroom that is full of mean but unrealistic threats toward other children and the teacher? Code I-1.5, P-1.1, P-1.2 Why did Cassandra emphasize to the children that the "mean talk" was only pretend? DAP 1E(1)

3. What do you think of the "talking with the teacher" consequence for deliberately hurting another child? In what ways is it different from a time-out? DAP 1E(1)

4. Should Cassandra have told Mrs. Johnson about her concerns and ideas without a scheduled meeting? What was missing from the telephone call that could have been part of a face-to-face meeting? Code I-2.1, I-2.4, P-2.4

5. Why do you think Cassandra decided to move Cory rather than Brent to another classroom? Code 3A(Introduction)

6. What do you think the advantages and disadvantages are of separating the twins into different classrooms?

7. If two unrelated children caused escalating mean behavior when they were together in the classroom, do you think Cassandra's approach should be different? Why or why not?

8. What would your response be to a parent saying "boys will be boys"? DAP 5D; Code I-2.7, I-2.8

9. Why did Cassandra make sure that the twins were made aware ahead of time of the plans to move Cory into a new classroom? Why did she provide the twins with playdough to play with during this talk?

10. Do you think it would have been more or less beneficial for the twins if Cory were moved right away rather than letting the twins know about the move a few days ahead of time? Why?

## SEPARATE CLASSROOMS

On the following Monday, the twins' parents took Cory to Stephanie's classroom and Brent to Cassandra's classroom. Brent was fairly quiet that first day and avoided hurting other children. Cassandra took a free moment to go next door later that morning and see how Cory was doing.

During the first week of the separation Cassandra asked her assistant to switch roles with her by preparing for and facilitating each new transition, freeing Cassandra to shadow Brent. Cassandra was successful in preventing Brent's lashing out and gave him as much attention as she could when he was behaving appropriately, depriving the other children a little, but only temporarily. Sometimes she played with Brent and invited others to join them. By the end of the second week since moving Cory to Stephanie's classroom, Brent was playing with the other children safely and was talking meanly only on occasion. Cassandra still kept a close eye on him to prevent the other children from being hurt.

Meanwhile, Mrs. Ortiz asked Mr. and Mrs. Johnson to come in to meet with her and Cassandra about helping Cory and Brent. Mrs. Johnson came to the meeting and listened as Cassandra and Mrs. Ortiz asked her to allow them to call in an early intervention specialist to observe the boys. The specialist could screen the boys to detect any special needs they might have and/or provide the family with suggestions for helping them adjust better to the child care and school environment. At the end of the meeting, Mrs. Johnson agreed to consider this.

Several days later Mrs. Ortiz informed Cassandra that at the request of his parents, Brent would be moved from her classroom into another teacher's classroom (not Stephanie's) the following Monday. Cassandra felt badly about this decision because Brent seemed to be making progress. Adjusting to another caregiver and classroom is difficult for most children and she believed it would be especially so for Brent. On his last day in her class, Cassandra observed a girl putting a dress-up cloak on Brent as they played, and noticed how he smiled blissfully at the girl's attentions. Cassandra wished that Brent could stay in her classroom.

Two months later, Cassandra was informed that Brent had lasted only two weeks in the new classroom before the teacher had asked that he be moved. She was told the twins were enrolled in a local school for children with special needs, a school that provides therapy for both children and families. Cassandra never learned any more about the twins.

## QUESTIONS

1. Why do you think Cassandra entered Stephanie's classroom to talk with Cory on the first day of the transition?
2. Why didn't Cassandra simply ask the other children to be Brent's friend and to play with him, rather than playing with him herself and then inviting others to join them?
3. Why do you think Mrs. Ortiz and Cassandra thought it would be a good idea to call in an early intervention specialist to observe the twins? Code I-1.9, I-2.6, P-2.4, P-2.15
4. Why do you think Mrs. Johnson asked Mrs. Ortiz to move Brent out of Cassandra's classroom? If you were the director, would you have agreed to this move? Why or why not? DAP 5D, E, F; Code I-1.3, P-1.1, I-2.6, P-2.4
5. Considering the later outcome for the twins, do you believe the decision to move Brent out of Cassandra's classroom was best for him in the long-run or not? Why?

# CASE

# 18 Heather Learns Through Play (3–5 Years)

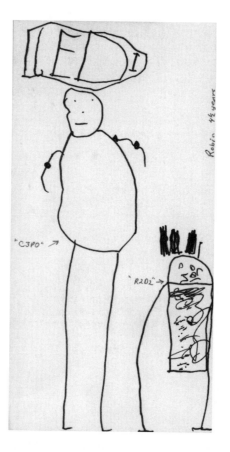

Tony is the lead teacher in one of two classrooms at a campus preschool center. The assistant teacher and four early childhood education interns also teach in the classroom. Each class has 20 children ranging in age from 3 to 5 years. Although it may be difficult to plan for all of the interests and abilities in such a diverse group, the teachers firmly believe the benefits of having mixed ages in the classroom outweigh the disadvantages. A great deal of learning takes place between these children of different ages just as it does in family situations. The older children model skills for the younger ones, and the younger children look up to the older ones for assistance when needed. In addition, there is usually a wide range of abilities even in a classroom restricted to certain ages, and this wider age range encourages the teachers and students to plan for this diversity in development and skills, allowing all the children to feel successful.

Several weeks have gone by since 5-year-old Heather Rogers joined Tony's class. She has adjusted easily to routines and new people and seems to be enjoying her time in the preschool. Heather often gravitates to the art activities and spends a great deal of time working carefully on her projects. Tony notices that Heather's artwork is advanced for her age and she is quite skilled at using a lot of detail in her drawings. Heather talks to the other children at the art table and is becoming friends with Zella, another child about her age who also enjoys artwork.

When Tony talks with Heather's parents about her adjustment to preschool, he mentions Heather's special artistic talent and how the new friendship is developing as a result of similar interests between friends. Mr. and Mrs. Rogers listen politely to Tony, but then express their concerns that Heather isn't learning what she needs to learn before going to kindergarten. Her birthday is in August, and she just missed the cutoff date to begin public school this year. Mr. and Mrs. Rogers talked to Tony about giving Heather more academic work to do.

One day when Mr. Rogers arrives to pick up Heather she is gluing nature objects on a collage at the table and another day she is painting at the easel. Mr. Rogers pulls Tony aside and asks, "Don't you have something to teach her the letters of the alphabet? She doesn't need to play with the younger kids when she should be learning!"

Tony tries to reassure Mr. Rogers that Heather is learning a great deal at preschool while she plays. He reminds him that next week they will be having a family night to explore the class's art curriculum, the value of **developmental play**, and parents' and teachers' ideas for the year. Tony asks Mr. Rogers if he will be able to come and Mr. Rogers says yes.

The following Thursday evening families gather in the classroom for the Open House. Art activities are set up around the room for children to do with their parents. The teachers and interns move among the various activities to engage in conversation and answer questions. In the center of each table are laminated information cards describing the links between that particular art activity and learning fundamentals across various disciplines, such as literacy, math, social studies, technology, and the arts.

After greeting the parents and children and helping them find activities to try, Tony floats around the room, visiting with parents and children at the various activities. He notices that Heather is at the tissue-tearing activity along with Zella and her mother. The children are busily tearing pieces of tissue paper and sticking them on large sheets of clear contact paper to hang in the window. The intern facilitating this activity talks about the warm and cool colors of the paper, the straight or curvy lines, and the different shapes they are tearing. The information card points out that this activity is great for expanding children's language and vocabulary and exercising their creativity and small muscle control. Parents comment on the colorful pictures being created and how each one turns out so different from the others. At the table next to them, children are measuring ingredients as they make some new playdough. This activity introduces children to measurement and physical science as they add water to dry ingredients and observe the resulting physical transformations. This exercises and builds on their intellectual abilities.

Families gather on the rug after about an hour of activity time and Tony discusses the evening's events with them. He explains in greater detail the academic value of each activity and answers parents' questions. Mr. Rogers asks, "Does painting help with learning to read?" Tony explains, "Children gain experience with, and are exposed to, a better understanding of print as they write their names on their pictures and have a teacher write a few words about the artwork on it or on a sentence strip to accompany the piece." Tony expands on this saying, "Children also exercise control of the hand and finger muscles they will need to write clearly. The way they visually organize the space on the paper helps children exercise thinking skills that will help them achieve success later in understanding mathematical concepts. The use of their imagination also exercises intellectual skills and helps them develop a sense of aesthetics. When we ask the children to tell us about their artwork, they exercise both intellectual and language skills needed in the process of coming up with a description in response." Mr. Rogers exclaims, "Good grief! I didn't realize all that learning goes on with painting! I guess it's good that Heather likes to paint."

Tony says he would like to have another Open House to look at other areas of the curriculum if parents are interested. Zella's mother asks about the block area. "My daughter has mentioned several times that she would like to play with the trucks and blocks, but 'only boys play there.'" Tony expresses dismay at this news and responds, "All centers are open to both boys and girls, but sometimes children experience emotional barriers to participating in certain areas." He then assures the parent, "I will observe to discover the reasons for this and work to help Zella and any other children who might feel unable or unwelcome to play in the block center. I sure don't want anyone to miss out on the many opportunities for learning that the block area provides."

Mr. Rogers expresses his interest in another Open House so they can have a better understanding of the values of all the activities their children enjoy at preschool. The children, parents and teachers finish up the evening with fun nutritious snacks and say good-bye.

## QUESTIONS

1. Why do you think Tony explains the connection of art to different disciplines rather than focusing just on the therapeutic and creative values of art activities? DAP 2D, 3D(1), 5E; Code I-2.7, P2.5

2. How can the teachers strengthen each child's competence by observing their interaction with art materials as related to various disciplines? DAP 2D, 3A(1)

3. How do you think the teaching staff works to establish reciprocal relationships between teachers and families in this setting? DAP 5A, 5D, 5E; Code I-2.4, 2.7, 2.8

4. In what way does Tony's practice of ensuring that each child feels successful contribute to the children's later school success? DAP 2F(5,6); Code I-1.9

5. How can Tony better address the concerns about kindergarten readiness like those of Mr. Rogers, and help parents become more knowledgeable and comfortable with the skills children learn through developmental play?

# CASE

# 19 Emiliana's First Report of Child Abuse (3–5 Years)

E miliana is a lead teacher in a preschool program sponsored by a large church, working with a class of 20 3- to 5-year-old children. She has an AA degree in early childhood education and has worked with younger children for several years. This job is her first job working with this older group of children and with this church program. Emiliana currently has an assistant teacher, Madeline, and an intern from the University, Deshane, working under her supervision, and from time to time one or two parents help in the classroom for a few hours as well.

Kylie is a 4-year-old in Emiliana's class. She is an active girl who is interested in almost every activity, especially the art activities that Emiliana sets out for the children every day. Emiliana enjoys Kylie's easy-going nature. Kylie's father is usually the one to bring her to school and to pick her up, and he often stays a few minutes and chats a little with Emiliana. Kylie often has a dirty face and uncombed hair when she arrives. Madeline is used to taking Kylie to the bathroom and washing her face and combing her hair when she first arrives.

Today the art activity is finger painting on large round pieces of paper. Deshane puts on Kylie's smock and rolls up her long sleeves so that she won't get much paint on them. As he does this, he notices that Kylie has several raw-looking circular red sores on one of her arms. Deshane asks Kylie what happened to her arm and Kylie tells him in a very quiet voice, "cigarette," and she tries to roll her sleeve back down to cover the sores. Deshane is not sure he has heard her correctly, but she won't give him any more information. He asks her to let him roll the sleeve up at least a little bit to keep it out of the paint. When he is finished getting her started painting, he leaves the activity and seeks out Emiliana.

When Deshane finds Emiliana playing tea party, he tells her he needs to talk privately with her. She excuses herself and takes him to a quiet corner of the classroom. Deshane tells Emiliana about the sores, what he thought he heard Kylie say, Kylie's reluctance to talk about how she got them, and her attempts to cover them up again. He tells Emiliana that he is worried that some form of physical abuse may have happened to Kylie. Emiliana thanks Deshane for telling her about it and assures him that she will investigate his concern and talk more with him after class.

Emiliana asks Madeline to monitor the entire classroom for a while, then goes over to the finger painting table and sits down next to Kylie. She starts talking with Kylie by verbally observing what Kylie is doing. "You are using a lot of yellow in this painting, Kylie. I like how it is mixing with the pink and purple." Kylie responds and the two chat a bit while Kylie paints. When Kylie is finished painting Emiliana helps her get cleaned up and, in the process, she sees Kylie's small, round lesions. Emiliana picks up a bag of playdough and asks Kylie to come with her to play at a small table, somewhat partitioned off from the rest of the classroom, a place where some of the children play during small group activity time. They sit down at the table and Emiliana gets out some of the playdough for Kylie to play with, telling her that she wants to talk privately with her while she plays.

Emiliana then picks up some playdough herself and starts rolling it around on the table. She talks about how much she likes to play with the playdough. Then she tells Kylie, "I saw some sore spots on your left arm and I am wondering how you got hurt there?" Kylie responds reluctantly, but after a little more questioning, she tells Emiliana that the lesions were "from cigarette." Emiliana asks Kylie who used the cigarette, and Kylie says that her mother did it. Kylie continues to play with the playdough for a minute or two while Emiliana thinks and tries to calm her own feelings. Emiliana tells Kylie that she is very sorry to hear that, then thanks Kylie for telling her about her burns and takes Kylie back to the main area of the classroom, where the children are just finishing cleaning up for snack time and going to wash their hands.

Emiliana is not sure what to do next. She goes to see the preschool director, Ms. Hayden, and tells her about the sores and what Kylie said. She tells Ms. Hayden that she thinks she should call **children's services** to report this. She asks Ms. Hayden if she agrees. Ms. Hayden tells her that she will need to decide for herself. Emiliana asks again, using different words, but she receives the same answer. Emiliana is getting upset since she can't understand why Ms. Hayden won't give her any more direction. Then Ms. Hayden suggests that she should talk to the Family Liaison, Angela, who has the most contact with the families. Emiliana checks the personnel board and sees that Angela won't be in her office until 4:00 P.M., so she goes back to the classroom where some of the children are finishing their snack and choosing books for the small group reading time. She sits down with the children and starts reading. The rest of the class time seems to go by very slowly for Emiliana.

After the children have all gone home and the classroom is tidied up, Emiliana talks privately with Deshane, letting him know that she is working on the issue of Kylie's lesions and again thanking him for being observant, questioning Kylie, and then telling Emiliana about what he heard. Emiliana also tells Madeline about what she and Deshane observed and heard from Kylie. Emiliana asks her assistant if she has noticed anything unusual about Kylie lately. Madeline replies, "No, but the day after Halloween I noticed that the scalp under her thin, blond hair was very red. It almost looked scalded to me but I figured it must have been from coloring her hair red for Halloween or an allergy to a shampoo, or something."

It is 4:00 P.M. and Emiliana goes to see Angela. She explains what has happened and asks for advice. Angela recommends that Emiliana do nothing. She says that if Emiliana reports the abuse, the family may withdraw from the program and that would be bad for Kylie. Angela says she thinks that the incident was probably an isolated one, anyway. Emiliana is very distraught now. She knows the law says that she is a mandatory reporter of child abuse, yet her coworkers, who are supposed to know more than she does, are not encouraging her to do this.

Emiliana goes home and cries. She has never reported child abuse before. Deep down she knows what she must do, yet she is afraid. She is afraid that she will get in trouble at work if she reports the abuse. She is also afraid that Kylie's father will guess or find out somehow that she was responsible for calling children's services. She is afraid that he will get mad and threaten her or her own children. She calls Ms. Hayden at home and tells her what Angela said. Ms. Hayden still leaves the decision up to Emiliana. After the children are in bed, she talks with her husband at some length. He helps her listen to her own sense of ethics, responsibility, and her concern for Kylie.

The next morning Emiliana calls children's services and makes her report. The social worker who takes her report, Bobbie, informs her that she will be coming to her class to talk with Kylie today and requests a private room in which to interview her. Emiliana informs Ms. Hayden of this and arranges for the private room. When Bobbie comes, she asks Emiliana to bring Kylie to the private room and stay with her and Bobbie during the interview but to let Bobbie and Kylie do the talking. Bobbie works hard to put Kylie at ease, and the subsequent interview is done in a very careful and thorough manner. Kylie tells Bobbie and Emiliana about her mother burning her arm with a cigarette and many other inappropriate and hurtful experiences that are ongoing in her life. These are very distressing to Emiliana, and she is now absolutely certain that her decision was the right one. Bobbie tells Kylie that what her mother did to her was wrong, that it was not Kylie's fault, and that her mother and father should not hurt Kylie. Bobbie says she will take Kylie to stay with a different family for a while to keep her safe until her mother is able to keep from hurting her. Bobbie also reassures Emiliana that her identity as the reporter is absolutely confidential.

Bobbie informs Emiliana and Ms. Hayden that she is removing Kylie from her home and is taking Kylie now to place her in a foster home while her family gets therapy. Bobbie will make sure that Kylie continues to come to preschool and Emiliana will see her again very soon. Emiliana informs her assistant and Deshane that she reported her suspicions of abuse and that children's services decided to remove Kylie from her home. The following week they meet Kylie's foster mother as she brings Kylie to class, and Ms. Hayden and Angela both thank Emiliana for calling children's services and tell her that she did the right thing.

Emiliana is still worried that Kylie's family will assume that it was her who reported the abuse and will be extremely angry with her. However, she doesn't hear anything at all from them. A month later Kylie's father is again the one to bring her to class, and he is his usual fairly chatty self, acting as if nothing had happened. Emiliana is grateful for that and chats with him in the same manner. The next time she suspects child abuse and therefore needs to report it, she is more self-confident and it is much easier for her to do what needs to be done.

## QUESTIONS

1. If you were Deshane, would you have asked Kylie about the red sores on her arm? When she replied quietly and refused to talk any more, was Deshane's subsequent behavior appropriate? Why or why not? Code P-1.8

2. Why do you think Emiliana left the tea party and immediately went over to sit next to Kylie, and then take so long to ask Kylie about the sores on her arm?

3. Why did Emiliana thank Deshane for telling her about Kylie's lesions and assure him that she was working on the issue? Code I-3a.1, I-3A.3

4. Why do you think Ms. Hayden acted the way she did in response to Emiliana? What were her responsibilities in this situation? Code P-1.8, P-1.9, P-1.10

5. How do you feel about the response Angela gave to Emiliana's questioning? Do you think Emiliana did the best thing for Kylie when she reported her suspicions of child abuse? Why or why not? Code P-1.8, P-1.9, P-1.10

6. After Emiliana told Madeline, Ms. Hayden, Deshane, and Angela about what Kylie told her, how did this then affect each of their own responsibilities? Code P-1.8, P-1.9, P-1.10

7. Was it reasonable for Emiliana to be afraid that Kylie's family might react violently toward her if they suspected that it was she who reported the abuse? How would you have felt in Emiliana's place?

8. How do you think Emiliana would have felt if she had decided not to report the child abuse to children's services? What do you think might have happened?

# 20 An Activity Close to Amanda's Heart (4–5 Years)

## FAVORITE CHILDHOOD SCHOOL MEMORIES

It is early February and Amanda Greenfield has been assisting Hana Serisawa, a preschool teacher with 20 4-year-old prekindergarten children enrolled at a private morning preschool program. Amanda started taking university classes in early childhood education last year and began her practicum experience at this center about a month ago. Amanda is enjoying her experiences in this classroom, especially as she becomes more involved with individual children and small groups of children. She also enjoys setting up and facilitating some of the activities that Hana has created for the daily curriculum. Soon Amanda will be planning activities that she will facilitate with the children.

As she considers her involvement with individual children, she recalls that when she initially arrives at school, 4-year-old Mia often greets her and accompanies her to the area where she facilitates her first activity of the day. As Amanda observes and engages Mia in a variety of **unstructured activities**, Mia demonstrates good muscle control in her fingers and hands as she manipulates a variety of objects, such as markers, pencils, brushes, glue sticks, scissors, and playdough. When Mia creates pictures, collages, sculptures, and other representations, Mia often asks Amanda, "What should I make?" Amanda may reply by asking her, "What do you like to create?" As Mia identifies several objects, such as people, animals, and flowers, she asks Amanda if she will draw these. After Amanda draws an object, Mia is eager to try to copy the object. She then shouts to others, "See this!" and points to her new creation. After Amanda says "Good job," Mia places it in her cubby and walks over to another activity.

As Amanda considers the kind of activity she would like to plan and facilitate, she thinks of Mia's eagerness to copy an example and her fine motor skills. She also recalls the kinds of activities that she and Hana have led over the past 3 weeks. She thinks about several playdough activities, block construction, the sand table with cups, molds, and pitchers, painting at the easel and on different types and shapes of paper and cardboard, the restaurant in the dramatic play area, making murals together, and looking at a variety of shells through a magnifying glass at the discovery table.

She admits that although she is enjoying these kinds of activities, her fondest early school experiences were those involving crafts. She remembers the special snowmen made out of paper plates, the caterpillars made out of egg cartons and pipe cleaners, and even dot-to-dot pictures of different shapes and objects. Although she has enjoyed the activities Hana has offered each day, she feels excited about having all of the children achieve a specific project goal. She concludes that if she can get all of the children to do a set of tasks, they will be productive learners.

She decides to identify a couple of activity ideas to develop and explore with Hana. Over the weekend, she thinks about the week before Valentine's Day. She fondly remembers making "Valentine

Friends" with her classmates when she was young and then viewing them on the bulletin board in a large valentine-shaped pattern. She is excited about this possibility and searches through her storage bins for her kindergarten creation. When she finds it, she sets it out on her table to view and ponder as she writes down what she will need for this activity. As she begins to plan, she realizes that she can also create a dot-to-dot warm-up activity to accompany the craft project that will show Mia and the other children exactly what a Valentine Friend looks like with its body shape, arms, legs, face, eyes, lips, and cheeks.

## QUESTIONS

1. Amanda is drawing animals for Mia during self-selected activities. How could she better encourage Mia's drawing skills and creative expression? DAP 2F
2. How may Amanda's use of the common expression "Good Job!" limit Mia's involvement and motivation in the learning process? DAP 2F(7)
3. Describe Amanda's motivation for recreating her Valentine Friends activity for the children in this classroom.
4. What do you think Amanda's activity goal or objective might be for the children?

## AMANDA'S PLAN

As Amanda thinks about this activity she jots down her plan on a note pad. She lists the materials she will need, as well as the directions for preparing, setting-up, and facilitating the activity as follows.

### "Valentine Friends"

#### Materials

25 sheets of 9 × 12-inch pink construction paper

2 sheets of 9 × 12-inch white construction paper

2 sheets of 9 × 12-inch black construction paper

5 sheets of 9 × 12-inch red construction paper

10 sheets of red tissue paper

3 new pencils, unsharpened

3 bottles of school glue

#### Directions

#### To Prepare Valentine Parts

1. Draw and cut out a template for a 9 × 9-inch valentine shape, 1-inch circles for eyes, ½-inch circles for pupils, lips, and eyebrows, 2-inch circles for cheeks, 10 × 1-inch strips for legs, 6 × 1-inch strips for arms, 3-inch circles for hands, 5-inch circles for feet, and 1 × 1-inch squares for highlights.
2. Trace and cut out the following.
   20 valentine shapes with pink paper
   20 pairs of 1-inch circles for eyes with white paper
   20 pairs of ½-inch circles for pupils with black paper
   20 lip shapes for lips and mouth with red paper
   20 pairs of eyebrow shapes with black paper
   20 pairs of 2-inch circle shapes with red paper

20 pairs of longer strips for legs with red paper
20 pairs of shorter strips for arms with red paper
20 pairs of 3-inch circles for hands with black paper
20 pairs of 5-inch circles for feet with black paper
140 $1 \times 1$-inch squares to highlight cheeks and lips with red tissue

### Setting-Up

1. To prepare a model Valentine Friend, glue and press the body parts onto a valentine shape and place it in the center of the table.

2. Set up five to six work areas for a small group of children around a table. At each space, set a valentine shape in the center with the corresponding body shapes placed uniformly around the shape. Place the glue bottles in the center of the table, one in the center and the other two at either end.

### Putting It Together

1. Show the children what the Valentine Friend looks like.

2. Show the children the body shapes around their valentine shape.

3. Invite the children to glue their body shapes onto the valentine shape.

4. Watch and encourage the children as needed.

5. As children finish their Valentine Friend pass out a handful of red tissue squares and show them how to twist a square into a circle with the eraser end of a pencil and then pinch and glue them onto the cheeks and lips for highlights and texture.

6. After the Valentine Friend has dried, display it in a large valentine-shaped outline on a bulletin board.

### Initial Warm-Up Activity

Ten minutes before the children do the Valentine Friend activity, pass out a "dot-to-dot" Valentine Friend worksheet to each child and invite the child to connect the dots by finding numbers 1–20 in sequence.

## QUESTIONS

1. Does this activity encourage young children to individually express their thoughts and feelings? Explain your answer. DAP 2F

2. Describe how you believe children with different skill levels will participate in the Valentine Friend activity. Predict how Mia will be involved in this activity. DAP 2F(4,5); Code I-1.2, I-1.3

3. Describe how you imagine the children will do with the dot-to-dot worksheet?

4. How developmentally appropriate are these activities for this class? Explain your answer.

5. What lessons do you think the children might learn, both positive and negative, from their experience with these activities?

6. What specific recommendations do you have for Amanda and her plans for these activities? DAP 2B(2); Code I-1.3

## AMANDA CONFERS WITH HANA

Amanda is excited and anxious about sharing her plan and childhood valentine example. When she arrives at the classroom she asks Hana if she can meet with her for a few minutes after school to talk about her activity plans. Hana is glad that Amanda is thinking about possible activities she can develop and facilitate in the classroom. After school, Hana asks Amanda to share her activity ideas.

Amanda takes out her planning notes and her childhood example and talks about how her possible plan has evolved. As Amanda talks, Hana listens quietly. Hana remains focused on what Amanda is describing, without commenting on different aspects of the activities. Then she asks Amanda, "For which child or children in this classroom would these activities be most appropriate? What areas of development should be emphasized?" Amanda quickly identifies two children, Mia and Sam, who enjoy creative, manipulative activities and tells Hana that she thinks the valentine and dot-to-dot activity would further promote their fine motor skills. Hana tells her that this key aspect of their discussion is missing from her plan and that she needs to include it with a stated developmental objective that represents the needs and interests of one or both of these focus children. Hana also asks her to specify other areas of development this activity could address for these individual children.

Hana knows from her experience and training that there are a number of limitations in the design and in Amanda's expectations of these activities, but decides to let Amanda experience them as she created them and then debrief and evaluate the outcome with her. As Hana considers this decision, she knows that many activities in her classroom are open-ended, child-directed opportunities and will allow the children a choice on Amanda's teaching day. Hana asks Amanda to think about why her childhood activity captured her attention as a child and to think about what the advantages and limitations are for this kind of activity. Then she tells Amanda to make a list of the limitations in the current design of this activity and to indicate how she can modify her plans to enhance the children's involvement in the learning process.

## QUESTIONS

1. Describe specifically the limitations you believe Hana is referring to in Amanda's plan. DAP 2B(2), 2F(5)
2. Describe modifications you would make to this activity that would make it more relevant to the needs of individual children such as Mia. DAP 2F(3-4)

## AMANDA'S TEACHING DAY

Amanda takes some time to reflect about Hana's questions. She feels that the Valentine Friend has many parts to be glued in precise locations as indicated on the model. She admits that she is quite exhausted after cutting out numerous body parts for each valentine shape. She decides to omit the twisted tissue squares to highlight the cheeks and lips. After thinking about the children's fine motor skill levels, she is unsure that many of them would be successful at this task.

Wednesday is the day that Amanda will offer the activity in Hana's classroom during the first hour of preschool when the children choose the activities they wish to do. She talks with Hana about the best location to set up the activity and decides that the large rectangular table near the sink and clean-up area will work nicely. The table is next to another one where children can lay their Valentine Friends to dry. At this point, Amanda remembers that she has the copies of the dot-to-dot worksheets and wonders where she can set them down for children to do before they participate in the Valentine Friend activity. She locates a round table nearby and sets out the worksheets by each chair. Hana asks her, "Who will facilitate this with the children?" Amanda replies, "No facilitation is needed, children have seen enough of these games and will know what to do."

As the children arrive and begin their play at different centers and tables, two children begin the dot-to-dot sheets and three children, including Mia and Sam, ask Amanda about the valentine activity. Amanda directs them over to the worksheet area and tells them to join her after they are done. When Mia asks her what she can draw on the sheet, Amanda replies, "Follow the dots with your pencil and you will see." As they draw lines on their worksheets, Amanda notices that all of them have lines, squares, circles, and other markings in a variety of locations on their sheets. She is surprised as she realizes that none of the worksheets shows an emerging valentine heart person. In spite of her disappointment, she invites them over to the next table to make their Valentine Friends.

As they begin, Amanda points out the model of a Valentine Friend on display and shows them their base shape and all of the individual body pieces to glue and press onto it. Sam squeezes about two tablespoons of the white glue onto the valentine shape and decides he is done after the eyes are glued on. Amanda tries to get him to finish, but to no avail. Mia places all of her pieces in the "correct" places and then asks to create a second one. A third child, Mike, glues the lips and cheeks onto the legs. Amanda tells him that is wrong and asks him to start again. This time Amanda puts the glue on the valentine base in the "correct" places and shows him, one at a time, where the different parts should be placed. Another child folds the legs and arms like an accordion, which gives them a creased effect. Amanda asks that child to choose other legs because she wants the Valentine Friends to all look like the model, since they will be on display on the bulletin board. Amanda has her hands full as she guides each of the other children to create a Valentine Friend that resembles the model. She thinks that maybe she should have limited the activity to only two children at a time. She is too busy to ask the children to work on the dot-to-dot worksheets, and only one more child tries this option.

## QUESTIONS

1. Overall, how would you describe Sam's, Mia's, and Mike's experiences with Amanda's activity? Consider each child separately.
2. How would you describe Amanda's facilitation style: a **child-centered, teacher-assisted,** or **teacher-directed** style? Explain your answer.
3. According to the design of this activity, what kinds of decisions do children have the freedom to make?
4. As you consider the plan and implementation of this activity, whose goal or objective is the emphasis or focus placed upon? Explain your answer.
5. How do you think Amanda is feeling about how the children participated in her activity?
6. As an intern, how would you feel in this situation?
7. As the activity was facilitated, what aspects made the experience more successful for these children? What aspects made it less successful?

## DEBRIEFING WITH HANA

After preschool, Amanda has the opportunity to discuss her thoughts and feelings with Hana about her experience in the classroom earlier in the day. Amanda describes how hard she had worked to prepare the activity and help the children do it, how she feels very disappointed that "so many children didn't understand what they were supposed to do," and how much help she had to give them. Also a number of the children didn't stay to finish their valentines and she "had been forced to finish the valentines for them" so she would have enough to make the big valentine shape as she had planned.

Hana asks Amanda how old she was when she first participated in this activity? Amanda thinks for a minute and then realizes that she was probably in an elementary school classroom. At first, she feels defensive. "Perhaps I was in kindergarten," she tells Hana. Then Hana asks Amanda what she thinks the children learned from the activity today. Amanda says that those who stayed to finish the activity learned to follow directions and learned what a beautiful valentine they could make. She feels that those who finished doing it by themselves learned self-esteem because they seemed proud of their valentines, and several children didn't need any help from her.

Since only some of the children felt good about their valentine, Hana asks Amanda if that means that those who couldn't do it the way she wanted might feel a little "not so good?" Amanda looks thoughtful. Hana asks if her primary goal for the activity was to produce the big valentine shape out of the children's work? Amanda says yes, adding that she thinks it looks very nice. Hana agrees that it looks very nice and indicates that she appreciates how much effort Amanda put into preparing her activity. Hana reminds Amanda that her primary goal, to create this "product," was not a goal related to the children's learning and development. Amanda says that the children really like having a nice "product" to show their parents what they can do. Hana agrees that this is true.

Hana tells Amanda in a gentle voice, "When working on such an activity the main thing for children is experiencing the 'process' of working with the materials, the social interaction as they do so, the vocabulary you and the other children bring into the discussion, and the opportunities provided for their own creative expression and for seeing the different ways that the materials can be put together by their peers. When you had the children make the valentines according to your model, the children were not able to learn as much as they could have if you had given them the freedom to put the pieces together in their own ways." Hana adds that, "Limiting children's options when offering a craft activity suggests several subtle or underlying messages that perhaps we don't want the children to learn. Showing only one way of completing the craft through the use of a model, when the materials can be used in many more ways, limits children's creativity. It is as if we were saying 'Don't be creative; don't express or follow through with your own ideas; there is only one way to do things that is correct.'"

Amanda covers her mouth with a hand and her eyes pop. She says, "But I never meant to teach that! Sure, I wanted them to do it the correct way, but I didn't mean for them to learn those things!" Hana smiles and tells Amanda, "I know you didn't mean that, and I know if you think about it more you will see that there are many 'correct' ways of doing things for preschool children. You did work very hard, you were very nice in your interactions with the children, you used a lot of vocabulary with the children, and they were able to socialize while they were working, sharing the different ways their families sometimes celebrate Valentine's day or other winter holidays. I look forward to your next activity."

Amanda looks relieved; she tells Hana how much she is learning from these experiences and that she hopes she can soon create another activity that is directly related to the developmental needs of specific children. Hana asks Amanda about changes she could make to strengthen the Valentine Friend activity. She does not mention the dot-to-dot worksheets, thinking she has been hard enough on Amanda.

Amanda replies that the next time she plans an activity such as the Valentine Friends, she will avoid worrying about the "product" and will concentrate on the learning that her focus child and the other children will gain from the activity "process." She will also think about what subtle messages the children might learn from the activity. Hana reassures her that these actions will be responsive to the needs of the children.

She also suggests that perhaps Amanda might want to consider the amount of preparation time she has invested in contrast to what the children will gain from the activity. Then Hana also suggests that perhaps allowing the children the freedom to participate in open-ended activities might feel risky when the outcome is uncertain. Amanda agrees with Hana's interpretation and feels affirmed by Hana's interest and support as she looks forward to future teaching experiences in this classroom.

## QUESTIONS

1. What key part of an activity plan enables a teacher to evaluate the effectiveness of the plan with individual target children? DAP 3C(1-3)
2. Would you repeat this activity in your classroom? If so how could you revise it so that it is more developmentally appropriate? DAP 2B(2), 2C, 2F; Code I-1.2, I-1.3
3. After the Valentine Friends dry, what would be an effective way to display these creations? What might the children learn from this?
4. What are some key points Amanda learned from her experience with this activity and the debriefing with her supervising teacher?

# 21 Observation Reveals the Issue (4–5 Years)

Mary Martin is a new high school Consumer Sciences teacher who teaches child development classes and runs a preschool program for students to gain hands-on experience. Mary is a former preschool teacher who recently graduated from a well-respected teacher education program with her secondary education credentials and a Consumer Sciences endorsement. She is a bit nervous about beginning her first year of teaching, but she is excited to implement what she has learned over the past 4 years of college. Mary has a neighbor and good friend, Doris, who teaches first grade in one of the elementary schools in town and she frequently talks with her in confidence about her teaching experiences. Doris is a great sounding board, and offers helpful suggestions and support for Mary.

During the first few weeks of the school year, Mary teaches the high school students about young children and how they will effectively participate in the preschool program. They discuss child growth and development, positive guidance approaches, observation techniques, and developmentally appropriate preschool curriculum. After a month of classwork has gone by, the students are anxious to start working with the children.

Eighteen 4- and 5-year-old children have been recruited over the summer to participate five mornings a week in the preschool program. Mary holds an Open House for the families the week before the preschool program begins. Students attend so they can meet the families and interact with the children while Mary talks with the parents. Mary welcomes the families, introduces the students, and invites families to look over the classroom after her presentation. She then talks about the preschool program and answers any questions they might have.

The event goes smoothly but later that evening, Mary reflects on her concern for one particular family, the Burtons, she met that night. Mrs. Burton talked with Mary privately at the end of the Open House about her 5-year-old son Logan. Logan attended another preschool last year and was held back from going to kindergarten this fall because the teacher and his mom felt "he wasn't ready." Mrs. Burton said last year he was too active to sit still to do the schoolwork, and he didn't even know his colors. She said she wanted Mary and the students to teach him his colors right away. Mary agrees she would like to work with Mrs. Burton to help Logan with his overall development, including his mom's goal.

The following evening Mary talks with Doris about the family event. They agree the Open House was a successful way to welcome families into the program. Mary discusses her conversation with Mrs. Burton and her concern for Logan's needs. Doris mentions that she tries to attend to all of her children's particular needs, and Mrs. Burton's remarks might help Mary work with Logan's needs right away.

For the next week Mary and the students work together to plan the curriculum for the first few weeks of preschool. They decide to focus on colors and are hopeful that this topic will be interesting for all of the children in the classroom and will be especially helpful for Logan. The students design special activities related to colors in different areas of the curriculum. For 2 weeks they plan to have a different "color of the day" by using books, activities, and snack foods focused on the particular color for that day.

Many of the children are excited to be in preschool and actively participate in the planned activities. However, when asked to try the table activities during choice time, Logan refuses, saying, "No, I don't want to." He also doesn't attend to the books about colors being read during circle time, and, in fact, he is often disruptive at large group time when the class is talking about colors. When asked about the colors of objects, sometimes Logan names the colors correctly and sometimes he doesn't. "Red? Orange? I'm not sure," he guesses. Logan pleads with the teachers not to tell his mom when he gets the color names wrong. He says, "Don't tell my mom! Please don't tell!" Some of the students are disappointed that Logan doesn't respond to their color activities the way they had hoped.

At the end of the 2 weeks Mary reflects on the results of the color curriculum and her observations of Logan's lack of participation. She talks with Doris one evening, who reminds Mary to think more about Logan's "**approaches to learning**." Is he intrinsically motivated to learn the color names and is he really interested in the color activities? How does this compare with his approach to other kinds of activities? Together they decide to take the focus away from colors for a couple of weeks. Instead, Doris suggests Mary move to more of an informal way of considering colors. The following week Mary talks with Mrs. Burton and suggests she avoid pressuring Logan to name colors. "Perhaps Logan is trying too hard to please adults and has a block against naming colors correctly," she tells Mrs. Burton. It is agreed that Mrs. Burton and the students will just mention the color names in ordinary activities at both home and school. The students avoid pressuring him to participate in the table activities, and instead they just label paints, vehicles, and blocks by their colors as they interact with Logan and the other children.

In addition, two students are given the task of observing Logan and recording his overall cognitive development over several preschool sessions. The students use **anecdotal records** rather than a formal checklist to ensure that Logan doesn't feel pressured to perform. The anecdotes document that Logan is skilled in problem solving using puzzles, counting more than 10 objects with **one-to-one correspondence**, and naming letters, numerals, and most colors. He knows the names of many colors when he uses them as he plays. However, the students noticed that he seems to consistently have trouble naming red- or green-colored objects. They also notice that, although Logan is among the more physically active children in the class, there are many activities in which he regularly stays engaged for long periods of time.

When the students share their observations of Logan's cognitive development with Mary, she is surprised and encouraged. Just as she expected it looks as if the pressure of naming colors correctly, when he often is unable to do so, may be causing Logan to have a block against naming colors. It also occurs to her that since he can consistently name some colors correctly but has difficulty with red and green objects, they might consider the possibility of colorblindness. Red and green colorblindness sometimes occurs, most often in boys and men.

Mary talks with Mrs. Burton when she picks Logan up from school, sharing the results of the students' observations and her own suspicions. Mrs. Burton agrees to discuss the possibility of colorblindness with Logan's pediatrician. After clinical testing, it is confirmed that Logan is red–green colorblind, and strategies for helping Logan adapt to this condition are suggested for home and school.

After learning of the test results, Mrs. Burton calls Mary to give her the news. Mrs. Burton mentions how guilty she feels about not catching the colorblindness earlier, and putting so much pressure on Logan for so long to accomplish something that was impossible for him—and how it influenced her decision to hold him back from kindergarten for another year. Mary consoles her in the best way she can, pointing out how resilient children can be—especially when they have a close relationship with a caring parent. Mary also points out that she feels Mrs. Burton is a wonderful parent who received some poor advice and was just trying to do the best she could for her son. Mary tells Mrs. Burton about one of her own parenting mistakes from when her own child was young. Then Mary says, "I think it would be perfectly okay to enroll Logan in kindergarten now, even though the school year has already begun. Have you given that any thought?" Mrs. Burton replies, "You wouldn't mind if I took him out of your program?"

"Oh no, not at all!" Mary replies. "Logan's needs come first! It is your decision to make but from my perspective, I think Logan is ready for kindergarten. It can be helpful for Logan to be placed with his age-mates during his elementary school years. Sometimes children can be unkind to a child that they think is behind a year. You might call the elementary school office and talk with the kindergarten teacher about Logan. The school office can give you information about enrolling him, if you decide that is what you think is best."

## QUESTIONS

1. In what ways do Mary and the students help Logan feel more secure and less stressed in the preschool environment? DAP 1E(1), 2B(3); Code I-1.5

2. Why does Mary have students do informal **anecdotal observations** of Logan's overall cognitive abilities rather than test him on his colors? DAP 2B(2), 4D, 4F; Code I-1.6

3. How does Mary show Mrs. Burton that she is sensitive to her concerns about her son's development? Is there anything you would do differently? DAP 2B(1), 5D; Code I-2.2

4. Logan's teacher told Mrs. Burton that he is an active child and therefore not ready for kindergarten. Do you agree with that conclusion? What characteristics of a kindergarten program would you recommend for Logan? DAP 4G; Code I-1.9, I-1.12

5. If Logan stays in the preschool program, in what ways might Mary and Mrs. Burton address kindergarten readiness and plan activities to help Logan develop at his own rate since he is older than the rest of the children in the preschool?

6. How can you explain Logan's behavior becoming more cooperative when the pressure of learning colors is removed? DAP 2B(3)

7. What do you think about the decisions made by Logan's former preschool teacher to encourage Mrs. Burton in holding Logan back from kindergarten? If you were Mrs. Burton, what do you think you would do now that the reason for his color challenges has been discovered?

8. Why do you think Mary shared with Mrs. Burton a time when she felt that she had made a parenting mistake? DAP 5A

# C A S E

# 22 Productive Play with Fairy Dust (Kindergarten)

Noah Aronson is outside in the play yard with his group of kindergartners. Gracie approaches him, dragging her feet, and looking down at the ground. "What's up, Gracie?" he asks as he squats down by her. "You are looking kinda' sad."

"Taree and Lian say I can't play with them!" Gracie complains.

"What are they playing?" asks Noah.

"They're in the sand box and they say I can't play with them!" she complains again. There have been several times this morning that Taree, Lian, or Gracie has come to him complaining about two of the three children excluding the third. Usually these three children work well together, but despite several attempts at problem solving with them this morning, they remain easily annoyed with each other.

"You girls are having a hard time this morning. Why do you think that is happening?" he wonders.

"I don't know. It's not fair if I don't get to play!" Gracie asserts.

"I think we need some fairy dust to sprinkle around so that everyone is not so grumpy! Wouldn't that be fun?" Noah suggests with a laugh.

Gracie looks at him for a moment with her brow wrinkled as she ponders this idea. Her face brightens and she announces, "I know . . . I'm going to make a 'Fairy Trap' so we can catch some fairies and get their fairy dust!" With great enthusiasm, she begins to gather some **loose parts** from around the play yard: some tires, some interlocking plastic pieces that form a large cube, and a couple of small aluminum ladders. From the sandbox, Lian and Taree watch her work. After a few minutes they walk over to where Gracie is building and ask, "Watcha doin'?"

"I'm making a Fairy Trap so we can get lots of fairy dust so we can sprinkle it on everybody so they won't be so grumpy!" Gracie explains.

"Fairy dust!" Lian and Taree look at each other with eyes wide and mouths open in astonishment. "How do the fairies get in?" asks Taree.

"Over here in this hole." Gracie points to a hole in the large cube.

"I know! Let's move the tires over here so the fairies will see this trail and walk right up to the trap," Lian suggests.

"Yeah!" the girls all agree. Noah watches as the girls all work together for another 15 minutes on the fairy trap project. They talk excitedly about their plans and with each new idea the fairy trap grows and becomes more complicated. When both Lian and Gracie have different ideas about where they should put the fairies after they are caught, there is a momentary disagreement. However, before tempers flare, they decide that there are going to be "sooooo many fairies in the trap" that they need two places to keep the fairies so both plans are put into action. Noah is glad to see that the irritations of the morning seem to be gone. With their high level of involvement, the girls can sustain this new play on their own.

"What about the trolls?" Noah hears Gracie ask. He is curious where this new play element will take them. "Oh, no! We don't want the trolls to get in. Trolls eat fairies," Lian announces with conviction. "Look over there!" Taree points at the white clover blossoms growing in the grass. "That's troll poison. We need to get lots!"

Gracie is unsure. She walks over to where Noah is now standing watching the whole play yard and asks, "Is it OK to pick those?" pointing to the clover by his feet. He assures her that it is OK to pick the clover because they don't want the clover growing in the grass. "The clover attracts the bees and we don't want bees in our grass because someone might step on a bee and get stung. We want to keep children safe. You can pick as much as you want but watch out for bees! Thanks for asking. Were you thinking about the rule we have about not picking flowers in the garden?"

"Yeah," Gracie answers running back to the other girls. "It's okay because we don't want bees, so we can pick them to poison the trolls." "Yeah," agrees Lian. "Bees like the clover and fairies do too because fairies have wings just like bees. But trolls don't. They hate clover! We need lots of clover poison to feed to the trolls so they will stay away." As the girls busily gather clover blossoms, Fabio and Chin-Hwa approach the fairy trap and begin to disengage the ladder from the construction. "Hey! The trolls are getting the fairies!" yells Taree, running back to where the boys are struggling to get the ladder out.

"We need this ladder and you're not using it. You are over there in the grass!" asserts Fabio. Lian and Gracie have joined Taree in defense of the fairy trap and Gracie pulls on the ladder, which by now is in Chin-Hwa's hands. "No! We ARE using it. We need it for our fairy trap!" On hearing raised voices, Noah moves closer to the play to observe if they need any help in resolving this dispute. "What's a fairy trap?" asks Chin-Hwa, still holding the ladder. "We're catching fairies, so we can get their fairy dust. See, we need this ladder right here," explains Gracie, pointing to a place in the construction. "See, the fairies come in here and then they have to go down in this hole," she says as she points to the space between rungs in the ladder, "and then we catch 'em!"

As Gracie talks, Chin-Hwa maintains a firm grip on the ladder, looking back and forth between Fabio and the girls. "No! We need this ladder over here, so we can climb up on the big tires. Ladders are for climbing on," asserts Fabio. "But if we don't have the ladder, the fairies will get out!" shouts Taree right in Fabio's face. Fabio's body gets very tense and Noah starts walking toward the group, still observing how the children are trying to resolve this problem. "I know! You guys can roll the little tires over there and climb up on them," suggests Lian. "No! Ladders are for climbing on!" reasserts Fabio. "You guys can use the tires to catch fairies. See . . . tires have holes. Fairies can get catched in these holes."

The three girls look at each other, unconvinced. Gracie stoops down to look at a tire lying on its side. She sticks her fingers into the interior of the tire and then looks up with a smile. "Yeah! We can put clover in this pocket and the fairies will come in and get it."

"But not the trolls!" shouts Taree. "Okay," agrees Gracie, looking at the boys. "You can have the ladder over there. That is where the trolls live." "Yuck! We don't want trolls. We're climbing up on a T-rex!" proclaimed the boys. "Okay, then grab some white flowers! Its poison for trolls," advises Gracie solemnly.

Before Fabio and Chin-Hwa leave, Noah steps over to the group. "Looks like you figured out the problem with the ladder," he says to everyone. "Yeah, they're going to take the ladder over there," Gracie states matter-of-factly. "You were all really listening to each other to find a way that everyone could be happy. Gracie, Lian, and Taree still get to make a fairy trap and Fabio and Chin-Hwa get to climb up on a T-rex! It took a long time but you guys really worked it out!" confirmed Noah. "Yeah, so now we have lots of fairy dust to sprinkle on everyone! We can even sprinkle it on the T-rex!" Gracie announced with glee.

## QUESTIONS

1. What skills were the girls practicing in the fairy trap play? What were they learning? DAP 1B, 2E(4)
2. What problems did they encounter in the play and how did they solve them?
3. What skills were used in resolving the problem about the ladder?
4. How did Noah see his role in the fairy play situation? How did he see his role in the problem-solving situation with the ladder? DAP 2E(3), 2G(3)

# 23 Helping Julian Adjust (Kindergarten)

## WHAT IS GOING ON WITH JULIAN?

Several weeks have passed since school started and Mingmei Wong, the teacher for a full-day kindergarten class of 25 5- and 6-year-old children, has been very busy. Now that the children are settling into the classroom routines, she decides it is time to focus more on getting to know the children better. Some of them are beginning to act out more often now than they did at the beginning of school, and Mingmei believes establishing better relationships with the children will help to prevent some of the children's misbehaviors.

As Mingmei reflects on her day-to-day observations of the children in her class, she realizes that 5-year-old Julian has been mostly playing by himself since the beginning of the year, interacting only when necessary with the other children playing with the unit blocks in the blocks corner and interacting very little with her. Mingmei decides she needs to observe Julian's behavior more closely during the following week.

Mingmei decides to make frequent anecdotal observations, being sure to capture Julian's positive behaviors, as well as those that concern her. She tapes up a piece of notebook paper in an inconspicuous place in her classroom where she can jot down brief notes during the day to remind her of what she has seen. At the end of each day, after the children have left for home, she quickly types up her observations based on these notes. Mingmei also currently has a college student intern, Rhiannon, and she asks her to make anecdotal observations of Julian too.

Julian does not talk much but focuses mainly on playing with the wooden blocks, the playdough, the sensory table, and on painting at the easel. He typically ignores the paper and glue activities, the manipulatives and games, the science table, the loft, the sociodramatic play sets, the dolls, and the housekeeping area. On Monday she observed Julian knock down the block structures made by other children, and once he grabbed a block and hit a child who was trying to take a block from a structure he was working on. After attending to and comforting the hurt child, Mingmei drew Julian aside, talked to him about how everyone must be kept safe in the classroom, asked him why he had hit the child and what he could have done instead. She realizes she will need to pay particular attention to her relationship with Julian and try to find out more about his background and needs. When she has time to spend Mingmei sits down near Julian at least once a day and makes comments or asks questions to engage him in conversation. When a good time arises, she will tell him about something in her home life, such as how sick her cat is these days and how sad she feels about that.

Mingmei has always planned to have some unhurried time with the children every day, when she can sit near them and be available for conversation, one-on-one or in a small group. Usually she describes verbally what a child is doing, making comments or asking questions. Sometimes she is just quietly present, ready to listen to the children's ideas. Most of the children seem to love this, and show their trust in Mingmei by sharing many of their daily experiences, thoughts, and questions with her.

Mingmei avoids actively teaching children during these informal conversations. Instead, she relaxes into the present, actively trying to be a good listener, to understand all that the children are trying to tell her or are telling each other within a conversational group. If at all possible, she listens long enough to hear the full train of related thoughts a child is sharing. Mingmei is as polite with each child as she usually is when talking with other adults. She often shares short stories about her own life and recent experiences that are of interest to the children. Mingmei knows that in this process she is building strong relationships with the children and between the children. She is building the children's self-esteem by showing them they are important to her. She exposes them to new vocabulary, exercises their speaking abilities, and engages them in prosocial interactions with herself and with other children. She helps the children get to know each other, as conversations that begin as two-way give-and-take often expand to involve a larger number of children.

Mingmei treasures these times, and structures her routine to allow her to sit down and converse with children during meals and snacks, during outside recess, and while she works with a small group of children during self-selected activity time. A few of the kindergarten parents take turns assisting in the classroom, and Mingmei relies on their help to allow her these special times to be with the children.

Mingmei's efforts to strengthen her relationship with Julian are beginning to pay off. At first he was resistant to talking with her, but gradually he is responding more and more to her attention and conversational prompts. In fact, he often asks Mingmei how her cat is feeling. One day Julian came to where Mingmei was sitting during self-selected activities and asked her to come and see the block structure he had made. Mingmei saw this as a clear sign that her efforts were producing dividends with Julian. Soon he stopped knocking down other children's block structures, but did continue to hit children on a hand or arm if they wanted to play with something he had gathered near himself, and he had more angry outbursts than most of the other children. He also cried much more intensely in response to a skinned knee one day than Mingmei thought was reasonable given the circumstances. But he did let Mingmei comfort him until he recovered his composure.

## QUESTIONS

1. What is the benefit for Julian of his teacher's thoughtful observations and responses? DAP 2B(1,2,3), 4A; Code I-1.7
2. What would Julian learn about himself if Mingmei simply gave Julian a time-out every time he made a mistake, and rarely interacted with him other than to punish him? DAP 2B(1); Code I-1.4, P-1.1
3. How does Mingmei's class as a whole benefit from her approach with Julian? DAP 1B; Code I-1.5
4. Why do you think the children seem to act out more often after the first few weeks of school?
5. How do you think establishing good relationships with students is likely to help prevent misbehaviors? Why? DAP 1C(1)
6. Name three specific strategies for helping children to begin to feel at home in the classroom.
7. What possible benefits do you think come from Mingmei's sharing with Julian something from her home life and her feelings about it? DAP 1B
8. What do you think may have been a reason for Julian's particularly intense crying bout in response to his skinned knee?

## TALKING WITH JULIAN'S MOTHER

Mingmei's observations are beginning to paint a picture of a boy who didn't seem to know how to engage with other children in their play, or perhaps he just didn't want to. Mingmei sometimes saw Julian with his head tilted down, seemingly paying no attention to what was going on around him. When other children would indicate their interest in playing with him, he would look away and often just leave the area. He loved running around during outdoor recreation time, but did so by himself. Julian was often late for class, and on these occasions his mother left quickly after she directed him into the classroom.

When Mingmei feels she has enough information from her observations and interactions with Julian, she e-mails Julian's mother, Ms. Parker, who had selected e-mail as her communication preference on Julian's intake form at the beginning of the year. Mingmei tells her that she has some questions and asks if they can arrange a time to talk with each other privately on the telephone. Ms. Parker agrees and the next evening Mingmei calls her. After the initial greetings, Mingmei tells Ms. Parker about a number of admirable things she has observed about Julian. "I am so enjoying having Julian in my class. Julian is already making detailed drawings in his journal, and often provides somewhat detailed descriptions for me to write down next to them. Sometimes he thinks of the correct letter to use for the beginning sounds and makes sure I'm recording that accurately! He always remembers to hang up his coat on the hook and checks to make sure it doesn't drop off. He can count by 10s all the way up to 100, too. I'm really impressed with how he regularly makes complex structures with the unit blocks and also with the *Legos.*©"

Ms. Parker sounds pleased to hear about these descriptions of her son, and then asks Mingmei what questions she has. Mingmei then describes the main reasons for her call. "I've noticed a few things that I'm wondering about. Julian sometimes seems to be feeling sad with no apparent reason for it, and he doesn't do very much playing with the other children. He seems to get angry fairly easily and sometimes he hits another child instead of using his words. These things worry me a little and I would like to help Julian. Could you perhaps help me to understand him a little better?" Ms. Parker is silent for a minute, and then in a very quiet voice she tells Mingmei that Julian's stepfather and she have recently separated, and that Julian had been very attached to his 4-year-old stepbrother who has left with his father. Ms. Parker talks much more and tells Mingmei of her marital troubles, her new financial problems, and how hard all of this is on Julian, about which she seems to feel terribly guilty. Mingmei listens sympathetically, and then she tells Ms. Parker, "I want you to be assured that I will keep all that you have told me confidential, but I want you to know that our school has a Family Support Office that is dedicated to helping families who are experiencing difficulties like you have described. I wonder if it would be alright with you if I give Ms. Olufson there your contact information? Then Ms. Olufson would call you to see if she can arrange to meet with you and look for ways that the Family Support Office could provide some help." Ms. Parker agrees to this. Mingmei adds, "It is particularly important to Julian's well-being for you to take good care of yourself. Research shows that your level of well-being is likely to impact his." Mingmei then compliments Ms. Parker for her strength and composure in such a difficult time, again mentioning that she is glad to have Julian in her class, and thanks Ms. Parker for her help before hanging up.

## QUESTIONS

1. What are the likely benefits to Julian of Mingmei communicating frequently with his mother? DAP 5E; Code I-2.2
2. How do you think connecting Ms. Olufson with Ms. Parker might benefit Julian? DAP 5G; Code I-2.9, P-2.15
3. What underlying messages do you think Ms. Parker may have received from her conversation with Mingmei? How do you think she felt after her conversation with Mingmei? Why? How might these feelings affect her interactions with Julian? Code I-2.9

4. Why did Mingmei tell Ms. Parker she would keep everything she heard confidential? Code P-2.13
5. How would you interpret Mingmei's observation that Julian sometimes did nothing while tilting his head down?
6. What do you think of the method Mingmei used to confer with Ms. Parker? Can you list the strategies she used in the process?

## USING THE INFORMATION TO HELP JULIAN

After her conversation with Julian's mother, Mingmei e-mails Ms. Olufson, asking her to visit Ms. Parker, and providing her with contact information. She also mails Ms. Parker an information sheet she has in her collection about understanding and helping children impacted by parental separation and divorce, published online by a University Cooperative Extension department.

Mingmei now believes that she has enough information to develop an informal plan for helping Julian adjust to kindergarten. She involves herself in play with the children whenever she can, whether inside or outdoors. Mingmei decides that she will often ask another child to come play when she is already playing with Julian, or invite Julian to play when she is playing with other children, as a way of facilitating Julian's increasing involvement with other children, especially during self-selected activities or outdoor recreation time. She will encourage Julian to participate in painting and other **expressive art** activities that occur regularly during self-selected activity time, and ask him to tell her about his work, especially when there are no other children close by. Mingmei will carefully encourage Julian to talk with her about the losses he has experienced.

Next Mingmei uses a **concept web**, putting Julian in the middle and around him the issues she now believes to be most pertinent for him: sadness and loss, confusion, guilt, anger, and loneliness. She also surrounds his name with some of his strengths: creativity, cooperation, an interest in learning, and a good relationship with his teacher. Next she thinks about each learning process in her kindergarten curriculum: emergent projects, self-selected activities, small groups, journals, story time, large group time, physical education, music, and outdoor recreation. Mingmei then draws an outer ring of ideas for helping Julian. She cannot involve Rhiannon in this step because it is important to keep Julian's family information confidential.

Mingmei decides to implement a social studies theme or project on families as soon as she can, which brings out the many ways in which families exist in this culture. She will involve Rhiannon in planning this project. It will include the fact that sometimes families have to cope with separation or divorce or other great difficulties, such as a shortage of money. She always involves the children in developing her emergent curriculum projects like this one and makes sure she includes all of the major challenges she believes the children are, or might be, experiencing. She plans to involve them in making a concept web for the families project. Perhaps they will make a small house and a set of apartments out of large cardboard boxes and make up short plays about families to act out. Mingmei decides to ask the school librarian and the parent who volunteers as class librarian to look for kindergarten-level books on these topics in the public library. She plans to read these books during story times. It is also Mingmei's habit to tell stories, as well as read them during story time, and she realizes that she rarely includes single-parent or divorced families in her stories. She decides to include a greater variety of families in her stories right away.

Mingmei plans to introduce a number of project-related words for the **word wall** and to encourage the children to use them when working on their journals. She keeps a few special dolls (persona dolls) of both genders on a top shelf in her room, each with different challenges. From time to time she brings one out for large group time when she wants to help the children think about feelings and interpersonal interactions. She decides that one of the boy dolls will be facing the challenge of parental separation. She will pretend to talk with the doll about how this feels. She will be sure to interview this doll not only for the families theme, but also a number of times during future weeks and months. She will also explore feelings of anger with the children, helping them learn how to express anger in safe, nonhurtful ways. She will explore other emotions related to parental separation, such as guilt, sadness, and helplessness, as well as ways to understand and cope with these emotions. She will build empathy in her children through helping them verbalize their responses and her own expressions of empathy for the doll.

Mingmei has a number of puzzles that show families, but these all show traditional families. She will ask one of the parent volunteers to try to find some puzzles that show different **family constellations** for the classroom. Mingmei thinks about having a self-selected activity about families, for which she will pull out her stash of old family magazines, and have the class work on a group mural collage of different family constellations. Then she remembers that she has been thinking about including an **antibias curriculum** activity about families and their differences. This involves having all of the children bring in pictures of their family members to post on a large display of all of the children and their families. She decides to include this activity instead of the magazine picture mural. She is certain that several other children in her class will benefit almost as much as Julian from these experiences, and the rest of the children will learn a lot as well.

Mingmei and Rhiannon will continue to observe Julian to assess whether their strategies for helping him are working. She also plans to e-mail Ms. Parker in a week to ask her if she believes Julian is feeling any better and what he tells Ms. Parker about his experiences in kindergarten. She plans to continue to stay in touch with Ms. Parker in this way. She will also suggest that Ms. Parker arrange for one or two of the children who seem to play well with Julian to visit him at home to play together. Mingmei has already distributed to all of the parents a voluntary class list of children's and parents' names, addresses, and phone numbers. She plans to make sure that Ms. Parker has that list.

## QUESTIONS

1. How do you think using a families theme helped Mingmei develop a curriculum that enabled children to make meaningful connections across subject-matter divisions, while also developing a curriculum that would address Julian's needs? Why is this appropriate? DAP: 2B(3), 3D(2), 4A

2. How does Mingmei plan to support Julian's "home culture"? DAP: 2J(2); Code I-1.10

3. What areas of knowledge and development do you think the families theme curriculum could involve children in learning? How? DAP: 3D(1)

4. How do you think participating in expressive art activities might help Julian? DAP: 2B(3)

5. Why doesn't Mingmei just ask Julian what his painting was, rather than asking him to tell her about it?

6. How is Mingmei's strategy of involving herself in the children's play likely to help Julian?

7. How might Mingmei go about involving the children in planning the families project, and why do you think she plans to involve them?

8. What would have been lost if Mingmei had not consulted with Julian's mother about his behavior? DAP 5A, 5B; Code P-1.4, I-2.6

# 24 Sharing Akil's Work Sample (Combined First-Second Grade)

Literacy is an important part of the curriculum in Evelyn Stuart's combined first- and second-grade class. She believes that the children will learn more by doing longer projects than from short daily lessons. She therefore has them create their own books throughout the year. This allows the children personal involvement with literacy and also stimulates and affirms their self-esteem and creativity. Evelyn also believes that an essential part of literacy learning is the connection between school and home, so she tries to include parents as much as possible in her big projects.

The children have recently spent the past month creating their own 10-page books around the song "A Hunting We Will Go." With this book she helps the children understand the concept of rhythm and rhyme and has them make their own rhyming verses to include in the book. Akil has fun making his own verses and illustrating each of the eight verses using different artwork.

The children write a page about themselves to include at the end of their book. Seven-year-old Akil writes about who he is, where he lives, his family and pets, the page in his book he likes the best and why it is his favorite, and the most difficult page and why it was so hard to do. His favorite page says, "A hunting we will go, a hunting we will go, we'll catch a little heart, and make it very smart, and then we'll let it go." Akil illustrates this page by drawing a heart person with a face and a blackboard with addition facts on it.

Evelyn has all the books bound and sends home invitations for an evening Open House. Akil is excited to show his book to his mother and grandmother. Akil and his family go to school together that night along with many other families. Evelyn asks the adults to make nametags for themselves and any other children they have brought, and she asks the children to use the ones they keep in their cubbies for special occasions. She has taken all of the children's chairs and arranged them in a circle on the carpet. She asks the adults to sit in the chairs and the children to sit on the carpet next to their families. She takes her regular chair in the circle.

Evelyn begins by thanking the parents for coming to the first Open House of the school year. She talks to the group about the plans for the evening: a focus on literacy and then playing some math games. Evelyn talks about her philosophy of education in simple, brief terms. "When children feel safe, both emotionally and physically, their ability to learn is enhanced. I expect the children to develop a sense of caring and belonging through an emphasis in class on thoughtfulness and respect for each individual's feelings—including mine. I often remind the children that everyone has unique backgrounds, challenges, preferences, abilities, and developmental timetables. Developing skills early is not the same as developing excellent skills. I tell the students that I expect that each member of the class will be valued and treated with respect.

"Each of us has many talents. Some of our talents are still sleeping and some of our talents are awake. I like to look for each person's talents, notice them, and encourage them. As you read your children's books with them, I hope you can look for the many talents that were used to create these beautiful books. When your children finish reading their books, ask them about their work, how the verses were created, and the techniques they used to illustrate the verses."

Evelyn asks the parents if they have any questions or comments for her before they begin this first activity. A parent asks if that means she won't be testing the children very often. Evelyn responds, "I use multiple approaches throughout the year for assessing children's progress, and simple tests are among them. I do not use testing often. For children to feel emotionally secure and to maintain positive **approaches to learning**, there must not be a constant atmosphere of being judged. When I do give tests, I use them to help children learn, as well as to help them assess their own progress and areas that could use more work. I mainly use ongoing observations and children's work samples as ways to document their development and learning. Their books are an example of a work sample that tells me a great deal about what your children are learning about literacy." As there are no more questions or comments, Evelyn excuses the children to take their families to their desks and read their special books with them.

Akil and the other children escort their families to their tables and read them their books. Akil's mother helps him with one of the words but Akil reads all of the others without help. Akil especially likes reading the page he wrote about himself at the end of the book. His smile beams up at his mother and grandmother and they admire his writing and his artwork enthusiastically. When it looks as if most of the parents and children are finished discussing the books and how they were created, Evelyn blinks the lights and invites everyone back to the carpet. Then children assemble in a line in front of the room, each with his or her book turned to a favorite page. The class sings "A Hunting We Will Go" by following all the children's favorite verses in the row. Parents and children clap and cheer for a wonderful shared experience, and then Evelyn introduces the next activity, the math games.

## QUESTIONS

1. How does Evelyn's learning environment protect children's emotional development? DAP 1E; Code I-1.4
2. In what ways does Evelyn address children's different levels of skills and knowledge? DAP 2F(4), 3C(3); Code I-1.3, 1.4
3. What strengths do you see in Evelyn's method of sharing children's work with families? DAP 5B; Code I-2.3
4. What value do you see in having the children read the book to their parents? DAP 5C
5. How is it helpful to have the parents discuss the making of the book with their children? DAP 5C
6. What do you think the children gained from reflecting on the process of making their books, which page they liked, and which page was the most difficult? DAP 2F(2)
7. Describe how you might apply Evelyn's literacy activity in your classroom.

# 25 Why Won't Luke Finish His Work? (First Grade)

## A PARENT'S VISIT

It has been 2 months since Dr. Aiyana Arkeketa became the Principal of Mt. Vernon Elementary School. Prior to this job, she was an early elementary school teacher for 12 years and she served as a director of a large child care center for 4 years before that. She has been very busy with the many issues involved in beginning the school year but now that things have settled down, she is getting ready to focus on becoming better acquainted with her teachers, their practices and curriculum implementation, and how the children are doing in her school. She has not invited the faculty to call her by her first name yet, but they and the parents have gotten into the habit of calling her "Dr. A."

Today she has a noon meeting with a parent, Elizabeth Remington, who called in last week for an appointment. When she arrives, Aiyana takes her wet raincoat and hangs it up on a coat rack, then provides Ms. Remington with a cup of hot spiced cider and offers her a seat at a round table in her office. Aiyana then closes her office door and sits down, talking about the stormy weather for a minute or two and how wet she got on the way in to work. Then she asks, "How may I help you, Ms. Remington?"

"Well, Dr. A., I'm concerned about my first-grade son Luke. He is in Ms. Wells' classroom. He already hates school! About a month ago, Luke told me he didn't want to go to school anymore. I asked him why and he told me it was too hard, but he wouldn't say any more than that. Of course, I insisted that he continue to come to school every day. Then Ms. Wells called me and said that Luke wasn't getting his work done. She asked me to punish or reward him based on a 'Behavior Report' she sends home with him every day indicating how much of his work he is getting done. I've been trying, but it just makes Luke feel even worse about school. Dr. A., Luke is a good boy. He has always been fairly cooperative at home, even more so than my older daughter. Lately, though, he is grumpy and unhappy, especially on school days. I have actually let him stay home on 2 days. He just seemed so stressed that I felt he needed a "mental health" day off from school to just rest in his room—no TV or special outings or anything. His grandmother came when I had to work. It seemed to help. I hope this wasn't wrong of me.

"I've talked with Ms. Wells about how unhappy he is, but she says he must do the work if he is going to learn. I know he is behind the other children in learning to read, but it just doesn't seem to make sense to put so much pressure on him that he is miserable. Now Ms. Wells is sending the work home with him as well. It is too hard for Luke and he really hates it, even when I help him a lot. He seems very bright, but has never been very good at memorizing the letters of the alphabet, unlike his sister, but he loves to be read to at home and he spends a lot of time with his books. I don't know what to do to help him!" Ms. Remington's chin begins to tremble and her eyes begin to form a few tears at this point.

Aiyana offers her the box of tissues she keeps on the table, saying, "I can see that you love your son very much and want what is best for him. I want that too. I'm very glad you came in to talk with me, Ms. Remington. I'll get you some water." Aiyana gets up and pours a cup of water from a large bottle she keeps in her office refrigerator, then gives it to Ms. Remington. "May I call you Elizabeth? Just call me Aiyana. I think your mental health days were okay. I don't think children should have to get physically sick just to get a badly needed break. However, I think we will be able to help decrease his stress in the first place. Elizabeth, please tell me more about Luke and his personality, what he likes to do and what a typical weekend day looks like for him."

Elizabeth smiles. "Well, he goes outside to play a lot on the weekends. He has always been very active. If it rains, he spends some time jumping on the bed we allow him to jump on. He likes to wrestle with his dad and go to the park. And of course he can't get enough reading. He loves for us to read to him, even his older sister. He also spends a lot of time just going through his books, looking at the pictures. We go to the library and get a lot of books from there—about 10 or so every few of weeks just for him. He would read through dinnertime if we let him. He loves his wood blocks and interlocking ones. He loves to build towers and make what we call "setups" where he organizes his toys in different ways, often on his block towers—and around them."

Aiyana responds: "It sounds like he is developing very well, Elizabeth, and you sound like an observant and caring parent. It also sounds like he has a body that needs to move more than many children, which is just fine but important to know about him. Thank you for sharing this with me. Elizabeth, do you want me to keep what you have told me this morning confidential, or is it alright if I talk with Ms. Wells about this? In either case, I will look into this more." Elizabeth expresses fear that Ms. Wells might be harder on Luke if she knew about the complaint. "Alright, we will keep this confidential—you must not tell Luke about this talk either, since children have a kind of gossip network just like adults do. It is very important that children believe that their parents respect their teachers—and vice versa. I will relate my observations to my general duties. Are we agreed?"

"I would really be thankful if you would," says Elizabeth. Aiyana responds, "Try not to worry. I think we will be able to help Luke to feel more successful and enjoy school. I'm sure that Ms. Wells has the best interests of all of her students at heart. Obviously, you have already talked with Ms. Wells about how Luke is doing. As for what you can do for now, avoid any more punishments or rewards for Luke based on the Behavior Report. Tell him you think he needs a break from that for now—please avoid telling him that I recommended it. I will begin looking into your concerns right away, but try to be patient. It will take a little time. There is always the possibility of moving Luke into another class if we can't help him to thrive in his current classroom. Usually that has some drawbacks, and I don't think that it will be necessary. Would you be able to meet with me again in 3 weeks?" They set up an appointment and say good-bye.

## QUESTIONS

1. Describe the strategies Aiyana used to build a relationship with Elizabeth Remington. DAP 1E(1), 5A, 5B, 5F

2. Do you think Aiyana should worry about Luke's apparent delay in learning to read as soon as some of the other first-grade children? List all of the considerations you think she should take into account. DAP 2F(4), 2J(1,4)

3. What are the advantages and disadvantages of allowing Luke to take a "mental health" break from school? Code P-1.1

4. Why do you think Aiyana takes time in the conference to visit with Ms. Remington informally and to ask about Luke's behavior at home? DAP 1E(1), 5E, 5F

5. Based on Elizabeth's description of Luke, how would you describe some characteristics of the parenting he may be receiving?

6. What do you think Elizabeth means by the word "read" when she says that Luke would "read" through dinnertime if they let him?

7. In what ways did Aiyana have Luke's developmental needs in mind as she discussed his mother's concerns during their meeting? DAP 5E

8. Why didn't Aiyana tell Elizabeth that she would just have to work out her concerns with Ms. Wells on her own? Code I-3A.2, I-3A.3, I-3B.1

9. Why does Aiyana agree to keep the information discussed at the conference confidential and not share it with Ms. Wells at this point? Do you think this is a good idea? Why? Code 2P-2.13

## OBSERVING LUKE AND HIS CLASSROOM

Later that day Aiyana asks the teacher, Taylor Wells, if she could observe her class for a few hours, telling her that it is time to become acquainted with each of the classrooms and the teachers' curriculum and practices (which is true). They schedule a time for Aiyana to observe the class for an entire morning on Monday of the following week.

When Aiyana arrives at the appointed time, she asks Taylor where she could sit, Taylor directs her to an adult-sized chair at the back of the classroom and then returns to her desk at the back of the classroom where she continues to work on some papers. Dr. Arkeketa looks around the classroom and begins taking notes. The children arrive, place their coats and backpacks in their cubbies, and start the morning sitting at their tables, working at composing words from a list of letters on the whiteboard, as well as writing a simple equation using three numbers also written on the whiteboard. Aiyana is surprised that Taylor does not greet the children or the parents who come to the door with some of them, nor do the children greet her. The pencil-and-paper activity lasts for about 15 minutes while everyone arrives. Aiyana walks around and notes that only 2 of the 13 children present are writing words on their papers. She looks at the names on the papers and locates Luke. He and a number of others are playing with their pencils or gazing around blankly. A few are whispering to each other.

When the morning bell rings Taylor goes up to the whiteboard and asks the children what words they have come up with. Each of the two children who were working successfully raise their hands and share the words they made. Taylor writes those words on the board. She then asks what equation they made with the three numbers. One of the two children tells her "$4 + 3 = 7$" and then the other child says "$3 + 4 = 7$." Taylor records both of these on the board underneath the three numbers without further elaboration. Then she asks the children to copy all of the words and equations from the board onto their papers. She gives the children 3 minutes to finish and turn their papers in to her at her desk at the back of the classroom, counting down the last 30 seconds as they attempt to comply. She tells them they should have at least six words written down. Aiyana sadly thinks about how little meaning this exercise must have from the point of view of the children, including Luke, who were unable to compose the words on their own to begin with. She thinks about what a waste of time the activity is for most of the children.

After turning in their papers, the children sit on the carpet for "calendar time," which lasts 25 minutes and includes about 5 minutes in which four children "share" about small toys and jewelry they brought from home. The subsequent calendar activities involve an **AA BB pattern** on the calendar, and a lot of different ways of counting related to the date and the number of days of school already past during November. Again, Aiyana thinks about how meaningless this exercise must seem to the children, who go through the same thing every day with only one more calendar day to add variety. She observes that there is an emotional aura in the classroom that she thinks is best described by the word "morose."

During this time Taylor calls on children randomly, drawing their names out of a basket and asking each one to stand in front of the other children and answer the math questions. When one child can't come up with an answer, she asks for a volunteer to come up and help. When it is Luke's turn he has trouble with the task and stares at the floor while the volunteer stands next to him and provides the answer. Aiyana is sure Luke must be feeling embarrassed in front of the other children.

Taylor gives each child three "good behavior" tickets for the day, reminding them that they will receive a piece of candy for each ticket they still have at the end of the day. Taylor then reads a section from the "story of the week" for about 5 minutes and then the children go to their tables and work on worksheets related to this part of the week's story. Most of the children spend the majority of the time drawing on the worksheets and doing only a little writing. This table work time lasts for 50 minutes during which the children are allowed to chat quietly, but not to visit with children at other tables. Taylor sits down at a small table and calls specific children to come over and sit with her so she can help them with their worksheets.

Aiyana observes that Luke has made some progress on his worksheet, but is currently drawing a picture of some airplanes and people on the back. He is also wiggling in his seat a fair amount, seemingly having a hard time sitting still. There are several other children who seem to be having trouble sitting still, and Aiyana walks around looking at their papers. These children have done only a little writing, and have focused on drawing pictures. When Taylor goes to check on Luke's progress, she tells him firmly that he must finish his work if he wants to go outside for break. He responds that he is working, then murmurs "but it is very boring," as Taylor walks away.

When it is time for their midmorning break most of the children scramble to get their coats on and line up by the door to go outside. Taylor keeps Luke and two other boys at their tables to finish their work before she lets them go outside for the break. Aiyana observes that Luke is the only one kept in for the entire 20-minute break. He is getting more and more agitated, pleading with Taylor to let him go outside. He loses one of his good behavior tickets at this time when Taylor becomes quite exasperated with him. Luke finally gives up and sits looking down at his paper, dripping a few tears on it.

When the children come back inside it is time for writing in their journals. They are asked to write four sentences, using invented spelling or checking the **word wall** for correct spelling, and to draw a picture with at least five colors. No talking is allowed during this time and Taylor plays some relaxing music for the children. This activity lasts for 55 minutes until it is time for lunch. During this stretch of time Luke gets into trouble for talking with his neighbors and getting up out of his seat several times. He loses the last of his two good behavior tickets. Another boy and several girls engage in similar behavior and the boy loses a ticket, although the behavior of the girls is ignored. Taylor appears to be feeling quite frustrated during her interactions with Luke. Aiyana feels sympathy for her, but even more so for Luke. She can certainly see why Luke hates school.

After the children have left for lunch, Aiyana asks Taylor if this is a typical morning and Taylor assures her that it is. Taylor goes on to explain that she has particular trouble with the student she kept in from break, Luke. She believes that Luke is very bright and should be able to do all of the work easily. She says that she has been working with the school counselor and that Luke's parents are helping put pressure on him, using a system where Taylor gives Luke a daily report card that he must take home to them. At first this seemed to make a little difference during October, but now Luke is back to his usual "dilly-dallying" ways of not completing his work. Taylor believes that Luke is an "underachiever" who is very bright and just needs to get over his stubborn resistance.

Aiyana makes an appointment to meet with Taylor after class a few days later. Then she returns to her office and types up the notes she made while observing Taylor's class, making sure to include her observations of a number of the children's behaviors and their progress on the assignments.

## QUESTIONS

1. What do you think about using behavior takeaway tickets to reinforce appropriate behavior in the first grade? What are the advantages and disadvantages of this approach for both the teacher and the children? How do you think a child would feel about losing a ticket in front of the other children? If a child often loses tickets, how do you think this might affect his or her peer relationships? DAP 1A, 1E(1); Code I-1.3, I-1.4, I-1.5, P-1.1, P-1.2

2. How do you feel about using candy as a daily reward in school? What else might be used to provide rewards when called for? DAP 1D; Code P-1.1

3. How much paper-and-pencil work time is best for students in the first grade? How would you determine this? DAP 1D

4. What other teaching strategies might be effective in helping children to learn the specific curriculum content? DAP 2C, 2E(1,2,3,4), 2F(5), 4A

5. Teachers often keep children in from the break to finish incomplete work. What are the advantages and disadvantages of using this technique during early childhood? DAP 1D, 2D

## MEETING WITH TAYLOR

When Taylor comes to Aiyana's office for their meeting, Aiyana welcomes her with an offer of coffee or juice. When they are settled down with their drinks, Aiyana thanks Taylor for the time she is taking from her other important work. She gives Taylor a copy of the typewritten notes from her observation. She starts her discussion by pointing out the many nice features she noticed in Taylor's classroom, such as the physical environment, how she gave personal attention to the students who were having the most trouble with their paper-and-pencil work, how she gave the children notice before the transitions, how she read to the children with expression, how she involved Luke's parent in her concern for him, how she played music for the children during their quiet work period, and how the children who finished their work were able to choose books from the shelves and read by themselves on the carpet. Taylor looks pleased, but cautious. She responds, "Well they aren't really 'reading' of course." Aiyana responds that there are many ways of reading as young children explore and enjoy books.

Aiyana asks Taylor if she is familiar with the concept of developmentally appropriate practices (DAP). Taylor replies, "Oh yes, I had a class on that topic when I was in college." Aiyana says that she has attended some workshops on implementing these practices in early elementary classrooms and that she has had some experience with implementing them herself. She tells Taylor that there is a great amount of research that shows that such practices are more effective for children's learning over the long run than the more teacher-centered practices of the past, and asks Taylor if she would be willing to work with her on implementing a number of these practices in her classroom and then assessing how the children do. Taylor agrees to do this, and seems excited at the prospect.

Aiyana explains, "As you know, in early childhood teachers need to focus on all major areas of children's development: language and literacy, math, but also social, cognitive, and physical development. These are all closely related, of course, with each one affecting the others. Each also affects whether a child has learned the fundamentals needed to succeed in learning the skills and knowledge content in which we expect them to become proficient as they progress through the elementary school years. Helping children develop in all of these areas and also developing a positive 'approach to learning'[1] are some of the goals of developmentally appropriate practices and should be our goals—developing the whole child."

"This sounds very familiar, Dr. A." Taylor comments.

"That's good," Aiyana says. "It is uncommon to see many developmentally appropriate practices in early elementary school, however, and that applies to our school, too. I think this is partly because with all the pressure on us to have the children meet certain standards, we don't trust that developmentally

---

[1]Hyson, M. (2008). *Enthusiastic and engaged learners: Approaches to learning in the early childhood classroom.* Published simultaneously by Teachers College Press, New York, NY and the National Association for the Education of Young Children, Washington, DC; National Research Council. (2008). *Early childhood assessment: Why, what, and how.* Washington, DC: National Academies Press. Retrieved November 30, 2008 from http://www.nap.edu/catalog.php?record_id=12446#toc.

appropriate teaching strategies will work well enough and soon enough, even though the research is clear that they do work very well. People worry about meeting standards and the "high-stakes" standardized testing that is required in third grade. Our state has reasonable, age-appropriate standards, but many other states require testing and even letter grades for students beginning in first grade. Such tests may show whether children have memorized the letters but not other critical fundamentals of early literacy, such as phonological and **phonemic awareness**, or love of reading. Standardized testing in early childhood fails to take into account the wide age range of typical development of the skills needed for learning to read and working with numbers in the abstract.

"Taylor, I would like to move toward more developmentally appropriate methods of teaching in our school. One way to do this is to keep trying to see things from the point of view of the children, and keep in mind their developmental limitations and individual personalities, strengths, and needs. For example," she explains, "the children were spending quite a lot of time involved in paper-and-pencil activities the other day when I was observing. During kindergarten and the **primary grades** most children actually do not benefit from large amounts of paper-and-pencil activities, especially when what they are working on is not particularly meaningful to them or is too difficult for them. Luke is a case in point. He probably would be more interested in finishing his work if he didn't have to spend so much time on it and if it was more meaningful to him. Also, I noticed that he seems to have a body that really needs to move. He sure had a difficult time when he missed the morning break!"

"I know, Dr. A., and I just don't know what else to do. He sure is more difficult after he has missed a break!"

Dr. A. continued, "Well, Taylor, I think that the less time he has to sit still, the less likely he will be to get into trouble. If he is a very active child, he is especially likely to have difficulty spending long periods doing paper-and-pencil exercises. Bright and creative children are likely to be even less tolerant than others of work they find to be boring. The need to move and boredom are two of the major causes of young children getting into trouble in a typical early elementary classroom. Although teachers have the best of intentions, the more pressure that is put on some children to hold still and do paper-and-pencil work for long periods of time, the harder they may resist and push back. In such a situation, they may learn that they fail while other children succeed, although they may be quite bright. Obviously, we don't want that to happen!"

Taylor laughs in agreement. Aiyana continues, "The most important traits and behaviors that children need to be successful in school comprise a child's '**approaches to learning**,' and indeed, research shows that they affect school success. Maintaining children's natural joy and interest in learning is one of the greatest challenges for teachers of early elementary school, especially with today's pressures for children to perform."

Now Dr. A. gets up and refills Taylor's glass of juice. She sits down and asks Taylor if she would be willing to work with her in making a few changes in her classroom that would help the school move toward using more developmentally appropriate practices. Taylor replies, "Of course. I would be happy to, Dr. A! I just need to know what to do."

Aiyana replies, "Well, it will be a little challenging but you will have my help and I think you will soon see a big difference in how engaged the children will be in learning and how much less trouble you will have with challenging behaviors." Aiyana asks if she may call her Taylor, and invites Taylor to please call her Aiyana, since they will be working together often. Aiyana explains that it is her job to help Taylor adopt these changes, and that she will also be working with all of the classrooms in one way or another over the rest of the school year.

Taylor takes several sips of her juice, sets it down, and asks Aiyana if she can borrow some paper. Then paper and pen in hand, she asks what Aiyana would like her to do. Aiyana smiles warmly and stands up to pull some books from her shelves. She hands Taylor a small book on developmentally appropriate practices and one on the learning value of hands-on activities. She sits down again and further describes and explains this approach.

"Moving to developmentally appropriate teaching will mean providing children with some hands-on learning experiences and activities that may appear more like play than learning. Some parents may object, and all will probably be curious about the changes they see. I will help you organize a meeting with them, perhaps with some dessert and a demonstration of some of the new activities, so that we can explain why they are valuable and answer the parents' questions.

"Anyway, young children need to be engaged in experiences and activities that are meaningful to them, age appropriate, and also challenging but achievable for the mix of individual skill levels among them. Again, this is about making sure they all learn the fundamentals upon which academic learning is built, ensuring their early success, and building a positive approach to learning and attachment to school. For example, a child may know the names of each digit and be able to count by rote to 100, but not be able to grasp that when you add three blocks to two blocks you end up with five blocks.

"The first dimension of DAP is 'Creating a Caring Community of Learners' and I think this dimension is actually the most important one. All of the others are affected by it. It means structuring your own interactions and your expectations of your students to ensure that each child feels that he or she belongs to the group and is accepted and cared about by the group. It involves the adults also, including teaching assistants and families, and even me," Aiyana says, smiling.

"Anyway, let's make another appointment to meet and talk more about this. Try to squeeze some time in to scan and read parts of those books before our next meeting." Taylor and Aiyana set a time to meet again on Friday of the same week. Taylor goes home and gives quite a lot of thought to how she could help the children feel that she cares about them, and get them to care about each other.

Later Aiyana thinks about the additional concern she has about the fact that Taylor was focusing on pressuring the boys more than she was the girls. She had noticed that Taylor also called on the boys much more often than the girls during the group time, a common mistake when teachers are not adequately trained. Gender equity will be a topic for a faculty meeting soon. Aiyana also makes plans to end the use of candy or other foods as rewards and also to end the school-wide good behavior takeaway ticket system.

## QUESTIONS

1. Why does Aiyana spend so much time observing Taylor's class? Code I-3A.3
2. Why did Aiyana work to spare Taylor's feelings? Code I-3A.1
3. About how long were the children required to be in structured work situations before and after the mid-morning break? Do you agree that this much time is likely to be difficult for 6- to 7-year-old children? Why or why not?
4. Why did Aiyana type up her notes and then give Taylor a copy?
5. Why did Aiyana start the meeting by sharing her positive evaluation of a number of characteristics of Taylor's classroom practices? Code I-3A.1, P-3A.1, P-3A.2
6. Do you know of a child who resembles Luke in some ways? Describe him or her.
7. Why didn't Aiyana tell Taylor during the meeting about her concerns with the gender-related issues, the candy, and the good behavior ticket takeaway system?
8. In addition to Luke, in what ways do you think the other children in Taylor's classroom might benefit from the changes she and Aiyana have planned? DAP 2E(1)

## FRIDAY'S MEETING

At their next meeting on Friday, Aiyana again makes Taylor comfortable and gives her a glass of juice. She asks Taylor how things are going for her and her class. Taylor tells Aiyana, "I have been thinking a lot about what you told me at our last meeting, and have been doing some reading in the books you gave

me. I never thought about the social relationships in my class as that important before, and certainly never thought about the parents as part of our classroom community. I have started trying to be more friendly with the parents when I see them. It is amazing how responsive they are! I'm really not sure how to get the children to care about each other, though. But I am trying to smile more at them and give them complements on their work. But will they respect me and obey if I'm not stern with them?"

Aiyana responds, "Oh yes, they will continue to respect you, as long as you continue to enforce the rules consistently but kindly. Don't worry. I am so happy to hear that you are already beginning, Taylor! The children will learn to be caring by watching you be caring, and there are some additional techniques you can use, such as referring to children's feelings using feeling words and expecting each child to take the feelings of the others into account in his or her own behavior. There is also the problem-solving approach to child guidance or discipline. We will talk about these techniques at another time. Today, I would like to talk about the overall characteristics of DAP.

"During preschool, activities should almost all be 'hands-on.' During kindergarten, a few more activities can be paper-and-pencil while most experiences and activities remain hands-on. During first grade, again a number of the daily activities need to be hands-on. Children still learn a great deal through play. At all levels, but especially during early childhood, most school activities need to be meaningful to the children, and they should include a range of levels of challenge and a variety of ways to work at them and be successful."

Taylor asks, "Aren't the worksheets and journals meaningful for the children? Surely they enjoy coloring the pictures!"

"That is a good question, Taylor. The answer depends on several things. Basically, let the children be your guide. For example, for a particular child, whether the topic of the worksheets is interesting depends on his or her interests and whether the worksheet is geared toward his or her particular ability to understand and complete it. When a worksheet is too challenging, it simply produces in the child feelings of frustration, bewilderment, and often a sense of failure. Researchers in child development point out that it is not uncommon for some children developmentally to take until ages 7 or even 8 years to begin to be able to read sentences, and this is often no reflection on their early experiences at home or their eventual reading and other cognitive abilities. Too much time spent with worksheets also translates into not enough time spent in other valuable learning experiences. Furthermore, frequent coloring of pictures in worksheets can interfere with children's confidence in their own ability to draw and color creatively.

"Most first-grade children still need appropriate experiences in early literacy fundamentals. These fundamentals must therefore be included in kindergarten and first-grade at a minimum. They are taught by using techniques such as reading big books together or books with copies for every child so they can follow along, learning about letters as parts of words and words as parts of sentences in stories, and demonstrating the different uses of print. At all times, the emphasis should be placed on the enjoyment of reading and the usefulness of writing rather than on the mechanics and accuracy of it. Those are important only because they increase our ability to enjoy the reading experience and enable us to write so that others understand us. Love of reading is an extremely important factor influencing children's long-term reading and educational success. In these contexts, learning the mechanics of reading and writing becomes more meaningful to children and strengthens their motivation."

"I never thought of it that way!" Taylor responds.

"I know you are very concerned that Luke is not being successful in your classroom. We will have to work carefully to try to restore Luke's interest in learning to write and feelings of being successful in school. I think if we work together to bring in more developmentally appropriate teaching strategies, you will find some that will really engage and benefit Luke and the other children in your class. After all, I believe we are more effective when we work to entice young children to learn, as opposed to taking a coercive approach. We need to work with the children to provide opportunities for their learning and to facilitate the process. One of the best ways to do this is called the project approach, which we will be discussing on another day."

Next the two teachers begin to discuss Taylor's daily schedule and what changes she might make right away, especially to lighten up on Luke and the other children by interspersing more hands-on activities throughout the school day and reducing the amount of time spent on paper-and-pencil work. Aiyana and Taylor set another date to meet again the following Friday to discuss and reflect about these and other curriculum revisions and adaptations in Taylor's classroom. Gradually, Aiyana will help Taylor make her classroom routines and activities more developmentally appropriate for first-grade students.

## IMMEDIATE CHANGES

Taylor is excited about working with Dr. A. on transitioning to more current and higher quality teaching practices. She realizes she hasn't been feeling that things were going very well so far this school year in her class. The first thing Taylor does after her meeting with Aiyana is to call Luke's family. When Elizabeth answers, Taylor tells her that she consulted with Dr. A. and they decided not to pressure Luke or the other children anymore to finish their paper-and-pencil work, because they aren't yet ready to be doing so much of it all at once. Taylor tells Elizabeth that she has learned that Luke will do better in the long run if he is not pushed any more right now. She also points out how important it is for him to have a positive approach to learning and feelings of success at school. Therefore, she will be working on helping him feel more positive about school by providing him with meaningful work in which he can be successful. She further points out that it will be best if he is no longer pressured about school work at home for now. Thinking about the caring community of learners involving families, Taylor thanks Elizabeth for her willingness to be involved with her son and his learning at school, and she asks Elizabeth how Luke is doing at home. Elizabeth is surprised at this question, but is happy to tell her that Luke will be very glad to be able to relax when he gets home from school.

After the telephone call, Taylor thinks about what she and Aiyana decided she should do right away. One change Taylor will make beginning next week is to encourage the children to relax and socialize when they enter the classroom in the morning. When it is a few minutes after time for school to start, she will guide the calendar activities on the rug. She will shorten the amount of time spent on the calendar until she identifies and utilizes more meaningful strategies for teaching math concepts. (Aiyana told her that she thinks she knows where to obtain some unit blocks right away for her class.) Taylor will use the extra time to do a quick cooperative game activity from a book Aiyana loaned her. Aiyana told her that these changes will help her build a caring community of learners, a positive approach to learning, and a strong attachment to school for her children.

Next she will read the story of the week, and the children will go to their tables to work on the paper-and-pencil activities related to the story as before. This is a part of a curriculum required by the school district. However, she will shorten the length of time she expects them to do this seat work and won't require the children to finish more than the one worksheet required by the shcool district. She will allow the children more freedom to talk quietly a little as they work and to help each other. Later, she expects to be able to adapt some of the activity options offered by the curriculum so that they are more hands-on and meaningful for 6- and 7-year-old children. She will no longer restrict the children from participating in outdoor break periods and getting the physical activity and social experiences that Aiyana reminded her they need for their physical and emotional development.

Instead of doing the journals after the break, she will switch that time with the social studies/science activities she has been having the children do in the afternoons, which will allow the children to be more active before lunch. In the afternoon, the journals and math blocks will be broken up by the music, physical education, and art time that is part of the afternoon schedule. Taylor thinks about how challenging it feels to be making these changes, but she also feels an excitement about implementing something new and seeing how the children react to it. She also has confidence that she will have the help of a kind mentor in Aiyana.

Aiyana said that some of the children might have a difficult time transitioning during the changes in the schedule, so Taylor will make a "picture & words" poster of the revised schedule to post at the children's level. She will tell the children about the changes in the schedule tomorrow, discuss them the following day too, and wait until Monday of the following week to implement them.

## QUESTIONS

1. Why did Taylor call Luke's family as the first step in the changes she is making? How well did Taylor's call represent partnering with parents? DAP 5B

2. How do you think Luke will react to the new changes? How do you think he will benefit from them? DAP 1E(3), 2J(1)

3. Do you think Taylor should talk with Luke about how she will no longer pressure him to finish his work? DAP 1C(1,3,4), 2B(3)

4. What do you think the reasoning is behind the following changes that Aiyana and Taylor will be making to Taylor's classroom routines? DAP 1B,1E(2), 2F(5), 3B-D
   a. Beginning the day socializing on the rug, then doing a brief calendar time
   b. Playing a cooperative game
   c. Having the children work on literacy activities for a shorter time, giving them more freedom while they work, and allowing them to help each other in appropriate ways
   d. Providing more hands-on types of activities during the literacy period
   e. Allowing everyone to go out to break for the entire break period
   f. Switching the post-break journals period with the social studies/science period

5. Do you think it is a good idea to wait to make the changes until the children have had a few days to get used to the idea? Why? DAP 1E(1, 3)

## MEETING AGAIN WITH ELIZABETH

When Aiyana and Elizabeth meet again, Aiyana asks her how Luke is doing. Elizabeth is quite excited to tell her of Ms. Wells' phone call and how Luke has been reporting changes that he really likes. "He says that he has been doing better and Ms. Wells reads more interesting stories to them now, and they get to play with blocks sometimes. He talks about the friends he is making who also like to play with the blocks. And they get to play board games sometimes, too."

Aiyana is very happy to hear this. She says, "Ms. Wells is relatively new to teaching and that means several things. One is that although she is well-educated, she hasn't had many opportunities for professional development. I simply shared with Ms. Wells some workshop information and materials I've received at professional conferences, and we worked together to make the classroom routines more developmentally appropriate. Another thing about a fairly new teacher is her enthusiasm for learning on-the-job and her enthusiastic dedication to helping her students be successful."

Elizabeth responds, "I am very happy to hear that, and Luke is much happier with school now. I don't have to push so hard to get him out the door in the morning. But is this going to help him learn how to read and be ready for second grade?"

Aiyana smiles and describes what the children are learning from these new activities. She explains that they will still be doing at least some of these things in second and third grades because they help children learn in ways that are most effective for their age-related and individual developmental levels. Aiyana then tells Elizabeth that she would like to get a Parent-Teacher Advisory Council started at the school, and asks Elizabeth if she would be interested in helping her to do that. The Council would provide a way of partnering with parents. It could help review school policies and ways in which they are implemented, and could improve communication between teachers and parents. Elizabeth looks pleased, agrees to consider this, and thanks Aiyana for everything. Aiyana asks her to "keep me posted on how Luke is doing."

## QUESTIONS

1. Why did Aiyana emphasize Taylor's strengths to Elizabeth? Code P-3A.1
2. Describe how this situation has become a success for Luke, Elizabeth, Taylor, and Aiyana.
3. If you were an intern in this classroom and you noticed Luke's improvement and enjoyment in new friends and classroom activities, what would you consider to be important teaching qualities and strategies to help children be successful?
4. In what ways has Aiyana strengthened the home–school relationship in this example? How is this partnership benefiting Luke, Elizabeth, and the school? DAP 5A, 5B, 5C, 5D
5. What specific role might a Parent-Teacher Advisory Council play at an elementary school? Why did Aiyana ask Elizabeth to be a part of it? DAP 5C; Code P-2.3

# Why Dante Succeeds in Second Grade (Second Grade)

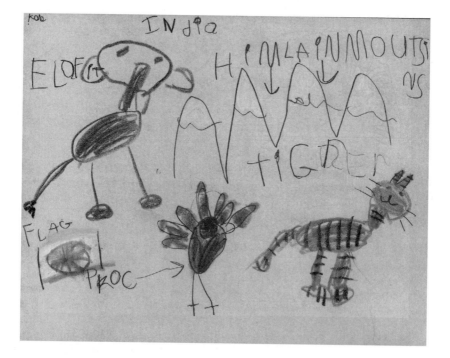

## DANTE'S FAMILY IS CONCERNED

It is fall and 2 years have passed since Dr. Aiyana Arkeketa became the Principal of Mt. Vernon Elementary School. She has overseen a shift toward the use of more developmentally appropriate practices in the early grades. She has also incorporated a focus on family involvement in the school, and has tried to make it clear to the families of the school that her door is always open for them to visit and communicate with her. Today she is expecting a visit from the family of second-grade student Dante Castillo and she makes sure she has cleared the books and folders off all six chairs she has set at the round table in her office. Shortly before the appointed time, Mr. and Mrs. Castillo arrive, along with Dante's grandmother, an uncle, and a 4-year-old girl, Victoria, who is one of Dante's sisters. The school's counselor has set up this visit, knowing the Castillo's through their mutual church, and having discovered that they had a concern about their son's education.

Aiyana greets the family and invites them into her office. She invites Victoria to play in the corner of her office where there is a small cozy rug and pillows with a basket of assorted toys and books. The adults have a seat at the round table and Aiyana brings out a tray of cups for juice and coffee. Once everyone has received a refreshment, Aiyana says, "Thank you for coming. I always enjoy getting to know the children's families."

Mr. Castillo replies, "Dr. Ark . . ."

"Just call me Dr. A., Mr. Castillo," Aiyana interrupts.

"Alright, if you are sure this is okay," Mr. Castillo replies. "I want to say that we are very grateful that you are willing to meet with us, taking your valuable time. It is very nice of you."

"I not only enjoy getting to know children's families, it is an important part of my job, Mr. Castillo. How is Dante doing?"

"Dr. A., I don't really know how Dante is doing at school. Dante regularly gets into trouble at home, although not so much lately. Yet, Mrs. Wells—Taylor Wells is his teacher—she tells me that Dante is doing well in her class, even reading at grade level. I know she is highly qualified, but I find that too hard to believe because that wasn't what first grade was like at all. He got into a lot of trouble last year. Also, he seems to be doing a lot of playing in his class this year. He talks about it. He never did that in first grade at Fairfield Elementary School before we moved here last summer. Should he be playing in school?"

"That depends, Mr. Castillo," replies Aiyana, including the other family members in her gaze. "I am glad to hear that he is doing better this year than he did in first grade! I want to discuss those concerns with you, but first, are there any other issues you are concerned about?"

"Well, Dr. A., Dante never brings home any homework," continues Mr. Castillo. "Ms. Wells says she doesn't assign it! So after school he just watches TV and plays videogames until we send him outside to play. But now the weather is getting too rainy and cold to send him outside. So all he does is sit in front of a screen. He should have homework to do."

Dante's uncle speaks up for the first time. "Dante is very smart, Dr. A. We think he could go far in life, even become a doctor or engineer. We want him to get a good education from the very first years so that he has a better chance of doing that."

Aiyana smiles at them. "We want that too, Mr. Castillo. But tell me more about Dante. What does he like to talk about? What kinds of books is he interested in? What does he do on the weekends?"

Mr. Castillo replies that Dante used to be a very active boy. He still plays soccer on the weekends, and he plays with some friends in the neighborhood, going to their homes to watch videos or play videogames or bringing them to his home. "That's what he likes to talk about, too—his videos. I think maybe some of those friends are having a bad influence on Dante. That might be why he sometimes hits his younger sister, and argues and is disrespectful at times. I don't know what kind of books Dante likes to read." Mr. Castillo asks his wife if she knows.

She responds, "He likes me to read to him when I have time. We read some picture books that he and his sisters have received from relatives. I like them too. They have some brown-skinned children in them, as well as white children."

"I am glad to hear that, Mrs. Castillo! I like those kinds of books, too. Now about Dante's education: I believe that Dante is likely to be getting a very good education in Ms. Wells' class. It is early yet in the school year, or you would have the opportunity to come to an evening demonstration of how Ms. Wells is teaching the children. She will be planning one in another month, I think. However, you are concerned right now and if you and/or Mrs. Castillo can find the time during the day, we could arrange for you to come and observe in Dante's classroom, and I can explain how our teaching methods work. Have you talked with Ms. Wells about your concerns, Mr. Castillo? No? How would you feel if I mentioned it to her? That way she will understand why we are observing her class, and she can answer some of your questions, too."

Mr. Castillo replies that telling Ms. Wells would be okay. Next Aiyana explains, "All of the kindergarten, first-grade, and second-grade classrooms are using 'developmentally appropriate practices,' which are teaching methods that research tells us help provide the children with the experiences they need to learn the key fundamentals upon which all academic learning is based. These fundamentals need to be learned during the critical early years, and are best learned through 'hands-on' experiences that seem like play, but actually are very important work. The fact that these activities are hands-on helps the children be thoroughly engaged in the learning experience. For example, let's talk about unit blocks. Do you know what they are like?" Seeing a negative nod of the head, Aiyana continues, "The blocks are all related in size. The small square one is one "unit," the next size is the same as two units, the next size is the same as four units, and the largest block is the same as eight units. In this way, when the children play with them they learn basic math and fractions, three-dimensional construction of patterns, and some basics of architecture. When the children build a high tower, they like to count the number of blocks they used. This helps build the fundamental understandings of how a number such as nine represents a specific number of items that when counted total nine, and that five is less. It helps the child visualize the items represented in that number. Many games are very useful for this as well. The children learn and retain much more this way, as opposed to sitting still for long periods working with pencil and paper, which is quite boring when you don't yet have all the skills you need. Being less bored may be why Dante isn't getting into trouble in school anymore. Ms. Wells' teaching methods may meet his age-, personality-and development-related needs better than before."

"But what about learning to read and write?" Mr. Castillo responds, sounding a little frustrated.

"At the same time, we are teaching spoken and written language basics, other basic mathematical concepts, science and social studies, and additional academic topics at a level that research tells us is best for this age group, and we allow some wiggle room in this to make the learning effective for each level of learning ability and development in our early childhood classrooms. The main thing to remember is that although it seems that children are having fun or playing, the children are learning in the best ways many years of research tell us they can. Teaching seems as if it should be simple, but actually it isn't if you want to do the best job for the children. I think you will understand better once you have observed the classroom, and I will explain in more detail. Do you think you could find the time during the day to observe in Dante's classroom?" Mr. Castillo looks at Mrs. Castillo, who smiles and nods.

"Yes, I think we could do this," he says.

"If you will consult your schedules, I will talk with Ms. Wells and we'll arrange a time for you. Will it be alright if my office calls you tomorrow?" Mr. and Mrs. Castillo nod their heads in the affirmative. Aiyana says, "I have a resource packet for families about this method of teaching, and I'll give you a copy. We can meet again after you visit the classroom so that we can discuss this topic more, alright?"

Mr. Castillo looks less frustrated and nods his head in agreement. Aiyana isn't finished yet, though.

"Now, about homework. I very much agree with you that Dante would be better off if he did not spend so much time watching TV or playing videogames. However, second grade is pretty early to have assigned homework from school. The children expend a lot of study-related energy in the classroom and really don't need to study more after school. However, that doesn't mean you can't give them home assignments of your own, such as 15 minutes reading an easy book with you or reading to a pet, or time listening to you read a book that interests them, or spending time with you in active play or work, practicing a musical instrument, or playing a board game or card game. These are all educational activities and strengthen family relationships, too.

"Second-grade children are typically also beginning to become quite interested in learning from their parents how to do the practical skills of ordinary living, such as how to do the dishes, how to repair a car, how to dust the furniture and repair the furniture—that sort of thing. So asking Dante to help with a chore, and teaching him how to do that chore, would be another excellent use of his extra time at home.

"Watching TV or playing videogames is very often an isolating activity. Educational videogames do exist but generally young children will learn more through time spent in active play, reading, or interacting with family members. Also, television and videogames are powerful teaching devices, but the content and underlying messages most programs teach are likely not messages you would want your children to learn. It may be that your son has learned some of the undesirable behaviors you mentioned from TV and videogames rather than from the neighborhood children. I recommend turning off the TV most of the time and planning specific times to watch specific programs you believe are best. It's called 'appointment TV.' You could let Dante and your other children choose from among several programs that you believe teach your family's values. The adults in the family could also choose programs that don't undermine your family's values if the children will be watching or listening. It really is okay to say no to TV watching and videogame playing. Children don't need to be entertained all or even most of the time, even though they often seem to think that they do. When children have to come up with something else to do around the home, it is quite surprising what wonderful and educational things they find, especially if family members are willing to help."

Aiyana asks the family how they are feeling about the ideas she has been discussing. Mr. Castillo replies that he has not thought about it this way before. Aiyana adds, "I have a resource on this topic full of good ideas in my file cabinet. I'll give you a copy in case you think you might be interested in changing Dante's habits in this way. It is a very good way to enrich his learning at home from his first and most important teachers—his family." Mr. Castillo raises his eyebrows at Aiyana's last sentence and then smiles at Mrs. Castillo, who smiles back.

"Do you have any more questions or concerns you'd like to talk about now?"

Dante's father says no and that he needs to get back to work. Aiyana summarizes, "Let's set up a time for you to come and observe Dante's class, and then arrange a follow-up meeting in, say, 3 weeks? I'll fetch those resource packets for you now."

After Aiyana pulls out the resource packets and gives them to Mr. Castillo, he makes a tentative appointment for observing the classroom and an appointment for the follow-up visit. Aiyana mentions that it would be best if only two family members observe at one time, so that the children are not overly distracted. Then Mr. Castillo, Mrs. Castillo, and the other two adults thank Aiyana. They help their daughter pick up the toys and books she has been busy with and depart.

Aiyana asks her secretary to make new copies for her files of the two resource packets she has given to the Castillo family. Then she e-mails Taylor about the concern Dante's family had and the tentative appointment Aiyana made with them to come and observe. She asks if the time is a good one for Taylor, and asks her to reply to the office assistant. Later, Taylor replies that the day selected is one in which the children will be going swimming during the mid-morning. The office assistant and she find another time and the assistant calls Mr. Castillo to ask if that will work. He says it will, so the day and time are confirmed. Aiyana e-mails the Castillo's asking that they inform Dante on the morning of the observation that they will be visiting to "see how your teacher teaches in the classroom." She also requests that if Dante acts up, they allow Ms. Wells to be the one to respond to it.

## QUESTIONS

1. Why did Aiyana invite the Castillos to come and observe Dante's class rather than just reassuring them that it was well taught or asking them to just wait until the Open House to get their concerns addressed? DAP 5D, 5E, 5F; Code I-2.5, I-2.6, P-2.2?
2. What dimension of DAP does having a basket of toys in Aiyana's office contribute to?
3. Why does Aiyana ask for permission from the Castillos before she tells Taylor Wells about their concerns? Code P-2.13
4. In what ways does the use of DAP help reduce the amount of boredom young children are likely to experience in school? DAP 2E(1,2,3,4)

5. In view of a large societal push for children's early achievement in school, why do some educator's continue to insist on the use of DAP? DAP Guidelines (Introduction)

6. Why doesn't Aiyana just have Taylor assign homework worksheets for Dante? DAP 5D

7. What does television and videogame use have to do with school achievement? Why doesn't Aiyana just tell the Castillos to forbid television viewing during the week?

8. How did Aiyana happen to have resource packets to give the Castillos in her files? Give three examples of other topics you think Aiyana might have collected for resource packets to put in her files?

9. What are some reasons why it would be best for the Castillos to let the teacher respond to any misbehaviors on Dante's part during their observation?

## DANTE'S PARENTS OBSERVE

At 8:00 A.M. on the following Tuesday, the Castillos arrive at Aiyana's office. Mr. Castillo has taken the morning off from work, and Mrs. Castillo has brought their 4-year-old daughter, Victoria. Dante has already gone ahead to his classroom. Aiyana takes their coats and hats and hangs them on her office clothes tree. She asks them if they would like anything hot or cold to drink, but they say no. Then Aiyana picks up the basket of assorted toys and books from her office corner and guides the couple to Dante's classroom. On the way, she reminds them that Dante may misbehave more than he usually does just because they are visiting, and that this is a common reaction for a number of children when their families visit.

When they get to the classroom and walk in, Dante is talking with two other early students. Aiyana introduces his parents and sister to Taylor, and directs them to sit in the adult-sized chairs she has placed next to a wall to one side of the classroom. She also lets them know that they are welcome to get up and look over the children's shoulders if they would like to at any time. The Castillos both smile in reply. Taylor also takes the basket from Aiyana and places it in a carpeted corner. She tells Victoria she is welcome to play there. Mrs. Castillo seems uncomfortable with this at first, but allows Victoria to play.

Several children are coming into the classroom. Taylor greets them, using their names, and introduces her guests to all of the children. They all say hello, accept Dante, and the newly arrived children go to their cubbies to put their coats away, and then join Dante and the other child in friendly conversation. Taylor says to the Castillos, "I am very happy to have you visit today. We usually start the morning at 8:15 with a brief circle time on the carpet, during which we do different things each day of the week. For example, yesterday we worked on the calendar and related patterning challenges. Today, we will sing some songs and make up a poem with rhyming words. Rhyming is an excellent **auditory discrimination** and literacy activity—I mean we will be exercising our abilities to discern sounds and engage in language composition. Tomorrow, we will add to our graphs of the rising and setting times of the sun, and the weather on Thursday. On Friday, we will review the progress we've made related to our current project.

"At about 8:35 we will review the story we are currently reading in our reading groups. Then we separate into our reading groups at 8:45. The other two second-grade classes and my class all combine into four reading groups according to skill level. We have a reading specialist who takes the small group that needs the most help, and each teacher takes one of the other groups. My reading group consists of the children who are reading right at the third-grade level and Dante is in it. We practice reading in several different ways, and do some paper-and-pencil work afterwards, mainly to work on reading comprehension and beginning writing using "guess-and-go" spelling. Twice a week, the fifth-grade students come in and help the children with their paper-and-pencil work. On other days, we have some 'family assistants' who take turns coming in and helping out.

"After reading we have morning recess from 9:45 to 10:05. Then we wash our hands and work on assigned math exercises, which I will set out during the break. Those family assistants who can stay like to help out with these exercises too. At about 10:45 we will start working on science and at 11:30 it's lunchtime and lunch break." Taylor points to a simple chart near one of the large whiteboards that lists the

| TABLE 26.1 | Ms. Wells' Daily Schedule, Second Grade |
| --- | --- |
| **Time** | **Activity** |
| 8:15 | First Circle |
| 8:45 | Reading Groups |
| 9:45 | Break |
| 10:05 | Math Activities |
| 10:45 | Projects (Science, Health, or Social Studies) |
| 11:30 | Lunch |
| 11:50 | Break |
| 12:25 | Quiet Story Time |
| 12:55 | Writing Workshop, Library, Technology |
| 1:40 | P.E./Music/Arts/Choice Time (Play and Hobbies) |
| 2:10 | Last Circle |
| 2:25 | Dismissal |

schedule and the times at which each component starts. Then she remembers that she has the schedule printed out in handout form for the coming Open House. She mentions that she will give Mr. and Mrs. Castillo a copy of the schedule as soon as she gets a chance today. Then she is interrupted by more students coming into the classroom and she greets each of them by name, and chats with some of them while others go to talk excitedly in small groups of two or three, scattered around the room.

## First Circle, 8:15 A.M.

The beginning bell rings and Taylor places a necklace microphone around her neck. She calls the children to the large carpeted area at the rear of the classroom for circle by singing a song. Many of the children join her in singing as they make their way to the carpeted area and sit down. Taylor asks what they should sing next, and a student raises his hand and suggests the "Hokey Pokey," so they all stand up and go through the motions as they sing the song together, then sit down again. Victoria comes and sits a little behind the students on the carpet and watches the circle time. Mr. Castillo frowns at Mrs. Castillo, who looks a little bewildered.

After the singing and movement, Taylor introduces the Castillos to the children, saying they are visiting today and may be looking over their shoulders a little. Next some of the children have brought an item from home to share that is related to the current classroom science project, which is "growing plants," and each one stands up in turn next to Taylor to tell about their object. As one girl is showing a large garden worm, many of the others start talking at once, and Taylor says, "Alligator, alligator," in a voice a little louder than usual. The children stop talking and listen as Taylor asks them to "help us out." The children listen more quietly as the last boy shares the envelope of seeds he brought from home. Then Taylor tells them it is poem time, and asks the students for a topic for the poem that would be related to their science project. Dante, giggling, volunteers "worms," and Taylor writes "worms" on the large sheet of lined chart paper she has taped to the easel next to where she is sitting. Mrs. Castillo worries that Dante has suggested such a silly topic for a poem, but is surprised that Ms. Wells has accepted it.

Taylor asks for words that the children think of when they think about worms. Each time she calls on a child, she writes the response on a large sticky note and places it along the bottom edge of the newsprint. There is much giggling during this process. Even Taylor laughs from time to time. Aiyana notices that all of the children are attentive and thoroughly engaged in this activity, including Dante and Victoria. In a whisper, she points this out to the Castillos. She also whispers to them that involving the children in such activities is a very effective way to keep them engaged and help them learn language arts and reading.

After Taylor has printed the five responses (dirt, tickle, dig, wiggle, long), each represented by a single word, she guides the class in writing phrases for the poem that refer to the thoughts raised by the children, asking them for guidance on wording and on rhyming as well. She takes her time and prints the words carefully. Finally, the poem fills the paper and the final phrase is finished.

*Worms are very long*

*In the dirt they wiggle*

*On my hand they tickle*

*And they make me giggle!*

Taylor guides the children in choral reading of the entire poem, pointing to each word as it is read. Taylor asks the children how well they think the poem turned out using a five-fingered vote, and the children vote by holding up zero to five fingers on one hand. Taylor laughs, points out the huge variety in the number of fingers held up, and notes that "beauty is in the eye of the beholder."

### Reading Time, 8:45 A.M.

It is almost time for the reading groups. Taylor asks the children what they remember from where they left off reading the story the day before. They respond individually, and then Taylor asks them to get their workbooks and head to their reading groups. About two-thirds of the children leave the classroom, while some children from the other second-grade classes file in and sit down at the tables near the front of the classroom with their workbooks. At the same time, two adults wearing visitor's badges enter the classroom and sit down at two different tables near the children. Meanwhile Taylor tapes up the poem on a low corner of the bulletin board so that the children can look at it and draw on it to illustrate it through the rest of the week, and then she picks up her book and goes to the front of the classroom. Aiyana whispers to the Castillos that this reading program is the same throughout the city's school district. Taylor says hello to the two family assistant "visitors." Several of the children have also greeted them. Next Taylor points to a large pair of construction paper lip shapes stuck to a construction paper stoplight near the red light, reminding the group that they may not talk out of turn during this time.

She suggests that they read the story from their workbooks, using "partner-reading," and calls on two children whose hands are raised. Taylor gives each a necklace mike, reminding them that, "If you make a mistake, it is no big deal." The two children read a paragraph aloud at the same time, Dante and another child receive mikes and read a paragraph, and then two other children are selected, and so on until the entire section has been read. Taylor helps them with a word from time to time during this process until the day's section is finished. Mr. Castillo beams with pride for Dante's excellent reading, even if it was with another child. He smiles at Mrs. Castillo and squeezes her hand. Victoria has been quietly watching and listening to the readers. Then she again becomes involved with the toys and books from Aiyana's basket.

### Comprehension, 9:20 A.M.

The story has been about some children, and Taylor asks, "What life skills could the children use to solve their problems?" A few of the students respond with suggestions, and then Taylor writes some of the words they brainstorm on the whiteboard. Taylor then moves the construction paper lips to the yellow light, indicating quiet conversation is allowed, and gets them started on their pencil-and-paper work at the shared tables. The children are to list the story children's problems on the left side of the page and potential solutions on the right-hand side. Taylor reminds the children that they may use **guess-and-go spelling,** but that they need to put the words in a sentence with a capital letter at the beginning and a period at the end. After a few moments, the Castillos watch some of the children take their papers to one of the family assistants for help with their writing. Taylor looks over other children's shoulders and kneels down beside a child to give assistance from time to time. The Castillos listen as she discusses the children's writing with them and helps them make improvements. Mr. Castillo gets up after about 5 minutes and walks around looking at Dante's work and over the other children's shoulders to see how they are doing, comparing that in his mind with the quality of Dante's writing. He is surprised that Dante seems to have written more words on his paper than most of the other children and that he also put all of them into short sentences. Mr. Castillo is not happy with Dante's spelling though. He also notices that the workbook asks the children to make specific drawings in certain areas on the page and Dante is busy doing that now.

Aiyana whispers to the Castillos that making drawings seems to be a "glue that helps to anchor" the related information in some children's minds. Then she excuses herself, letting them know that she has to get back to her office for a little while, but that she will return soon. The Castillos listen especially closely when Taylor kneels down beside Dante to give him some help. They are amazed at the quality of his questions and that he seems so grown up here.

About 10 minutes after the children started their paper-and-pencil work, several of them ask Taylor to check their workbooks. When she checks them, she sometimes closes and picks up their workbooks, and at other times seems to ask them to add or change something. When their work is accepted, the children go to the book shelves and choose a book to look at there or select one from a box of books all the same size. Mrs. Castillo notices that there are quite a number of books that look like public library books among those the children have selected, and some of those actually have titles in Spanish. The children take the books to the carpet area, lie on their stomachs or find a pillow by the wall, and begin reading. Some read the same book together and others read by themselves. After a few more minutes one of the family assistants walks with a child to the small sofa and rocking chair in a corner near the book shelves, sits down, and reads a book with one or more of the children.

The Castillos notice that sometimes after one of these children finishes a book, he or she asks Taylor to use one of the two computers in the classroom, then opens a program that allows the child to choose a book title and then take a comprehension test. When Dante wants a turn with the computer, Taylor suggests that he invite his parents to observe his work there and he motions for them to come over and watch, a little proudly. The Castillos are impressed and very happy to see Dante doing so well. The Castillos are surprised next when Taylor looks out the window and exclaims, "Alligator, alligator! Come look at the kindergartners wearing the jet packs they made!" Most of the children get up and go look, and the Castillos do also. The kindergartners indeed look quite amazing walking and prancing past the windows in their colorful cardboard jet packs. Then the second-grade students go back to their work, smiling and laughing with each other on the way.

## Telling Time, 9:40 A.M.

"Alligator, alligator," Taylor says a little loudly. The children look up at their teacher and Taylor asks them what time it is. She does this by referring them to the large old-fashioned clock on the wall, pointing out where the short hand and the long hand are pointing, and asking what each means. The students raise their hands to answer and, one at a time, the group decides what time it is and that there are 5 minutes until time for morning break. They start putting books away, going to the coat rack to put on their wraps and boots, and gathering by the door to the outside, chatting in normal voices.

Taylor opens the door as the bell rings and the children head out to play, although it is raining lightly. Dante comes over to his parents and gives his mother a hug and then he, too, goes outside, along with one of the family assistants. Taylor turns and smiling, says to the Castillos and Victoria, "Thank goodness for boots! It is getting quite wet outside. Victoria, you have been so quiet and cooperative. Thank you!" Taylor removes her necklace mike and introduces the remaining family assistant, a student's grandfather, to the Castillos.

## QUESTIONS

1. What do you think about Taylor's focus on the calendar activities only 1 day per week rather than the more traditional 5 days a week? What is she accomplishing by doing this? DAP 2F(3)
2. Why would Taylor distribute the daily class schedule to the children's families? In what ways might it benefit them? DAP 5B
3. What do you believe the value of music and movement might be for second-grade children? DAP 2D, 3B Why do you think Taylor uses it at the start of First Circle? DAP 1B
4. Taylor asks the children to bring only items or stories related to the current class project for sharing and no toys. Why do you think she does that?
5. Why does Taylor make light of mistakes as she starts the reading group? DAP 1E(1)
6. What is another name for "guess-and-go spelling"? What are its advantages and disadvantages?
7. Why do you think the children are encouraged to draw as part of their paper-and-pencil work time, in addition to what Aiyana told the Castillo's?
8. Why do you think Taylor invited the children to interrupt their work and come to look at the kindergartners in their jet packs? What is the benefit for the second graders? DAP 1A, 1B

### Break, 9:45 A.M.

Taylor tells the Castillos, "I need to spend this time setting up the math games and exercises but I can answer questions while I'm doing it. You are also welcome to go to the teacher's room and get something to drink and a snack. It is just across from the office." She hands a list to the grandfather, who opens a cupboard and starts pulling out several puzzles of various sizes, setting two of them down on a table and one on the carpet. Mrs. Castillo goes over to the reading corner and begins reading a book in Spanish to Victoria. Mr. Castillo asks, "What are these puzzles for? I thought the children had math next."

Taylor answers, "Oh, yes. Math comes next. The puzzles provide the children practice with spatial relationships and the use of logic. Puzzles also help the children develop an eye for detail and visual cues—or clues. These math exercises help the children learn the fundamentals of math, while having fun. This also helps them develop a positive attitude toward math that will last for many of them for a very long time. The activity I'm setting up now is called "pom-pom jacks".[2] This is a little like old-fashioned jacks, but it includes making estimates and testing them. It also helps children visualize specific numerical sets—or same-numbered groups of items." The Castillos watch Taylor set down a hula hoop on the rug, distribute a bag of small pom-poms inside of it, and place a timer next to it. The grandfather sets out one game that involves play money and one that involves pies made out of laminated wedges with a fraction written on each piece. At one table area, Taylor sets out three open boxes with sheets of paper in them. The Castillo's go over and examine the sheets. In each box, there is a pile of worksheets with about 24 addition and subtraction problems on them. The sheets in each box contain a different level of difficulty from the sheets in the other boxes. There is also a set of dominos, some **pattern blocks**, and a game that uses two dice and a large construction paper chart with glue and different colored square pieces of construction paper. Taylor finishes by setting down laminated cards with different children's names near each of the games, consulting a notebook as she does this. She also sets out three names in the carpeted area near some shelves filled with unit blocks, then moves the construction paper lips to the green light.

---

[2]Adapted from Copley, J. (2000). *The young child and mathematics.* Washington, DC: National Association for the Education of Young Children, in cooperation with National Council of Teachers of Mathematics.

## Math Exercises, 10:05 A.M.

The children come in from outside and take off their boots and wraps, putting them up in the coat rack area. Then they go line up to wash their hands at one of the two available sinks. A student at each sink takes charge of squirting hand soap into each waiting child's hands so they can rub it around while they wait to finish washing at the sink. After washing, the children find their name cards, sit down, and start working. Taylor talks with a child who seems to have had a mishap during the break. Then she sits at the table with the worksheets and begins to help the children there. Dante is at a table with two other children and the grandfather assistant who is there to help them. The grandfather instructs the children on what they should do.

Aiyana comes back into the classroom shortly after the children do and sits down again next to the Castillos. Mr. Castillo tells Aiyana that Dante had a very difficult time with math in first grade and really didn't like it. "I am surprised at the idea of making math fun. Dante has always loved working puzzles—he is very good at it, but I never thought puzzles could help him with math." Aiyana smiles in response and invites them to go look over the children's shoulders. Mr. Castillo goes over to watch Dante working. Dante mixes up the two dice and tosses them down on the table, getting a side with 1 pip and a side with 2 pips. He then takes a 1-inch blue square and pastes it on the chart above the blue number 3 on the horizontal axis. The child who rolled the dice just after Dante did was counting the pips on both of the dice, which were 6 and 5, respectively. Next that child glues a yellow square above the number 11. The third child rolls a 3 and a 5. She counts the pips and glues a green square above the green number 8. Then Dante rolls the dice again. Aiyana explains that Dante and the others are producing a vertical bar chart showing the likelihood of rolling any particular total number using two dice. They are working on understanding the concepts of probability and graphing, as well as practicing visual recognition of number sets and the concept of adding them together. "Too often, children just memorize addition facts based on numerals without really understanding what the numerals actually mean."

Mrs. Castillo goes over to the blocks area where Victoria is helping the three students who are building a complex structure. She tells Aiyana that she is surprised that the two girls and boy are including Victoria in their play. Aiyana replies, "Taylor has established a caring community of learners. This is extremely important, partly because it contributes to positive **approaches to learning,** which are very important to children's long-term success in school. With the blocks, they are learning cooperation, spatial relationships, fractions, architecture, and creativity." Mr. and Mrs. Castillo continue to walk around looking over the children's shoulders, thinking about what the children might be learning as they play enthusiastically. Mr. Castillo thinks, "I haven't yet seen Dante misbehave. This kind of learning must agree with him."

## Science Project, 10:45 A.M.

Taylor says, "Alligator, alligator" again, then says that they only have 5 more minutes to finish up what they are doing, put the games away, and gather on the rug. It takes a little longer than 5 minutes for all of the children to come to the rug, but Mr. Castillo is amazed at how most of the children who finished first went to help the children who were not done yet, some with a little prodding from Taylor when they sat down on the carpet early. Once most of the children were sitting on the carpet, Taylor clapped a complex rhythmic pattern and the children echoed it. Taylor repeated this several times as the remaining children finished what they were doing and quickly came to the carpet. Taylor said, "Very good! It is time to listen right now. Notice that I've moved the lips back to the red light. Remember to raise your hand when you want a turn to talk and wait for me to acknowledge you.

"I've noticed that the two types of grasses you each planted in the plastic cups have all come up and are quite tall. It is time to do some observations and 'mowing.' We are going to be scientists now.

We're going to draw our planted grasses and then write down what we see on our science sheets. When we draw the grass, we need to use the best colors we can to reproduce its actual color. When we are drawing for art or fun, we can make things any color we want, but when we are being scientists, we try to draw things as accurately as we can. We can't use words like 'cute' or 'nice' because we can't measure that. What kinds of words will be needed? Think about when the woman from the Agriculture Department came and talked with us." Aiyana notices that Victoria is playing on her own with the blocks, but looks over at the other children from time to time. Then Mrs. Castillo goes over, sits down, and joins her block play. Aiyana excuses herself again and leaves the room. The students are now coming up with words that Taylor prints on the whiteboard: length, long, smooth, bumpy, curly, green, dark, light, brown, dirt, soil, rye grass, alfalfa.

"What if you think of something later? Is it okay to tell me and I'll add it to the list? Yes," she agrees with the children's answer. She speaks to two girls who are whispering to each other busily. "Help us out, girls. First we are going to measure the height of the grass above the soil level using a ruler. Since we are being scientists, what units of measure are we going to use? That's right, centimeters. So be sure that you are looking at the centimeters side of the ruler." Taylor holds up a ruler and demonstrates seating one end on the soil and looking at where the tallest leaf of grass comes on the ruler. The two girls are whispering to each other again. Taylor says, "You need to be focusing this way, my friends. Each of you please sit somewhere else now." The girls get up and move to opposite sides of the group on the rug, apparently having had to do this before.

"You'll notice that the rye grass has grown a lot taller than the alfalfa. Now I'm going to mow my grass with the scissors," Taylor says as she holds up the planter with about 5 inches of grass growing out of it. "When I do that, I want to cut low enough to make sure I cut both types of grass. Remember to measure it before you cut it. Remember not to squeeze the grass too tight. What might happen if you do that? . . . That's right. It might die. Are there any questions?" There are two questions, and then Taylor excuses the children to go to the window for their grass plantings and then to their tables. She asks three of the children to hand out the rulers, the scissors, and some paper towels because the grasses have been watered recently. Taylor then hands out sheets of paper with an outline of the plastic cup in which the grass is growing, with some lined space to the side of it. Each table already has a basket of crayons in the center, and the children start distributing the crayons around the table.

The children set to work fairly quietly. Taylor has moved the lips to the yellow light. Some are helping others. Taylor starts helping one child right away, then moves to stop another from cutting his grass before measuring it. She is kept busy answering questions and monitoring how the children are doing. She says "alligator, alligator" again and holds up an example of how one student used some yellow, as well as green in her drawing of her grass. Taylor points out how this detail helped to describe the color of the grass better than only using green.

Mr. and Mrs. Castillo confer together quietly around 11:10 and then go over to speak with Taylor. They thank her very sincerely for letting them observe. Mr. Castillo says that he now feels very happy about how Dante is learning in her classroom. Mrs. Castillo thanks her for letting Victoria play during their visit, too. She asks if she can return the toy basket to Dr. A's office and Taylor thanks her for that. They say good-bye and the Castillos wave to Dante and leave the classroom. They return to Aiyana's office, put the toy basket away, and Mr. Castillo thanks Aiyana, telling her how much he has learned and that he is feeling much better now about Dante's schooling. He has one last question. He wonders about the time in Taylor's printed schedule that is labeled "play and hobbies." Aiyana points out that there is a different activity during that time each day of the week. On Fridays, it provides an opportunity for Taylor and the children to relax, be creative, engage in pretend play together, show each other their hobbies, or practice putting on a play—a literacy activity—and just about anything else they haven't been able to squeeze into the earlier part of the week. Mr. and Mrs. Castillo thank her and Victoria does too. Aiyana shakes Victoria's hand and says, "I am looking forward to seeing you in kindergarten here next year, I hope." Victoria tilts her head down shyly and smiles.

Aiyana reminds the Castillos that they are always welcome here. She also provides them with a list of the various ways families can become involved in the school, pointing out that family involvement in a child's school tends to help the child be more successful. Then she asks the Castillos if they still want to meet for their previously scheduled 3-week follow-up meeting, and Mr. Castillo says he doesn't see any need to do so unless Dr. A. would like to. She says, "Let's cancel that meeting, but my door is open and I'll keep an eye on how Dante is doing. Thank you for coming in and observing today." They all say good-bye, and Aiyana smiles and thinks about what a nice family Dante has, and how proud she feels of Taylor and how far Taylor has progressed as a teacher in the short time they have worked together.

## QUESTIONS

1. What fundamental mathematical concepts do you think the second-grade students might learn from playing with the dominoes? The pattern blocks? The game involving play money? The game involving pieces of pie?

2. Why does Taylor facilitate a brainstorming of words that might be used to describe the grass plantings and write them out on the board? Wouldn't she have a better idea of how skilled the students are by avoiding helping them in this way? DAP 2F(5), 3C(1,2)

3. What are the pros and cons of allowing children to help each other with their work?

4. Why did Taylor stop the child from cutting his grass too soon? Would it be better for him if she had let him suffer the consequences of his mistake? DAP 2F(5)

5. What do you think the learning and other benefits for the children might be of Friday's "play and hobbies" time (see Table 26.1)? DAP 2E(3)

6. What are the benefits and purpose of Taylor and the children clapping a complex rhythmic pattern? What skills are the children exercising?

# 27 Involving Children (Second Grade)

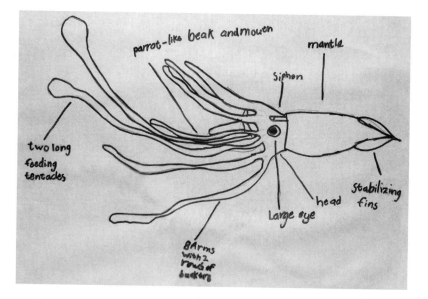

## WILLIAM AND NASHAWNA AND THE OCEAN ANIMALS PROJECT

It is the beginning of the spring term and Frank Edwards' second-grade class has just finished studying "families and traditions" for social studies. It is an **antibias** project as well. It is time for a new project, one that focuses on life science. Frank chooses a project about ocean animals, with which he has had a lot of success in the past. One of his students, 8-year-old William, has a history of early medical problems, which have set him back. He is actually at a beginning first-grade reading level and goes to the learning laboratory several times a week for extra help. Over spring break William's family took him to the coast. They spent a lot of time on the beach and a whole day in an aquarium there. The aquarium had a beautiful collection of jellyfish that impressed William immensely.

On Monday morning, as the children make their way to the carpet for first circle, Frank puts on a necklace microphone and sings a "come to the class meeting" song he has made up to a rhythmic tune that is popular with the children and involves much knee slapping and tongue clicking. William and his friend Cohen sit down close to Frank. They grin and slap their knees and click their tongues to the tune. Once all of the children are seated, Frank finishes the song. Then he tells the class, "Today we are going to begin our life science project on ocean animals, and we will start today during our science and health time." William is thrilled and whispers to Cohen how he loves jellyfish. Cohen whispers back that he would rather study horses. Many of the other children are whispering to their neighbors about the study topic and Frank asks the children to raise their hands if they have something to say. William is first to raise his hand. When Frank calls on him he says, "I went to the 'quarium last weekend, and saw lots of stuff 'bout the ocean. I like jellyfish and Cohen likes horses, so I think he could like learning 'bout sea horses 'cause sea horses live in the ocean—I saw 'em."

After reading, recess, and snack, it is science and health time. The children are sitting at their tables, four or five to a table, with two sitting at the desks in the loft because it is their turn to do so. Frank asks the two in the loft to come down to their usual tables for the next activity. He announces, "We are going to do some brainstorming about ocean life. I am going to give you some sticky notes to share at your table. I want each of you to take a sticky note and write down something related to ocean plants and animals. You may use as many sticky notes as you have words for, until you run out of them. Stick them around on your table, until you are done. Let me know when you are done and I will tell you what to do next. You may use guess-and-go spelling if you want, and you may help each other with spelling as well. Remember to write only one word per sticky note, and remember that each of you should write down your own ideas—no one person's ideas are better than any others right now."

William is excited and when he gets a sticky note, he draws a picture of a jellyfish. Then on the next note, he draws a picture of a sea horse. Next he draws a sea star and then pictures of gills, fins, and a picture of a fish's mouth with large, sharp teeth. William tries at first to get the attention of Frank or Mrs. Santiago, the parent helper, to help him write the words, but they are helping other children. At the same table, 7-year-old Nashawna, whom Frank considers an advanced learner, is busy writing the words whale, dolphin, seals, salmon, octopus, crabs, clam, sea lion, sea gull, and penguins. When their table runs out of sticky notes after about 10 minutes, William tells Frank. Frank comes over and tells the table group that they should now work on sorting the sticky note words into categories: placing words that describe similar things in a group by themselves and other words into their own groups. Frank suggests they might think about body parts, what and how the animals eat, where they live, what their enemies are, that sort of thing. He tells them they can use more sticky notes if they need them. He goes to each table as the children are ready for him to tell them about this next step. One table starts to group their words according to the colors of the animals, but soon change their minds as they notice what the other table groups are doing. The classroom is very noisy as the children discuss and do the sorting activity. Frank notices that every child is engaged, although Susie is absent again. He reflects on how she misses several days most weeks since her family became homeless. She does good work when she is present. He is disappointed that the connections that the school's family support team made for her family have still not solved their need for housing.

After it appears that almost all of the table groups have finished most of their sorting, he claps out a simple rhythm, which the children quickly take up until all have quieted down. He stops and speaks to the group. "Now we will start making our **word web**. Table 3, who wants to tell us what groups you sorted your sticky notes into?" Nashawna's hand goes up immediately. Frank calls on her. She talks about the categories on which her table finally agreed for the sorting task. Frank writes the categories on the whiteboard. Then he asks for Table 5's categories, continuing until all of the tables have reported their categories and he has written all of them on the whiteboard. There is much erasing and rearranging, and he allows lots of room between the categories. He has used all three adjacent panels of the whiteboard, keeping the writing low enough to be within reach of the children.

Frank tells the children, "After I'm done giving you directions, each of the table groups may transport *their own* table's sticky notes to the whiteboard word web we have started and stick them close to the word that we used to label the category in which each belongs. Work only on *your own* table's sticky notes and respect your neighbors' right to transport their own notes. I want each of you to walk slowly and remember to be courteous and take turns as you need to at the whiteboard. When you are done, you may return to your tables and continue to work on today's drawing assignment until the lunch bell rings. If you don't have time to finish moving your sticky notes, I'll let you finish while I start the chapter book read-aloud after lunch. Now, who can tell me what the instructions are that I just gave you?" Several children raise their hands and Frank helps them bring out each of the steps he has just outlined, including the reminder to walk slowly and be courteous. Then he says, "Okay, you may start now."

As William is putting up his sticky notes, a nearby child, Roger, notices William's use of pictures instead of words. Roger, who has joined the class only recently, teases William about needing to use pictures because he "doesn't know how to write." Nearby, Nashawna says, loud enough for Roger to hear her, "That's okay, William. Those are good pictures. Roger doesn't know our class very well yet, but he'll learn that 'we all have special ways we do things, and they are often different,' right William?" William smiles at her and says, "Right! Like Mr. Edwards always says."

Later, during math time, Frank conducts the class through some word problems involving graphing and multiplication using several different ocean animals the class had come up with on the word web.

At the end of the day, Frank takes several close photographs of the word web with all of the sticky notes on it as part of his strategy of ongoing assessment. Then he prints out several copies of the pictures and gives a set to the school librarian with a note to let her know what kinds of books the children will be looking for during their library time on Thursday. He e-mails a set to the class families' newsletter list to let them know what they did that day and posts prints on the family bulletin board for those families without e-mail. He thinks about who he might contact in the community to come and talk with the children about ocean animals, and decides to plan a trip to the coast aquarium about 50 miles away, assuming there are enough field trip funds left in the school's budget.

During science and health time the next day, Frank asks each table group to make additional sticky notes of any new ideas they may have thought of and to place the notes in the best category on the word web. He asks the children to think about where in or near the ocean the animals live, what they need to eat, who their enemies are, and where they fit in the food chain. He gets out several bins of small books he has collected over the years about oceans and related animals, and encourages the children to start reading through these as best they can. He asks the children to look for more information about their own favorite animals and to alert their table mates if they come across information about their favorite animals.

When there are about 10 minutes left before lunchtime, Frank calls the children to attention and tells them, "I will be expecting each of you to choose just one animal to study, and come up with a project report in the form of a display chart. When everyone is finished with their charts, all of them will be displayed in the hallway outside our classroom. Each chart will focus on an ocean animal and will have five components. One component is a title that I will help you make using the computer. Another is a real photo or copy of a photo of the animal. Then you will need to do a hand drawing of the animal with all of your animal's body parts labeled. You will also need to come up with five or six true sentences about the animal—all in your own words. It can't be something you copy out of a book, like you have done before. For most of you, it will be the first time you will be expected to do this, but I have confidence that you *can* do it, and of course you will have help. When these parts are all done, each part will need to be glued to a colored frame cut from construction paper. Now, raise you hand if you have questions." William is a little worried about the idea of all the writing, but he is so excited about the project that he doesn't worry for long. Then it is time for the children to wash their hands and go to lunch.

Sometime during the first week of the project, Nashawna writes the words for the pictures on William's sticky notes. During writing workshop one day, Frank points out that there are a number of different spellings among the sticky notes for the same word. He asks a table team to research what the **standard spelling** is and to correct the sticky notes for each of these words. He also asks the teams to look closely at all of the words to see if they look "right," and if a word doesn't look right, to see if they can find the true spelling and either verify or fix the spelling on the sticky note.

Over the next 6 weeks many of the classroom activities are related to the ocean animals project. Having finished reading the book about family history during his 30-minute chapter book read-aloud time, Frank begins reading a junior science book about the ocean. He likes to read different types of books to the children, from fiction to biography to poetry. The children always doodle or draw pictures at their tables while they listen. Today, William often draws simple pictures of marine animals during this time. Nashawna draws more detailed pictures while she listens, and she also writes down some words and phrases from time to time, using guess-and-go spelling. William sometimes asks either her or Cohen to help him spell the names for the pictures he has drawn. Frank always encourages the children to give each other help when they can.

For one activity, Frank tells the class they will make an "ABC book" about ocean animals. Each child draws a letter out of a hat and must think of an ocean animal that begins with that letter. Then the child needs to draw a picture of the animal and write a sentence telling something about it on the same page. Once the pages are laminated and all put together in alphabetical order, their ABC book is finished. It becomes a very popular book the children love to read.

The class is able to take the field trip to the aquarium, and this lends a whole new excitement to the project and many more words on sticky notes are added to the web. They also have a speaker come to talk about different kinds of whales and the challenge of protecting some of them from extinction. The word web keeps growing and filling in with words, especially over the first 2 weeks. At first the web changes every day as the class finds good reasons to reorganize, add more sticky notes, or add another section. As the weeks pass, changes are needed less often (see Figure 27.1).

As Nashawna learns more, she becomes interested in blue whales. She finds that the school's library is limited and the junior search engines the school permits are also limited in this area. Her parents help her do some additional research on the internet and in the city public library. As she continues to learn more, she realizes that the word web needs to be reorganized in one section. She talks with Frank about it, and he encourages her to go ahead and do the reorganizing. Whenever she finishes an assignment early, which happens often, Frank allows her to pull out her project materials and continue her work on it. It is clear, he reflects more than once, that her approach to learning is highly positive—she is easily engaged, curious, persistent, and really seems to enjoy the process. Nashawna also seems to be having some influence on William's approach to learning as well. Frank records some related anecdotal observations and adds them to his file for each child to document their learning.

Again, Nashawna finds a place in the web that needs reorganizing, separating the cnidarians out of the mollusks group, and Frank points out to the children that he didn't know about cnidarians before. "I feel so lucky to have this job, because I'm always learning new things!" He also likes to point out the mistakes he makes from time to time, modeling for the children that making mistakes is normal and not to be feared.

After about 4 weeks, Frank copies down all of the categories on a very long piece of butcher paper with Nashawna's help, using different colors for different sections, and posts that on a long section of wall, again low enough for the children to be able to see and reach it. Then he asks the children to move the sticky notes to this mural. In the process the children find several sticky note words that had originally been placed in the wrong category.

Frank sets out two boxes on his desk. One is labeled "not finished" and the other "finished, needs frames." The children clip their papers together when they are done working on them for the period and place them in the "not finished" box, which Frank then files in each child's hanging folder. After the children have gone through the peer- or teacher-review process, and have fixed all of the pieces, they write on the back of each piece what color of frame they want and place these in the "finished, needs frames" box. Frank then cuts the frames, clips each together with the piece it will frame, and then clips the group together and places them in the child's hanging folder. Once a child has glued the finished work to the

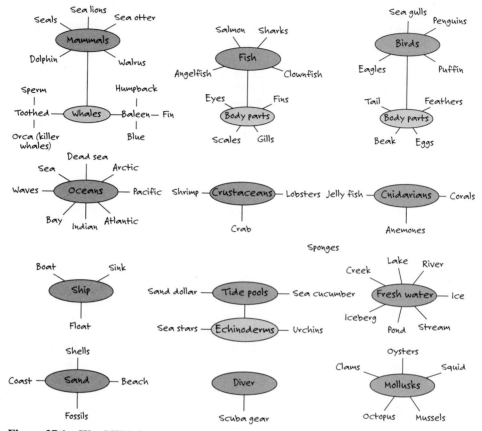

**Figure 27.1    Word Web for Ocean Animals Project**

frames, Frank gives him or her a piece of poster board on which to arrange the work and then glue it down as the final step.

While William works on his project, he often refers to the sticky notes on the word web mural. They help him figure out how to spell the words connected with his pictures. Frank reflects that a number of the children seem to do better at writing if they draw a related picture first. William has chosen a "man-of-war" jellyfish for his report. It has been about 6 weeks since the project started, most of the children have finished their reports. Both Nashawna and William are still working, however. Frank allows 2 weeks for the last children to finish, mostly during the "writing workshop" period. Nashawna has amassed so much information that she has to pick and choose the parts she wants to include in her report, and she has a difficult time deciding. When William is ready for the peer-review process, Cohen, Nashawna, and his other tablemates help him go over his rough draft, change the **invented spelling** to true spelling, and decide how to fix one of his sentences that is incomplete.

Eight weeks after the start of the project, all of the children have finished, including Susie, who had to finish with a less in-depth report than she was capable of due to her continued frequent absences. All of the poster board reports are hung in the hallway. The children receive a great many positive comments about them from parents, teachers, and staff members. Frank is very happy at how proud the children are, and he arranges the photographs he has taken of the process on some poster board and tacks that up on the bulletin board in the classroom for family members to see. He also includes these photographs and captions in a small assessment report that will be part of his year-end assessment of the progress the children have made over the school year. Next it is time to prepare the children to lead their family conferences.

## QUESTIONS

1. Name three benefits for the children of the ocean animals project curriculum. In addition to specific information about various ocean animals, what aspects of biological science were the children likely to learn? DAP 3C(2,3), 3D(1,2,3)

2. What benefits might result because of the way in which Frank involved the children in generating the word web for the ocean animals project? How would a simple brainstorming with all of the children as a group, calling on them one at a time as they raised their hands, and writing their ideas on the whiteboard, been different? DAP 1B, 2(introduction), 2E(1), 2F(1,2), 2G(3)

3. What were the advantages of allowing children to use invented spelling rather than insisting on true spelling in the web-generating strategy? DAP 2F(5), 3C(2)

4. Why did Frank make a point of reminding the children to be courteous and walk slowly when they moved their sticky notes from their tables to the board? Why do you think he asked the children to repeat his instructions? DAP 1C(3)

5. What does Nashawna's response to Roger's put-down of William, about drawing pictures on the sticky notes, tell you about how Frank builds a caring community in his classroom? DAP 1A, 2J(3); Code I-1.3, I-1.5, I-1.8

6. What do you think Frank could do to help Susie, given her homeless situation? What would you do? What do you think the school family support team did? DAP 5G; Code P-2.15

7. If there had not been enough funds for a field trip to the aquarium, what other types of field trips or guest speakers would have helped make the ocean animals project feel more real to William and the other children? DAP 3D(1,2)

8. When Frank introduced the chart report requirements to the children, name two strategies he could have used to make the requirements more clear to the children from the outset. What are the pros and cons of using a model in this situation?

9. What are the benefits of rearranging the sticky notes as more is learned during the project? Why didn't Frank just correct their placement and correct the spelling himself right away? DAP 1B, 2F(2)

10. What items might you keep in William's portfolio to document his progress during this project? DAP 4D, E, I; Code I-1.6, P-1.5, P-1.6

## WILLIAM LEADS A FAMILY CONFERENCE

Now that all of the children's ocean animal reports are finished and hung in the hallway outside of the classroom, it is time for Frank to help the children prepare to lead part of the teacher and parent conferences. The first step is filling out the *Self-Report Cards*. These have been constructed by the second-grade teachers and have seven different categories: spelling, daily oral language, handwriting, reading, writing, math, and work habits. Each category has a number of descriptive sentences with an underlined spot for the child to write in a symbol for *doing great*, *needs work*, or *making progress*. For example, under *Writing*, the descriptive sentences include the following.

_____ I am thinking of new ideas to write about.

_____ I am planning my writing before I begin.

_____ I am sounding out words and using guess-and-go spelling.

_____ I am working hard on illustrations.

_____ I am proofreading my writing and making changes.

Under *Work Habits*, the descriptive sentences include the following:

_____ I am listening when I need to be.

_____ I am following directions.

_____ I am working alone when I need to be.

_____ I am finishing my work.

_____ I am doing neat and careful work.

_____ I am working well with others.

_____ I am managing my time.

_____ I am organized and responsible.

_____ I am solving my problems when I should.

_____ I am trying hard in school.

Frank has the children fill out their self-report cards by putting them up on the overhead and working through each section, one sentence at a time. The children work at their tables and fill out the self-report cards as Frank goes over them. He reminds them that each should decide for himself or herself which symbol to use to score each sentence. Frank collects the cards so that he can check how each child is taking responsibility for his or her own learning, a major goal of this process. He will consult with some of the children about their self-assessment if he thinks that will be helpful to further this goal.

On the following day Frank passes out copies of the "Family Conference Road Map" that each child and family will use to progress through the steps of the conference. He guides the children through the map, showing them what they will need to do at each step along the way. One of the steps is reading a book sample out loud. William chooses a section from one of his favorite books about jellyfish. Frank makes sure the children have plenty of chances to practice reading their samples during a time when there are two parent volunteers available to assist in helping them do this.

Frank tells the students that he plans to talk with each child and his or her family for the first 15 minutes. He tells each child privately what he will say about him or her. He points out, "Everyone has something they need to work on, something to set a new goal for." After the first 15 minutes, the child will lead the conference using the road map for the next 45 minutes while Frank moves on to talk with another child and family. There will be five tables and other families will be coming and going. One of the tables will have the ABC Ocean Animals book that the class made, along with two of the math games the children have been playing. Also there will be snacks and beverages at the back of the room. The class has helped plan what those will be.

On family conference day, William and his mother arrive at 10:30 A.M. William is very excited. He has dressed in some of his best clothes. Frank is just finishing up with Cohen and his grandmother, directing them to an empty table, with Cohen smiling and carrying his own conference folder. William waves, but Cohen is focused on his grandmother. Frank greets William and his mother warmly and directs them to an empty table. William and his mother, Mrs. Fields, sit down. Frank picks up William's conference folder and sits down with them. He says, "Thank you so much, Mrs. Fields, for coming today. First, I would like to ask you if there is anything in particular you would like to discuss or any questions you have for me?"

Mrs. Fields says, "I just want to say how much William likes school this year and how happy I am about that! I have also really appreciated the books you are sending home with him for us to read together."

Frank replies, "I'm happy he is interested in the books and that you are taking the time to read to William. I'm sure William appreciates it too, huh, William?"

William nods vigorously and smiles. He listens to them talk some more, but isn't paying a lot of attention, since he knows what Frank is going to say about him. Frank is talking about social issues: how William gets along with others, how he practices his life skills in class, and how he is progressing slowly but steadily. William is thinking about his part of the conference that is coming up. Soon it is time, and Frank slides William's conference folder across the table to him, shakes hands with Mrs. Fields, stands up, and smiling, leaves William in charge.

William checks the road map. He has drawn some pictures on it to help him remember what the writing says, and Nashawna told him to circle the words he knew, which he did. Frank's instructions to the class were to ask the parents to help, but William wanted to do it himself. The first task was to tell his mother how he learns to spell words the best, and to show her his spelling score graph. The graph was the next page in his folder. After they discuss these things, it is time for William to show his mother how he works on two sentences, correcting the errors in them. Next he shows his handwriting sample sheet, and compares it with the one he did in the fall. The two sheets are clipped together, and his mother seems really impressed when he shows them to her.

Then it is time for his reading sample, and he pulls out the book section he has practiced. He reads it all, with his mother helping him with only one word! He is very proud of himself. Then he shares some of the best worksheets he has done during reading group time. He shares his writing folder and his math folder. He is supposed to tell his mother what a fraction is. He had drawn a picture of a pie with one piece cut out of it on his roadmap. He tells his mother that a fraction is like a piece of a whole pie, when the pieces are equal. He hopes he is remembering that correctly. William is glad when it is time to play a math game with his mother. He sees that one game isn't being used, so he gets it and teaches his mother how to play. They play one game and that is lots of fun, with his mother laughing at her own mistakes. Then he shows her the ABC Ocean Animals book and he reads many of the pages all by himself, partly from memory. His mother helps with some of the words on the other pages. There is another book album full of pictures of other class activities, but William can't wait to show his mother the ocean animal posters in the hallway, and especially his poster. She is full of compliments and he beams in response. Then he takes her back into the classroom to sit again at their table. Out of his folder he pulls his rough drafts for the report, including his list of facts, and the rough draft of his writing that showed the corrections he made and explains them to his mother. Then he pulls out the last piece in his folder. It is a card and an envelope. He asks his mother to write a "secret note" to him and place it in the basket on Mr. Edwards' desk. William asks her to print it to make it easier for him to read, and tells her that Mr. Edwards said she should not tell William what she says in the note. William will get to read it tomorrow at school. Then it will be a surprise.

On the next day Frank passes out the envelopes with the families' notes to their children. William asks Nashawna to help him read his. The note says, "My dear darling William, I am so proud of you today! I am very pleasantly surprised at how much you have learned this year. I know it is because you are willing to work hard and really *want* to learn. I am so impressed! Love, Your Mother."

Nashawna sees how touched William is and gives him a hug. Then she shares with William the nice words her father wrote in her note. The entire class seems to be very happy for the rest of the day.

## QUESTIONS

1. What do you think the advantages of a self-led family conference might be for the second-grade children? DAP 4A,D,F; Code P-1.5
2. Are there any changes you might make to the example lists for self-assessment provided for the children in this section? Assess your own work habits using the example provided.
3. Frank goes to considerable trouble to help the children prepare for the self-led conferences. In addition, of course, he has to prepare his own part of the conference. Do you think it is worth the

children's time to prepare for the conference? What do you think the benefits are for William? What are they likely to be for Nashawna? DAP 2B(1,2), 2F(1,2,3,4,5,6); Code I-1.6

4. Why is it important during a family conference to ask family members about any questions or issues they wish to discuss? What underlying message does this communicate? DAP 5B, 5C, 5E

5. What do you think the benefits of self-led conferences are for the parents? Code I-2.7, I-2.8, P-2.7

6. Look up the second-grade learning outcomes (standards, goals, or benchmarks) for your state school system. In what ways would an ocean animals project or student-led family conference help children move toward meeting some of those outcomes? DAP 3B(3)

# 28 Lecia and the Standardized Tests (Third Grade)

It is an unusually cold winter morning in an inner city neighborhood. "Good morning, Lecia," says Shareece Hamilton to the tall 8-year-old girl as she walks into the classroom through the entry door at 8:05 A.M. "You got a haircut, Lecia. It looks very nice!" Shareece welcomes the children in her third-grade class one by one every morning. She believes that making this initial connection with eye contact and a personal greeting starts the day off warmly for her and the children.

"Thanks, Ms. Hamilton, my mother cut and styled it." Lecia goes to her desk, gets the week's homework sheet out of her backpack, and drops it into the box on Shareece's desk. She gets out a few other things, hangs up her backpack and coat on a hook, and sits down. She looks at the list on the blackboard Shareece keeps to remind the children of the things they need to do to get ready for the day. Lecia gets up and sharpens her three pencils, returns a book to the classroom library, and starts thinking about the morning's first assignment Shareece has posted on the board. Shareece is still talking with some of the students by the door. Maliha comes in and talks to Lecia while she gets settled at a nearby desk. After another 5 minutes, the morning bell rings and the children all go to their desks, hang up their packs, sharpen their pencils, and start working on the morning's assignment. The words Equation of the Day are written on the blackboard and the number 63. The children know from past experience that they are to write a number of equations that equal 63 using the mathematical operation symbols plus, minus, times, and/or divided by. This assignment allows the children to do simple to complex work, challenging them to exercise the skills they already have while leaving room for trying out more advanced skills. What they do on these assignments also helps Shareece keep tabs on where their skills in math computation are, and how they are progressing.

Shareece is not looking forward to her day. She must prepare the children for the national standardized testing that is required in a few weeks. Late in the spring there will be the same national test to take again, and then also the state test the children are required to take. These tests are hard on the children, she knows, and make many of the families uptight. The school principal, Mrs. Bailey, is already urging the teachers to review math, since the school's mean score on the national test was particularly low last fall in math compared to the national norms for that test. The fact that the population the school serves suffers greatly from poverty and unsafe neighborhoods, and that these circumstances contribute significantly to lower test scores, cannot be considered. Nor can the high mobility of the population be considered, the high levels of nonnative speakers of English, the large number of children with special needs, or the lack of funding for smaller class sizes and textbooks. Mrs. Bailey doesn't want to make these problems any more visible than can be helped, either.

After about 5 minutes, Shareece claps a complicated pattern that the children echo until everyone is looking at their teacher. She then asks for volunteers to share the equations they made up and writes them herself on the board, sometimes illustrating the smaller steps for those students who might need that help. Next the children all get up, place their papers in the box on Shareece's desk, and walk to the carpet to sit down together for the morning's class meeting. Lecia sits next to Maliha and Linjun. They are chatting quietly together when Shareece sits in her low chair and rings a little bell to get the children's attention. Then she starts, and the children join in by saying their beginning affirmation. "We gather here to learn and grow, each in our own way, respecting and caring for one another—go!" At the word "go," the children all stomp their feet on the floor rapidly, making a low booming sound. When the noise dies down, Shareece goes through the housekeeping tasks of the morning, such as taking roll. Then she begins the main discussion of the morning's large group time, standardized testing.

"In about 3 weeks, you will be required to take some standardized tests using the computer lab. You may or may not remember taking these tests last fall during the second week of class. In these tests, there is a question and then a list of several answers. You choose the best answer to the question, and then click on it. I will be reminding you about test-taking strategies several times in the coming weeks, but the main thing I want you to remember is that all you are expected to do on them is to . . . what do I always tell you about your math tests?"

Several of the children answer together: "Just do your best!"

Shareece says, "That's right! That is all you have to do—do your best." A child who is late walks into the classroom and puts his backpack at his desk. "Good morning, Alejandro. Did you check in at the office? Good! Please join us. We are talking about the standardized testing coming up." Shareece turns back to the other children. "This year, I am using several other ways of assessing what you are learning. Who can think of one way?"

Maliha raises her hand first and says, "Our Portfolios?" Shareece agrees and reminds the children that she keeps the best samples of their work, along with photographs of their group work and accomplishments, in their portfolios. "What else?" Shareece asks.

Rashan raises his hand and offers, "math tests?"

"Yes, Rashan, that is one way I keep track of your progress but also I look at the work you turn in regularly—this morning's work, for example. Can anyone think of some other ways I keep track of your learning?"

Lecia is not feeling good. She hasn't done very well on the math tests so far this year. If Ms. Hamilton needs to remind them of how to take the test, it must be a really hard one, she thinks. Breezy raises her hand, and when called on, says, "You are often writing in a notebook and looking over our shoulders during DEAR[3] time."

"That's very good, Breezy. Yes, I keep track of your progress in reading that way and there are other ways, too. You know that sometimes I just watch what you are doing when you play a game or work on a project, and I take photographs or write notes on paper that record what I see you are able to do. I keep track of all of these things in a large file folder I keep for each of you. So I have a number of different ways to keep track of your progress in school. These are useful because they all help me to decide on the best ways to teach each of you—what you have already mastered and what you need more time, help, and practice to learn. The standardized tests we have been talking about are just one more way of tracking how you are learning in school. We will work on reviewing test-taking techniques this afternoon after lunch, and then we will go to the computer lab and work on a sample test. You can ask questions then. I see Mrs. Garvey and Ms. Muriyama are here now. It's time for reading." Shareece thinks, as she gets her materials for reading time, how much longer the school year seems to the children than it does to her. The fall testing seems almost like yesterday to her—much too soon to start testing again.

---

[3]DEAR refers to "drop everything and read."

Lecia keeps thinking about the standardized tests all morning. Ms. Hamilton made it seem as if it wasn't too important, but Lecia isn't so sure. She is afraid she will do poorly and her grandmother will be angry and disappointed in her, like she was when her cousin Jeron didn't do well on something they called "The Test" where he lived in the South last year. He was in third grade then, too, and Lecia remembers that he was held back from going on to fourth grade because of The Test. However, he moved here to live with her and her grandmother last summer and is in the fourth grade after all. Lecia wonders if the test she will be taking will be like The Test. Then she remembers that Linjun isn't too good at speaking English yet because she came from China just about a year ago. How will she do on this test?

After lunch Shareece has the children go to their desks. She puts up an overhead of some test questions she made up that are in a format similar to what the computer tests contain. "I am going to talk about some techniques for taking tests now," Shareece says. "First of all, read the questions carefully. Take your time. For these tests, you will be given as much time as you need to complete them. Let's read this question first. What do you think the answer is?" Shareece goes through a number of test-taking guidelines, using the examples from the made-up test on the overhead. She recommends reading through all of the answer choices carefully, seeing which ones you can eliminate because you know they are wrong, choosing the one you think is the best answer, and then reading back through the question and the answers one more time to check that the answer chosen is still the best one. "Sometimes the computerized tests don't allow you to go back, but this one does as long as you do so before the end of the testing session. Also, remember to go to bed early enough the night before the tests so that you can get a good night's sleep. We'll go over these guidelines again next week before you take the tests. Today we will go to the computer lab and you will be taking a short sample test. Remember it does not count. It is just for practice." She has been answering the children's questions throughout this discussion. She now asks if there are any more questions before they go to the computer lab. Lecia asks, "How will I know if I do alright on the test?"

Shareece replies, "Your family will be notified of the test results. You are going to do great. Just do your best and you will do fine." She looks at the whole class. "You all will do fine. Some of the questions will seem fairly easy, and others will be quite difficult. The purpose of the test is to measure where you are in your progress, and what your skills are, on the day that you take the test. Therefore it has to have enough difficult questions so that none of you will be able to answer all of the questions correctly. Don't let those hard questions worry you. Remember our chant: learn and grow, each in our own way! Your progress in school and learning is a journey—not a race! You will do fine if you do your best in your very own way."

Maliha asks, "What about Linjun, Ms. Hamilton? She doesn't speak English that well yet." Linjun looks at Maliha and smiles and looks down at her hands shyly. Shareece replies, "There will be someone to help her translate the questions into Chinese during the actual test. Didn't that happen last fall, Linjun?" Linjun smiles and nods uncertainly. "It is very thoughtful of you to worry about her, Maliha." Shareece makes a mental note to talk with Linjun's father about the testing and with Mrs. Bailey to make sure there will be enough funds to pay for the required translator.

After a few more questions, Shareece dismisses the children and they line up by the door. She sends Isaiah, who has autism, and Danny, who has attention deficit hyperactivity disorder (ADHD), to the learning lab for their practice sessions, since they will be taking the tests there. The specialists in the learning lab will help them take the tests, a small portion at a time, with the accommodations they need, including taking the tests on paper with a blue or green transparent cover, or orally, or in a study carrel, or with whatever accommodations each child needs. Fortunately, the school has four skilled special education teachers and a large number of children with disabilities. Shareece's mother, a recently retired special education teacher, would sometimes express her frustration about how schools with high enrollments of children with special needs would have lower mean scores and thereby be penalized because the government requires all of the children to take the same test and all of the children's scores to be included in the overall mean score, which then serves as the assessment of the school's performance.

Shareece agrees with her mother that the practice doesn't help build support for high-quality special education programs in the schools, and penalizes schools, like theirs, that have high-quality programs that are in great demand.

Shareece guides the other children, all in one line, down the hall to the computer lab. One boy starts to pick on the girl in front of him, and Shareece moves him to the end of the line, just to the side of where she is walking. Shareece sighs. Last fall, they did not prepare the children for the test at all, but brought the children into the computer lab and told them to just answer the questions on the computers as best they could. They decided this was the best way to minimize the stress for the students. The national test was given during the second week of school. The teachers didn't want to scare the students with testing after only a few days in school. That didn't seem to be the best way to start the school year. The teachers' focus during the first few weeks of school was to create a warm, caring classroom environment in which learning is exciting, meaningful, and engaging, so that the students would want to come to school each day. They knew how important children's positive **approaches to learning** are for their future educational success.

But the winter is another matter. Shareece's relationships with her students are strong and they have grown a lot over the months. The winter scores will be compared to those measured in the fall to assess the progress the children have made. In some of the topic areas the scores will inform her teaching emphasis. At least the stakes aren't as high as for the spring testing, in which the public school's reputation and funding, and, in some cases, individual teacher's salaries, will be hanging in the balance. It is a lot of pressure, and try as she might, she can't prevent it from being felt by the children. At least Mrs. Bailey and the district administration are trying to keep this pressure from causing the school to push the upper grades' curriculum down into third grade. This would put even more pressure on the children, cause more of them to feel like failures, and perhaps cause them to lose their natural enthusiasm for learning.

The line of third-grade students reaches the computer lab and all the children go in. The computer lab assistant, Mr. Matos, has prepared the computers so that all is ready for the children to sit down and take the practice test. Shareece tried to get some parents to come today and help the children get accustomed to the computers and the sample tests, but those who might have been able to come were not feeling very confident about using computers, much less training the children. Many of them are very proficient in using their telephones for instant messaging and e-mail, but not at using the computer. So it is up to Shareece and Mr. Matos today. She has asked her students Breezy and Montell, who are advanced and very good with computers, to help, but not until they finish their own sample tests. They would not, of course, be able to help the other children during the real testing. Many of the students need to learn how to scroll down the page, since that is required in some of the tests, but is not a common move in the computer games most of the students play at school.

Lecia sits down at one of the computers, and sees the first question of the test staring back at her. Her mind just seems to freeze up. She can't read any of the words. She doesn't know how to start. Tears start dripping down her cheeks, and she puts her head in her hands. Shareece, who is helping Maliha, sees this, excuses herself, and comes over to Lecia. Maliha comes too. Shareece kneels down and gives Lecia a hug, patting her back while she cries into Shareece's sweater. When Lecia is calm enough to talk, she tells Shareece about how her mind just froze up and wouldn't work for her. Tearing up again, she tells Shareece how angry her grandmother was with her cousin Jeron when he didn't do very well on a test last month. Shareece hugs Lecia again. Then, Shareece gets up and says to Lecia, "Let's go back to that corner and talk a little more," pointing to the corner farthest away from the other students. Shareece knows that Maliha is a good friend of Lecia, but she says, "Maliha, it is very caring of you to come over to see how Lecia is doing, but I'll take care of her now. I think you need to go back to your practice test. Raise you hand and Mr. Matos will help you if you need it."

Shareece listens a while longer to Lecia's feelings about the test. When it seems that Lecia has said about all she has to say about the issue, Shareece tells her, "If you would like, I'll talk with your grandmother about the tests, Lecia. I'll try to help her see that it is only a snapshot in time of some of the pieces of knowledge that you have learned this year. I'll tell her how hard you work in class and how smart I think you are. Would you like me to talk with her?" Shareece nods her head and hugs Shareece again. Shareece says, "In any case, I think you will do well on the tests, Lecia. Let's go back into the computer lab and give it another try, okay? I'll help you."

Lecia sits down again at the computer. Shareece sits down next to her. She uses a piece of paper and covers the bottom part of the screen so that only the first question is visible. She reminds Lecia that this test is just practice, and asks her if she will read the question out loud. Lecia slowly manages to read it. Shareece says, "Good. That's the first step. What do you think the answer is?" Lecia thinks and finally verbalizes an answer. Then Shareece says, "Good. Now let's read the first of the answer choices the test offers you to choose from." She moves the sheet of paper just a little to reveal the first answer choice, and asks Lecia to read it. Lecia does, a little more confidently than previously, Shareece thinks. She asks, "Does that sound like the answer you gave me before? No? Good, let's read the next answer choice." Shareece and Lecia continue to go through the first several practice questions this way until Shareece feels that she can leave Lecia to work on her own for a while. There are many children with their hands up waiting for help, but luckily Breezy seems to have finished her sample test and is helping one of the other students. It looks as if Montell is about finished, too. Shareece and Mr. Matos and the students do their best for the rest of the sample test session.

The following week, Linjun's father, Dr. Jin, comes to Shareece's classroom after school at her invitation to talk about the standardized testing. He is very concerned about it. In China, standardized tests are extremely important, he explains. They are the gatekeepers that determine what kinds of further educational opportunities will, or will not, be open to the children. He is worried about how Linjun will do, given that these tests are not available in Chinese and Linjun's English is not very good yet. Shareece tells him that there will indeed be a translator for Linjun. Unfortunately, it will not be someone she knows, so that might cause her to feel a little more nervous. Also, family members or friends are not allowed to serve as translators. She reassures Dr. Jin the one thing she hopes will be reassuring, that although in this state the third grade testing does affect some of the children's placements, very few educational opportunities are closed off by a single test in the United States.

Shareece does not explain that the grouping of the children that is done in the subsequent grades in her school is affected by the children's standardized test scores. However, so far Mrs. Bailey has made sure that this placement also takes into consideration the other, more authentic assessments made by each teacher throughout the year. These are the assessments that track children's abilities in all of their complexity over time, rather than a simple snapshot of a few pieces of what the children know and can do. Shareece hesitates, but adds, "This testing is currently one way in which children are identified for the talented and gifted programs, and the third-grade tests are the first opportunity for the children to qualify. This program offers qualifying children some enrichment activities during the school year, but is experiencing severe funding limitations right now." Dr. Jin nods his head and is very polite, but Shareece senses that he is not happy about what he has just heard.

Shareece spends the next 2 weeks making sure the children know their math vocabulary and problem solving, because she knows that the standardized math test relies heavily on terms such as perpendicular, parallel, and trapezoid. She has the children working on math word problems, reminding them to underline the important parts, draw a picture, and go back and check their work. She also guides the children through a review of literary terms, such as alliteration, synonyms, antonyms, homonyms, homophones, contractions, apostrophes, and plurals, and similar terms they will need to know to understand what the test questions are asking. The day before the test begins, Shareece uses a set of funny sample questions she made up. When she uses them to review the test-taking strategies with the students, they laugh and laugh all through the session.

Shareece includes a note about the testing in her weekly family newsletter that goes home with the students on Mondays and includes the week's homework assignments that usually involve the families.

She lets the families know about the dates of the testing, recommends lots of tender loving care for the children during that week because the testing can be quite stressful, and points out that the purpose of the testing is *mainly* to check on how well the school and teachers are performing. In the spring she faces an ethical conundrum: whether or not to also tell the children and their families that the standardized test scores may help determine where they are placed in future classes and whether they will be included in the talented and gifted program. Telling them would make the testing even more stressful for the children. In the newsletter, she points out to the families that the teachers have additional ways of assessing each child's progress, which will be shared during family conferences. Shareece also invites the families to contact her if they have any questions or concerns.

During the week of testing Shareece drops the weekly homework assignment and provides the children with work that they can do confidently: primarily art, easy board games, and self-selected reading, to occupy them during the periods of time when the children are not in the computer lab. She also brings in nutritious refreshments to help them keep up their energy and nurture their spirits. She is exhausted along with the students, as she is required to help in the computer lab much of the time when her students are still working there. She is allowed to help the children read the math questions, except for the numbers and symbols, and that keeps her very busy. She has asked the children to let her know when they are about to finish a test so that she can close the test down for them, hoping to keep them from seeing the total scores shown on the final screen. When the students have seen these in the past, some of them have gone back to the classroom and compared scores with each other, clearly resulting in some feelings of failure and jealousy among many of the students.

During the following weeks, the District Test Coordinator lets Shareece know that he wants 10 of her students to be coached on specific topics and to then retake the test. Shareece knows that some of the same students likely will be asked to take the test a third time, for the sake of raising the mean test scores for the school and for the district. There is nothing she is able to do to prevent this, but she makes sure that this extra instruction is as developmentally appropriate as she can make it. Unlike some of her peers, she has faith in the educational power and effectiveness of a developmental approach. And she will not be a willing partisan, if she can help it, to robbing these third-grade students of their childhood and love of learning. She does ask for the breakdown of her class scores in the different math strands that the test includes, so that she can use the information to inform her teaching.

Shareece is required to present the results of the individual tests to each student's family during the early spring family conferences. She always postpones this until the end of each conference because if she doesn't, all that gets discussed is the tests. She has worked to build a trusting relationship with the children's families. Child-friendly family nights, weekly newsletters outlining interesting assignments, phone calls, and often involving the families in the weekly homework assignments have contributed to this. She now relies on that trust to help families understand the worth of her authentic assessments of the children before she reports the results of the standardized tests.

Linjun's test score was not as high as Shareece knew it should be. Shareece does her best to explain to Linjun's father that it was no reflection on Linjun's abilities, just a very cloudy snapshot of a very small piece of all the knowledge and abilities Linjun has. Shareece believes that the translation of the questions was likely not exact enough, or clear enough, to avoid reducing Linjun's test score. Shareece points out that Linjun will most likely do better on the spring tests.

Shareece fears she will have a hard sell with Lecia's grandmother, but is pleasantly surprised. On the night she meets with her, Shareece finds that emphasizing how hard Lecia works, mentioning her many positive authentic assessments, and describing the standardized tests as only snapshots in time of a few of the pieces of knowledge that Lecia has learned, along with pointing out Lecia's hard-won reasonable scores, are quite convincing for her grandmother. After this conference Shareece sighs with relief.

When Shareece gets home that night she serves herself a large bowl of ice cream, sits down in a comfy chair, and reflects that at least, like her students, she has done her best and that will have to be good enough.

## QUESTIONS

1. Think back to your early grade school years. Write a paragraph about your childhood memories of taking standardized tests.
2. Why do you think Shareece asks the children to come up with some ideas for the other ways she uses to assess their progress, instead of just telling them herself? DAP 2F(2)
3. What additional advice can you think of to give the children about test-taking strategies?
4. Why do you think Shareece made up funny questions and answers to use for the final review of test-taking strategies? DAP 2B(3)
5. What other ways can you think of to help reduce the stress of testing experienced by the children or to help them cope with it? Code P-1.1
6. Do you think Shareece should have told Linjun's father that the standardized test scores are considered when placing the children in certain classes during the subsequent school years? Code I-2.2, P-2.7
7. What were some of the advantages for Shareece and the children of the trusting relationships she worked to build with the families during the early part of the school year? DAP 5A; Code I-2.2

# GLOSSARY

**AA BB pattern**  An array of items that is different in at least one characteristic, such that two similar objects are followed by another two objects that are similar to each other but different from the first two objects; this order of items is repeated again, perhaps many times

**Accommodations**  Specialized staff services, tools, furnishings, equipment, and technology that support and assist a child who has special needs with specific targeted tasks documented on a child's Individualized Family Service Plan (IFSP)

**Anecdotal observation**  A recorded observation that describes one or more children's behaviors and/or interactions over a very brief period of time

**Antibias curriculum**  Curriculum that is designed to help children overcome and work against harmful biases, commonly held in the larger society, related to the ethnicity, culture, gender, sexual preference, abilities, appearance, and other common characteristics of groups of people

**Approaches to learning**  A child's emotions and behaviors related to learning, such as interest, pleasure, intrinsic motivation, creativity, self-regulation, flexibility, initiative, and persistence, that influence the child's long-term success in school

**Auditory discrimination**  The ability to hear and discern different sounds, usually those involved in a particular language

**Child-centered**  An approach to teaching and curriculum that is guided by the interests and abilities of the children, along with the program goals; a learning environment that allows a child many choices in the direction of his or her play or interaction with materials and equipment and with other children and adults; not teacher-centered, in which the teacher makes most of the choices and children spend most of their time listening to and following a teacher's instructions

**Children's services**  Public service agencies dedicated to helping children and their families, such as child protective services, that often have different names in different regions

**Cognitive processing skills**  Involves the mental abilities of the child's brain to take in information through the senses, then organize, store, retrieve, utilize, and create new information. These mental functions are used as a child encounters experiences in daily life

**Concept web**  A method of concretely showing relationships between primary concepts and secondary or tertiary ideas by connecting single words or phrases with lines to show relationships between them, often used for curriculum planning and often involving children

**Curriculum web**  A concept web used for planning curriculum, also referred to as a word web, especially when used with children

**Developmental play**  Play that involves tasks that help children practice and extend developmental skills, individually or as a group

**Down syndrome**  Down syndrome or trisomy is a chromosome disorder in which all or part of an additional 21 chromosome is present. This abnormality causes mild to moderate cognitive and physical growth impairment. The incidence of this disorder is 1 in 800 to 1000 births and is often diagnosed during pregnancy or at birth

**Dramatic play**  Children engage in this kind of pretend play as they take on imaginary roles; they may use real or symbolic objects to enhance their play; some common themes include being animals, monsters, housekeeping, driving, grocery store, and superheroes

**Early interventionist**  This person is a state-licensed professional who works as a partner with parents and families of children with special needs; the early interventionist assesses the development of very young children (0–3 years) who have been referred and writes an IFSP to target delayed cognitive, language, speech, social, and fine and/or gross motor developmental skills (see accommodations); the plan is developed in collaboration with parents, teachers, and appropriate therapists to provide supportive services and activities that can enable the child to improve important skills

**Emergent curriculum**  Curriculum that emerges at a point in time in response to one or more children's expressed or observed interests, or due to an unplanned opportunity for engaging children's interests and learning

**Expressive art**  Art activities experienced by the child through open-ended exploration and experimentation with art materials including paint, paper, glue, markers, crayons, brushes, clay, cardboard, and many other possible materials and items

**Expressive language**  Language produced by the child verbally, including skills related to articulation, sentence structure, self-talk, conversation, and vocabulary

**Eye–hand coordination**  The organization of eye and hand movements working together to accomplish fine motor tasks

**Family constellation**  The makeup of a family in terms of ages, gender, and relationships; for example, a family made up of an unmarried mother, her male partner, her grandmother, and three children, two older boys and a girl who is the male partner's daughter

**Fine motor skills**  Skills involving the ability to use small muscles in the hands and wrists, feet, or face and other parts of the body to perform tasks that require precise movements, such as making a drawing, speaking, or kicking a ball toward a goal

**Guess-and-go spelling**  A descriptive word to convey to children the idea of invented spelling or phonemic spelling (see definitions below)

**Individualized Family Service Plan (IFSP)**  A document that describes and evaluates the special need(s) of a child (based on assessment) and a timetable of recommended goals and objectives and supportive staff and therapist services

**Invented spelling**  A learner's way of representing a word based on his or her knowledge of some of its phonemic sounds and the letters that represent those sounds; also known as phonemic spelling

**Learning centers**  Specific areas of the classroom learning environment in which children interact with equipment and materials to enhance their developmental skills, often in areas of special interest (dramatic play, reading and listening, observing nature, carpentry, sensory play, drawing and writing, etc.)

**Learning process**  Acquisition and organization of knowledge and skills based on the child's interaction with materials, equipment, and other children and adults

**Loose parts**  Objects and materials that are available for children to play with and move around as they wish to construct play environments, especially in outdoor playgrounds

**Manipulatives**  A variety of smaller-sized objects that encourage fine motor control skills such as grasping in various positions, holding, pushing, lifting, squeezing, balancing, and cognitive skills such as counting, spacial awareness, patterning, seriation, classification, and representation

**Obstacle course**  A sequence of gross (large muscle) motor tasks often involving equipment such as climbers, tunnels, hanging bars, balance beams for climbing, crawling, swinging, and balancing

**Occupational therapist**  A therapy specialist who provides activities and tasks for children who have demonstrated difficulty in small muscle or fine motor tasks

**One-to-one correspondence**  The concept that when counting, each number corresponds to one, and only one, item

**Pattern blocks**  Small blocks with a number of different geometric shapes and colors, with which children can make various patterns, designs, and other representations

**Phonemic awareness**  The ability to discern each of the specific sounds within spoken words, a precursor to making connections between letters and their related sounds

**Phonological awareness**  The ability to discern the sounds involved in spoken language, which begins in infancy and is later demonstrated and enhanced through experiences with rhyme and alliteration

**Physical therapist**  A therapy specialist who provides activities and tasks for children who have demonstrated difficulty in large muscle or gross motor movements to promote strength, coordination, and balance

**Primary grades**  Often defined as first, second, and third grades in elementary schools, but definitions vary

**Project approach**  Similar to integrated learning, a project approach involves a focus on a particular topic that stimulates related learning activities extending into many of the major developmental and curriculum content areas

**Receptive language**  A child's ability to hear, listen, understand, and accurately interpret the speech of another

**Self-selected activities**  Activities, materials, and play opportunities freely chosen by the child

**Shadowing**  Constantly observing and staying close to a particular child who is being shadowed, often for the purposes of helping the child and/or preventing a problem behavior

**Speech articulation**  The production of consonant and vowel sound patterns utilizing muscles of the tongue and mouth and structures such as teeth and the roof of the mouth

**Speech therapist**   A therapy specialist who provides activities and tasks for children who have demonstrated difficulty in producing sounds necessary for speech communication

**Standard spelling**   The true or conventional spelling, as opposed to invented or phonemic spelling

**Teacher-assisted activity**   A child's engagement in an activity is supported or enhanced by a teacher using strategies such as asking open-ended questions, making helpful comments, helping with materials, and providing demonstrations

**Teacher-directed activity**   A child's behaviors in an activity are dependent on a teacher's instruction and supervision

**Time sample method**   Observing and recording children's behaviors at frequent, regular time intervals

**Transition meeting**   A meeting of staff, parents, and specialists, associated with the child's Individualized Family Service Plan (IFSP) or Individualized Education Program (IEP), who review and discuss the child's progress toward goals and objectives to best prepare for events such as completing preschool and beginning kindergarten

**Unstructured activities**   Activities in which children are encouraged to utilize materials or props without instruction in self-directed play

**Word wall**   An area in the classroom where words that have been introduced, are of current interest, and that the children are often asked to write are posted in large letters so that they can be easily seen

**Word web**   Another term for concept web, usually used with young children involved in constructing a curriculum plan around a particular topic, a process often referred to as webbing